FREEDOM
FIGHTER

FREEDOM FIGHTER

Joanna Palani

with

Lara Whyte

Atlantic Books
London

First published in Great Britain in 2019 by Atlantic Books,
an imprint of Atlantic Books Ltd.

2 3 4 5 6 7 8 9

A CIP catalogue record for this book is available from the
British Library.

Paperback ISBN: 978-1-78649-435-1
Trade paperback ISBN: 978-1-78649-436-8
E-book ISBN: 978-1-78649-437-5

Printed in Great Britain by CPI Group (UK) Ltd,
Croydon CR0 4YY

Atlantic Books
An Imprint of Atlantic Books Ltd
Ormond House
26–27 Boswell Street
London
WC1N 3JZ

www.atlantic-books.co.uk

I dedicate this book to the many girls and women, especially in Kurdistan, who are still fighting for the sexual revolution in the Middle East.

Contents

Prologue: Between Two Buildings   1

1   Daughter of the War in the Desert   21

2   Growing Up Kurdish   34

3   Rights Before Rules   49

4   Journey into Syria   65

5   Aleppo Begins to Crumble   75

6   The Real Revolutionaries of Rojava   101

7   The Friendly Agents of the PET   133

8   The Martyrs of Kobani   151

9   Stuck in the Mountains   182

10   *Peshmerga* Poster Girl   209

11   Pregnant Little Girls   226

12   Over Borders, Under Scrutiny   252

13   Evolution of Tactics   268

14   Selfies on the Manbij Frontline   285

15   Munitions and Mind-Games   313

16   Aftershocks   334

Acknowledgements   353

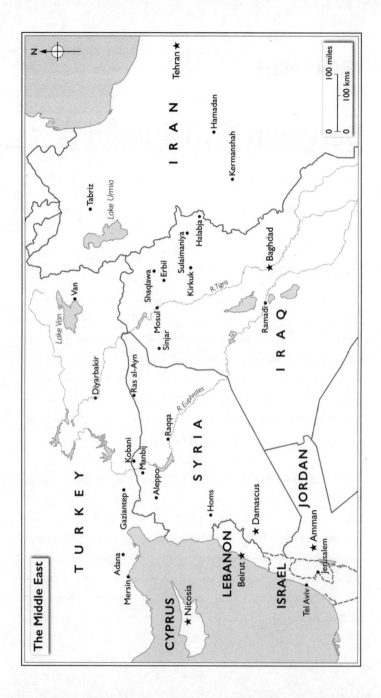

The Middle East

Between Two Buildings

September 2014

We'd been without food inside our house in Kobani in northern Syria for more than three days when I decided it was time to go and try to find some. I couldn't call where we were staying a 'safe house' because there wasn't one building in the city that was safe from ISIS at the time. Selected on the basis that it was one of the oldest houses we could find, it had thicker walls than the newer, half-finished buildings that make up much of the city. Bullets pass easily through cheap concrete and blast-stone buildings, but they struggle more with older, handmade walls.

I woke up cold after a night sleeping upstairs huddled in between two YPJ girls I had befriended, Amara and Bercem. It was our third night spent camped together as a trio in the room our unit used as a bedroom, but I had been tossing around and I knew the others were annoyed. Shortly before midnight Bercem put her leg over mine, and the warm weight of her had forced me to be still long enough to get to sleep. I woke up with my arm curled around Amara, but the breeze from the window closest to us, reaching my back, told me that Bercem was no longer behind me. I slept in my uniform, as we all did, and this morning marked eleven days without a shower. I slowly made my way downstairs to our yard, where some of the younger girls were already up, piously cleaning weapons, and through to our kitchen to make myself some tea, as my stomach knotted with hunger.

The Women's Protection Units, the YPJ, fight together with the men; and we all make up the YPG. We believe that women and men are equal, so we fight together for the freedom of the Kurdish people and the destruction of ISIS. There were sixty-four of us fighters spread across four houses in the south of the city of Kobani at the time, and fifteen stationed in our house. Our four locations were near the central market; and we were close enough to each other to send commands and move swiftly, when need be. We shared one fresh-water tap in the yard and our house was divided into three rooms: one for cooking, one for sleeping and resting and one room to go to the toilet. 'Toilet is out of bounds until further notice,' my commander explained over breakfast. 'We don't want *Daesh* to be alerted to our position by the stench,' Ameena added, and a few people laughed as our commander tried to raise a smile. Breakfast was sweet, hot blackberry tea and sugar. There was no bread left, and the logistic supply trucks – we just call them 'logistics' – had been delayed and blocked from getting in again. Opposite our house was an abandoned kebab grill, and that particular morning the faded pictures displayed in the windows felt like torture.

There was no power, so at night we sat together in the candlelight, drinking tea and talking politics, but for the last few nights the only thing on our minds was food. Supplies had become increasingly scarce as the summer passed, and by the time our unit – or *tabur*, as we say in Kurdish – arrived in Kobani, they had dwindled to virtually nothing. With Turkey to our north and ISIS everywhere else, we were effectively blockaded, or something very like it, but no one wanted to show they were scared, so we continued to behave as normal. We didn't expect to be attacked as quickly as we were in Kobani, as we thought ISIS would focus on cities near the oil fields such as Kirkuk, in the very heart of Kurdistan. So the siege was unexpected – if there really is such a thing in war, because a soldier should always be prepared for the unknown. Looking back and seeing the mistakes we made in Kobani is like having a ticket for a train that's already left the station. It's a painful and fairly useless exercise. We couldn't do anything more than stand our ground and fight with what we had.

We had been waiting for weapon supplies to arrive so we could push forward, but they had yet to materialize, so I spent long evenings on guard patrol on the roof of our house, watching through the cracked scope of my AK rifle as ISIS erected their black flags closer and closer to our position. They had been moving fighters into the region all summer long: they wanted to be seen internationally as being on Europe's doorstep. We shared our weapons among our unit, mainly cheap, black-market semi-automatic assault rifles, and munitions were at a premium as we were short of materials. Every morning and evening our AKs would be lined up and cleaned, as if polishing them would suddenly transform them into proper equalizers. There was sometimes some shuffling to get one of the better AKs, but we have a culture of sharing, so more often there would be a long conversation over who should have the less reliable weapon:

normally the more experienced fighter. The gun I was eventually assigned had a broken bayonet holder, so I had to fashion one of my scarves around it to hold my knife securely in place. We were depending on a fresh logistics shipment, as there were far more ISIS soldiers than us and they had far better weapons. When US planes did eventually drop weapons from the Iraqi *Peshmerga* forces to us, many landed in areas recently taken from us by ISIS, who were everywhere.

My fellow fighters were girls and boys often far younger than me, and I was proud to fight with them. We were defeating the greatest evil the world had ever seen, and I was prepared to die with a smile on my face and my head held high, just like the rest of them. Many of the people I was with had grown up in the Kurdish mountains and had been in combat training for years, which made them remarkable fighters. Though some were younger than me at the time (I was the grand old age of twenty-one in Kobani), most had already been in battle for many years. Life for many young Kurds in the Middle East doesn't give you much: a Kalashnikov, a hatred of fascism, a love of freedom and memories of a loved one killed for the crime of their birth.

I had woken up that morning feeling sore, and went up to the roof of our house to find out what trucks the Turkish soldiers were letting through the border; again it looked as if they were letting drivers for ISIS through, while blocking ours. Kobani lies right on the border and our vantage point enabled us to see who was coming towards us. Using the scopes from our rifles, we would look hungrily at the truck drivers to see if they were coming to us. The passing trucks looked like they were bringing charity supplies to some of the thousands of refugees and those displaced by the conflict, but they weren't – they were supplies for ISIS combatants. YPG units around Kobani followed the trucks and could see they were not going to the refugee areas. There were no refugee areas in Kobani; only combatants. We would watch ISIS fighters unload the vehicles and try on new camouflage gear sent over from Turkey. Supplies never came into our hands – only theirs. We knew this because the civilians were leaving the city through our areas; they didn't go along the roads where the trucks were coming, because they knew these trucks were connected to the army of death they were fleeing.

I wondered at the time if the Turkish NATO soldiers noticed the same as we did, or if they let them go on purpose. Today I know the Turkish soldiers knew what they were doing. They didn't let any Kurdish civilians from Kobani flee, but they let ISIS supply trucks through. We saw that the trucks contained food, dates and bread, and we were starving. Two days previously, Cengiz, a chef from Istanbul fighting with the YPG, had boiled together some leaves and grass with the final supplies of our sugar as a meal. *Heval* Amara and *heval* Bercem had a little taste of it and explained it was sort of like a dolma leaf, which is popular in the Middle East, and I tried it, initially thinking I enjoyed it. After a few mouthfuls, however, I knew it wasn't doing me any good, but in lieu of other food I had to keep eating. Every night the conversation would be dominated by the amazing meals Cengiz promised to make when the supplies of tomato and potato arrived. We were hearing that the European countries were supposed to be sending weapons, but no one had any evidence of it yet. 'Maybe the Europeans are sending some pizza and McDonald's, when they send us those weapons,' I joked. At times we became giddy with hunger and adrenaline, but when I made this quip I caught the eyes of one of the older men, who looked worried, and it made me stop laughing.

Our leadership was already well aware of the lack of weapons, and the poor state of the ones we had. But we, the YPG, refused to leave Kobani. As Kurdish fighters, we believe that freedom is more important than our individual small lives. We fight on regardless. The previous evening the Turkish volunteers sat with their mouths watering as Cengiz listed the best ways to sauté a potato or roast a tomato – I don't speak Turkish, so Amara translated for me, until I asked her to stop. I resented having to learn Turkish; I am a Kurd, yet I have to learn the language that replaced Kurdish as part of a campaign of cultural and actual genocide. I know speaking a number of languages is a benefit, but Turkish is not my language and I found it hard to communicate with the others because of this.

There was a Swedish volunteer with the YPG, so he and I indulged ourselves by listing the foods we missed from Europe, while Bercem would tease us for our 'Western imperialist' upbringing and tastes, telling us the variety of food choices available within modern capitalist culture – what we call 'the system' – is absurd.

For the past three days and nights I had been sweating out some kind of fever, which made me annoying to sleep beside. None of the Kurdish volunteers were quite as sick as I was, which was embarrassing, and even the Swedish *heval* (how we fighting Kurds call each other – meaning 'friend' or 'comrade') – was holding up better than me, despite this being his first-ever time on the frontline.

I found Bercem after our morning assembly, drinking tea, and we discussed the mission to go and find some food, as incoming and outgoing fire boomed in the background behind us. We were in a constant state of alert for incomings and outgoings, and the threat of artillery attack was always near. We needed to stay rational and focused, and in order to do so we needed food. She urged me not to go, but I figured I'd rather be killed by ISIS than die of hunger from eating dirty old leaves. It was hard for me to see my comrades suffering, and we needed food before anyone else got sick. On missions, we go together in threes: when the YPJ and YPG are working together on missions, it is normally two YPG members and one YPJ, or two YPJ and one YPG. Every member of the YPJ is also a member of the YPG, but the YPG are not members of the YPJ: we are the female fighters only. Four of the guys volunteered to go with me, including the Swedish *heval* I had spoken to, but I kept looking straight ahead and stayed in line, as my commander picked the two who would accompany me: *heval* Cengiz, the chef, who at thirty-two was one of the oldest in our group, and *heval* Levant, a tall guy of twenty-three who mostly kept to himself. Both were Kurdish Turks from Istanbul.

We didn't have a radio and were low on ammunition, but as I gathered my broken AK and prepared to leave, I felt determined but somewhat resigned. We had nothing to lose, and I didn't really care if I died, because I knew we would all die if we didn't eat. In Kobani, if you stayed in the same place for long, you would die: ISIS knew our spots and we were so close that at times we could hear them pray. It was early afternoon and the sun was high in the sky when we left, but I knew it would be cold later. I was always the wrong temperature in Kobani – shivering with the cold at night or sweating with a fever. We crept as quietly as we could between the houses, avoiding the main streets and obvious places where we thought ISIS might have a good vantage point.

The Chechens who had joined the ISIS forces were leading the march towards the city, and we knew one wrong move could put us in full view, so we kept low as we darted between the densely packed buildings. The structure of the streets and buildings gave us lots of places to hide, but made us more vulnerable to injury from debris. We knew they had shoulder-launched surface-to-air missiles, which are basically point-and-shoot bombs that can destroy buildings, and really good-quality rocket-propelled grenades (RPGs). Their weaponry was far superior to ours, looted from US-backed Iraqi soldiers who had abandoned their posts all over northern Iraq that summer, and it was the best in the Middle East at the time.

They had no allies inside Kobani, unlike other places, so we didn't fear coming across families, and by this stage most of the civilians had left. Those who refused to leave helped the YPG, even though we asked them many times not to get involved. We informed them honestly about the great risks they would take by getting involved, but they wouldn't hear of it. They would yell that they refused to leave the city of Abdullah Ocalan (our Kurdish nationalist leader and founder of the PKK political party) for the Turkish puppies, which is how they refer to ISIS. In the YPG, we call ISIS *Daesh*. We tried to stop civilians from joining us, but it was their decision to make; ours was to support them in clearing the Turkish puppies out of the city. It was for them that we fought.

The streets were quiet, save for the incomings we could hear in the distance. Being so close to *Daesh* meant this was a normal sound, nothing to fear. There was no one around; only abandoned cars, and confectionary stands emptied of their wares. The people had left in so much of a hurry that many of the doors we came across were unlocked. After the siege ended, Kobani was reduced to rubble, but as we walked around, it felt like a very beautiful ghost town, with us three as the apparitions.

Kobani was the first city to adopt the ideology of Abdullah Ocalan – the city is linked to Ocalan from the 1980s, when he lived there. We would not be giving up his city. Putting my finger on my trigger as I walked, I ventured slowly through the streets with the other two and we fell into a formation: Levant in front, me in the middle and Cengiz behind. I knew ISIS had thermal-imaging equipment, from my guard duty of standing watch on top of our building, whereas we barely had binoculars, so when night fell around 8 p.m. we discussed going home empty-handed.

'We can't venture much further,' *heval* Cengiz warned, as we huddled inside the hall of what I think was an old newsagent's.

'We can't go back with nothing,' *heval* Levant said, which surprised me; he was quite shy, but the strength of his resolve was clear. They both looked at me expectantly.

'Let's just keep going,' I said quietly, 'but carefully,' before telling them to lower their voices. We wandered into a more suburban area with no working street lights and walked silently, listening to the punctuation of gunfire from other areas of the city, the frequency of which rose steadily as the sun set.

We heard some gunfire around dusk coming from the east of our location, so we suspected the Chechens were making another evening advance. As we headed west, I rifled through my uniform, hoping to find extra ammunition. I didn't know exactly where we were, as none of us were familiar with the city, but we figured we would take another route home now. We didn't have the cover of darkness to protect us, and we were worried about leading enemy fighters back to our house, so we slowed down a little to let our eyes adjust to the twilight.

It was hard to tell at times whether the houses were half-built or half-destroyed, but I knew our fruitless search was becoming more dangerous, the further away from our base we ventured. I was beginning to accept we had been unsuccessful when suddenly a barrage of bullets rang out from the opposite side of the street. There had been rumours that the Chechen snipers had started using gigantic 23mm-calibre bullets. The deafening sound told me their cartridges were certainly more expensive than ours. Huddling as close as I could to the ground, I tried to identify the different arms being used: my initial hope that it was another YPG battalion out 'hunting' faded fast. They must have been tracking us, as they were extremely close and we were outnumbered, and in the panic *heval* Cengiz and *heval* Levant hid inside the different houses they were searching, while I dived down to the closest shelter I could see, a small confectionary stand on the street in between the two.

My first instinct was to return fire, but as I gripped my rusty AK, with my scarf still keeping my knife in place, and steadied my breath to prepare to shoot, I realized this wasn't going to be possible. I had little ammunition and no vision, but worse than this, had I fired from my position I would have alerted the snipers to my precise location, which would bring them to me and the others. Trembling, I placed my hand on my heart pocket, where we all keep our final ammunition, in the event of being captured. The firing paused for a second and I ran towards the building closest to me. I knew this wasn't smart; when a group shoots at you and then suddenly stops, they are probably waiting for you to make a move. But I had no choice – I had to move. It was either move or die.

Sure enough the shooting began again, and I felt my heart pound as the bullets flew close to my ears. I wasn't thinking; I was in pure survival mode. Something took over and I managed to get to the building where *heval* Cengiz was. Entering the hall, I could hear him breathing heavily. It was difficult to see how badly injured he was in the darkness, but I could hear a gurgling in his throat, so I ran over to clear his airways. I couldn't ascertain the full extent of his injuries, as we were both trying to keep as quiet as we could. I tried to stop the bleeding from his chest, but it was pumping out all over us both very fast. He was losing too much blood and I needed help to get him to safety, but I also had to check on *heval* Levant. I looked Cengiz straight in the eyes and said in a clear, hushed voice, 'I will get *heval* Levant and bring him here, but you need to keep breathing, *heval*. We will leave together.'

Hearing a brief pause in the shooting, I ran the short distance to the next house. As I entered I could hear *heval* Levant moaning in the darkness. He was shot in the back through his shoulder and was panting loudly, but the noise was reassuring because it meant his breathing was okay. Hearing this, I realized that *heval* Cengiz was the more seriously injured, so I had to run back into the street to his hiding place. The shooting moved closer and was suddenly much louder and appeared to come from higher up, in frequent, erratic bursts. I raced as fast as I could, with bullets flying around me. I believed their new position put me outside their line of sight – as I couldn't see them. I knew where I was going; they didn't. So I just kept low, concentrated on my footwork and ran.

I reached the house where *heval* Cengiz was sheltering and was trying to calm myself so I wouldn't make any mistakes, as there wasn't time for that. Listening to the sounds of the gunshots to try and locate the snipers, I made my way towards *heval* Cengiz, who couldn't walk and was barely breathing. He was too heavy for me to carry alone, and *heval* Levant couldn't help carry him or support any extra weight as he was injured himself, although he could stand up and walk. Caught between these two injured men, I knew *Daesh* were making their approach. The shooting subsided briefly and I could hear the rough Chechen dialect of the soldiers ringing out behind me. I groaned so loudly that *heval* Cengiz noticed, as I could tell the soldiers were on the same side of the street as us, but that they had circled behind our building. None of us were in view, as we were inside the buildings and the firing had stalled, but I realized it was only temporary. They knew our positions and we had walked into their ambush.

I went slowly over to *heval* Cengiz, knowing that my movements could be heard. If he was going to die, let *Daesh* take us both. I would rather be with him and fight to the end – I didn't want him to be alone. In our movement, we don't leave each other, to save ourselves; we are one, and our strength is our unity. I knew he couldn't shoot because of his injuries, but I still could, so there was a small chance we could make it out alive. When we say we fight for love and friendship, this is what we mean: we fight for each other.

'Where is *Daesh*?' he whispered gently to me with his broken Kurdish as I stood above him to hold his head in my arms.

I looked into his eyes and saw flecks of green I hadn't noticed before. 'They've stopped shooting and are close by. They are probably listening right now,' I whispered as lightly as I could. I was kneeling right beside his ear, but I couldn't afford to risk making a sound. He struggled to breathe and his eyes couldn't focus on me. I could see the pale whiteness of his face as the blood drained out and onto the floor. Everywhere was wet and sticky. A pool began to form around us on the cold tiles, as we looked at each other again.

'*Bercho* – go,' he said to me. 'Go see *heval* Levant,' he insisted.

'I have already checked on him,' I whimpered, but he kept saying, '*Bercho, bercho.*' He managed to look me straight in the eye, and I knew what he was telling me to do.

I scrambled out of the room to the doorway and paused for a moment before planning the journey back across the street. Although it was quieter, the risk now was that ISIS were waiting for me to leave the house – if they had, as I suspected, seen me run towards it. In war, mistakes equal death.

The unmistakable ping of a pin from an old Russian pineapple hand-grenade landing behind me interrupted my thoughts. It was like glass breaking. I turned round and threw myself to the ground as it exploded, because I didn't know exactly who had thrown it. Initially I thought it was *Daesh*, but as I covered my ears and eyes while the debris from the building began to fall away around us both, I had a sinking feeling that it was my *heval.* Coming up for air seconds later, the smell behind me told me it was definitely Cengiz who had thrown the pin. He had placed the grenade in his mouth and blown his own head off. The smoke and dust from the settling concrete made it difficult to see what was going on, and I had to cover my face with a scarf to stop coughing. The smoke lifted to reveal a hole in the wall near his right shoulder. Cengiz was dead. There was blood everywhere, and he was not in one piece any more. The stench of his flesh caught in the back of my throat and I struggled not to vomit. Looking through the hole in the wall, I could see my escape. Looking back at Cengiz, I knew he had made the choice to kill himself to save all three of us from being captured. In my heart I had understood what he was telling me, when he had insisted that I go check on Levant. I knew the choice he had been contemplating: either one of us died or all three of us were captured and killed. These were the kind of impossible choices we made in Kobani.

I scrabbled through the remains of his body to find his ID card. The lower half of his body was exactly the same, his shoes were still neatly tied, but the top half was a gaping mess of yellow and red. It was only when I took his ID card that I learned his real name, instead of the *nom de guerre* we had known him by. From all over the world we fought together in Kobani, and Cengiz gave his life not only to save me and Levant, but to rid the world of the evil of *Daesh.* I wish I had known him better, but what he did for me describes who he was, and I remember him as a hero.

After racing back to Levant through the hole in the wall, we hobbled across the street towards where the firing had initially come from – but this was now in the opposite direction from the

Chechens, as they had switched sides. *Heval* Cengiz had given us precious seconds, as *Daesh* had to retreat long enough for us to escape. I held Levant by the waist and we ran as fast as he could. Stopping in an alleyway, I was attempting to bandage his wounds using my jacket, as he had bled through his, when we heard another group in the street opposite ours. We both dived for cover, into the same house this time, but as the voices became clearer, it was Kermanji – the Kurdish dialect the YPG use to communicate – that we heard and not Arabic. Exhausted, I immediately shouted as calmly as I could for help. I could hear my voice shaking, as I emerged slowly from our alley to explain that we were lost, Levant was shot and we needed help to get back to our base. In the YPG we work in small self-sufficient groups, so because this group didn't know us they half-heartedly went through our safety protocol motions; taking away our weapons, they checked our IDs and radioed our commander. Levant was given some pain relief and we were brought a small plate of food and some sweet tea, which was all I could manage.

Their driver, a young local guy from Kobani, drove us back, thanking us for coming and asking me questions about Denmark and Europe. Not in the mood to talk, I pretended my Kermanji wasn't good enough to understand him and stared out of the open window, looking at the sky and thinking about Cengiz. In Kurdish we have the phrase '*Sehid namirin*', which means 'Martyrs never die', and I repeated it over and over again, trying to let the final image I had of his corpse release itself from my mind.

We arrived back, debriefed our commanders and announced the death of *heval* Cengiz, and I went to the sleeping room to lie next to Bercem and Amara. In the yard below, one of those closest to Cengiz sang our martyrs' songs gently throughout the night. In Kobani we always sang, and someone always played the guitar. Everyone was upset, but I was quite numb. The others were making an effort to talk to me, though, and I had a lot of questions about Cengiz: Did he have a family? Did he have a lover? Would his family be prosecuted, now that he was dead? Did he have a successful life? What did he give up for our movement? What did he give up for me? Would his family ever know what he had accomplished in Kobani? It's unusual to see Turkish people joining the YPG, the Syrian Kurdish movement. It's a rare act of solidarity between a Turk and a Kurd.

Food supplies eventually arrived the next day. We finally had those tomatoes and potatoes. '*Heval* Cengiz would have cooked us a feast,' Bercem said quietly as she was tasked with providing the food for our *tabur* that day and I helped her prepare. I threw up my food after eating that first day; and my shit, which up until then had been green, was completely black. Something was seriously wrong.

Levant, injured to the extent that he could no longer shoot, was smuggled out of Kobani on the same lorry that had brought our paltry food supplies, and crossed the border into Turkey as a civilian. I have not seen him since. I hope the Turkish state doesn't jail or execute him for fighting with the YPG against *Daesh*. The next day, after Bercem's cooked breakfast, I was summoned to a meeting with my YPJ commander, who told me it was time for me to leave the frontline and Kobani. It was impossible for me to think about leaving when I was there; as far as I was concerned, there was no such thing as life outside the siege. I didn't want to go and tried to refuse, but she said I could go to either Turkey or

Iraq: my stomach had swollen up and I needed to see a doctor. I could return afterwards, she promised.

I travelled back through our base in Rojava, our area in northern Syria, and made my way into Iraq. I slept for almost the entire journey, curled up in the back of a truck that seemed to operate as a taxi service for local farmers. Hidden under a pile of blankets as I crossed the border, I slept and sipped my bottle of water, feeling sick, sore and delirious.

Arriving in Erbil, I had a few days of sleeping in a bed and being served food as I rested. I went to the doctor's, but didn't tell them where I had been or what I had been doing, as I didn't trust them. I just told them I was visiting from Denmark and wasn't feeling well, after eating something that didn't agree with me. Which wasn't a lie. Though I felt like a failure at the time, being sent away from Kobani saved my life, as I missed the terrible winter that followed that starving summer. Friends of mine who survived there until the end say it wasn't until the start of winter that they began to call Kobani our Stalingrad, but it's hard for me to imagine how life could have become more difficult.

In Erbil I knew I was lucky to be alive, but I was sick with worry for my friends who had remained, and I felt this cloud of guilt and shame descend on me that I just couldn't shake. Cengiz was the last person I saw die in Kobani, but he wasn't the only person I lost in that fight. Girls as young as fourteen and boys as young as twelve died in that battle; this is not our policy in the YPG, but how could we stop them fighting for their lives?

As I recuperated in Erbil, every day on social media I would read reports from different rumour mills, and new martyrs' pictures made by the YPG would be posted in tribute to those who had died. I became fearful of checking online, as I didn't want to see who had died. But of course I had to know. I went online every single day, and frequently. I think this was when I first became addicted to social media, as it was my connection to my friends. Our *tabur*, called *Tabur Berivan*, was demolished – pushed back by *Daesh*, cut off by Turkey and undermined by the glacial speed and infighting among the international coalition.

In the darkness of Kobani we eventually defeated *Daesh*, despite the best attempts of Turkey to prevent us. By January 2015 we had cleared it of their black flags and dark hearts. We lost more than 1,000 fighters in Kobani, though the official death-toll reported in the international media was much lower. It was the first major battle that the YPJ contributed to, with a bravery the world hadn't seen from our army before. We fought fearlessly, along with the men, and accounted for about one-third of the fighters, but more than one-third of the deaths. For the women of the YPJ, it was not only about defeating *Daesh*, it was also about creating a new society in the Middle East, with new laws and cultures that value and respect women as equals. Many of the girls I fought with died for this, and several fighters – like Cengiz – blew themselves up in order to save their friends.

Shortly after I left Kobani, Arin Mirkan, who was a mother of two, committed suicide when her group was surrounded on the hill of Mistanound. She did this to save her friends. Her explosion allowed the other girls to escape when they were completely surrounded, and her *tabur* survived because of her heroism; she was their commander, and she died so they could live. These deaths are not our methods as YPG fighters, and the difference between us and *Daesh* is that they fight in this way to die for a promised paradise with glory and greed, but we fight so that others can live under our own democratic terms. The heroic act of Arin, and many like her, is the symbol of true friendship, which is everything in our movement. She valued the love of her friends more than her own life. That's why we say, '*Sehid namirin*' – 'Martyrs never die' – because the memory of them will live on for ever. They are the reason we are still here.

Those who ran out of ammunition were less lucky and were captured by *Daesh*, who tied their hands together and lashed them to the back of a car, then drove them through the city. It was a brutal public execution, and the civilians cheered – most likely because of fear, but it was an ugly thing to see.

I spent just over two weeks in that filthy old house in Kobani, and three years later my body is still recovering from what happened. Of the fifteen of us, only five from my *Tabur Berivan* of YPJ and YPG survived. I am the only YPJ fighter from my unit who made it out alive. For this I take absolutely no pride. I'm supposed to be one of the lucky ones, because I survived.

I'm still here, breathing the air of freedom that my friends gave their lives for, and I want to use my voice for those who lost theirs: the many hundreds of young Kurdish volunteers from Bakur (Turkish Kurdistan) who swam across the river, risking their lives on the way to the city that would become their grave; those who fought for love and friendship, and whose names will never be known. Even though press from all over the world were watching us, they didn't really *see* what was actually going on. They were recording us on their cameras like they were shooting a film, and we could see them looking at us and doing nothing to help. They were so close we could see them without binoculars, but they weren't as close to us as we were to *Daesh*.

Those watching us through the lens of their cameras could hear the bombing and shooting from the safety of the blockaded border, while I was hearing the screams and calls for help from my friends. They saw burning buildings, but my view was different: I watched the burning bodies of my friends.

CHAPTER ONE

Daughter of the War in the Desert

I f Kurdistan was a country, it would be one of the most populous states in the Middle East, with thirty million people scattered between Iran, Iraq, Syria, Turkey and Azerbaijan. This is just the official toll, the real number is believed to be as many as fifty million. Turkey and Iran refuse to acknowledge their Kurdish populations, and therefore don't count correctly the number of Kurds living within their borders, so it's hard to know for sure how many we are.

My family was originally from the eastern part of Kurdistan, in the western part of Iran, which we Kurds call '*Rojhelat*', meaning sunrise. In the YPG, our area in northern Syria is the western part of Kurdistan and we call it '*Rojava*', meaning sundown. In Kurdish we also use the words *Rojhelat* for east, and *Rojava* for west. *Bakur*, our northern area, means 'north' in our language, and geographically is situated in south-east Turkey. *Bashur*, our southern area, is in the northern part of Iraq and we use this word for south.

Most Kurds speak Kermanji, which is spoken in Bakur and Rojava. Some Bakur Kurds still speak the original Kermanji, called Zazaki, but also different dialects, such as Sorani, Badini, Feyli, Kalhuri and Hawramani, which are also spoken in Rojhelat. Originally my family spoke Kalhuri, but now we speak Sorani or a kind of pidgin-mixture of both. Because of the different dialects, it's pretty common for Kurds to struggle to understand each other.

My grandparents are both children of the Mahabad Republic, the first and only independent state declared by the Kurds in January 1946, and destroyed by the Iranian regime in December that same year. Along with their parents, my grandparents supported the Democratic Party of Iranian Kurdistan (PDKI) when it was formed the year before. As the first Kurdish armed movement to become an official political party, the PDKI was established to promote democracy, social justice and gender equality, rejecting monarchy, theocracy and autocracy. Supported by the Soviet Union, the PDKI ran our republic for the five years leading up to the official declaration in 1946. The PDKI continue to train *Peshmerga* (our word for fighter, which translates as 'one who stands in front of death') to defend Rojhelat from the Islamic regime of Iran. After our nation was destroyed by the Shah of Iran in December 1946, many PDKI leaders were executed, but the party remained in existence. My grandfathers met while my family was still inside Iran, as they both served as *Peshmerga* fighting against the regime of the Shah in 1967. This is how my mother and father would later come to know each other.

My mother's family farmed the mountains outside Kermanshah in the countryside of Serpeli-Zahab, which is right on the border with Iraq. Even within this small region there are several dialects: Kermanshani, Kalhuri, Sorani and Feyli. Working as an informal cooperative, her family produced food and reared animals to trade. My mother didn't go to school in Iran or Iraq – her education comes from Denmark. My father believes the lack of women's education is one of the reasons why Kurdistan still doesn't have its own nation state, and he was educated very well by his family along with his brothers in Iran, but his studies were cut short by the war. All of the sons in his family, just like my mother's, became *Peshmerga* as soon as they were old enough. This led to several relatives and friends being executed and killed inside Iran, so my father had to leave.

While my father's family is mainly Sunni Muslim, one of his brothers was a Christian – which didn't bother his family, but made him even more of a target for Iran's Revolutionary Guards. He would sneak around to attend services run by the American Church groups that existed inside Iran. He was abducted many times, but he could not confess to crimes that he had not done, so his captors would eventually grow tired and release him. They tortured him because he was a Kurd, first and foremost, but also due to his belief in a Christian God and their belief that he was an agent of 'the Great Satan' – America. Kurds are mainly Sunni Muslims, and the regime remains a Shia theocracy. To be a Kurd in Iran at the time – male or female – was to be an enemy of the state, and to be Sunni inside Iran still remains very difficult.

My mother's father was a *Peshmerga* commander and captain for the former president of Bashur, Mala Mustafa Barzani. He was also a farmer, who would take animals to trade in the markets inside the old souks of Kermanshah, our city in Iran. Our area, also called Kermanshah, has the highest Kurdish population in Iran and extends far beyond the city, almost from the city of Hamadan towards Tehran, and to the border with Iraq on the other side. It is home to Shia and Sunni Muslims as well as Circassians and Christians, which makes it unique as a region inside Iran. Although the city suffered in the Iran–Iraq wars during the 1980s, the people of Kermanshah are relatively open-minded for the Middle East. Different cultures live peacefully together, as they are all threatened by the regime. Young people especially look west for their hopes for the future – devouring American media, fashion and popular culture – or at least the ones I know do.

My mother thinks she was eleven when her family fled on foot from Iran into Iraq. As she never went to school or learned to count, she isn't even sure when she was born: she thinks it was 1971. She has a very conservative view of how a family, and especially women, should be. She married my father when she was fourteen years old, in a match arranged by my grandfathers, who met again when their families were both living in the Al-Tash camp in Ramadi, after they fled Iran.

Marrying young remains very normal in my culture, and in my family. Back in my mother's day – which is not so long ago really, as she is not yet fifty – girls would be married as soon as they had their first period. My mum used to say it was for our own sake, because waiting longer would mean a girl was more likely to have physical contact with a man, which, in my mother's opinion, is a fate worse than death. As our mother, it is up to her to police our sexuality and ensure that we protect the family name until we are married. The younger this happens, the better. I am twenty-five now, and my not being married is a source of discomfort for my family. We talk a lot about girls in our community, and as a girl gets older and remains unmarried, rumours about her start. People look down on her, and talk badly of her mother for not being 'woman enough' to raise girls properly. Everything we do right, our father takes the credit for, but for everything we do wrong, our mother takes the blame.

A woman being independent, or living alone, is treated suspiciously by the community. After a certain age – normally late teens or very early twenties – marriage prospects for girls like me shrink, and offers of marriage start coming in from older, divorced or disabled men; those with lower status. If you are unmarried after twenty-five, in the community I grew up in, most likely your fate is to stay unmarried or to become a man's second wife or mistress. In the Islamic world it's estimated that one in every five men practises polygamy, and sadly many men in Europe practise it, too. If, like me, you are not a virgin, your prospects are worse still.

In the 1980s, when my mother was growing up, the Iran–Iraq war was fought mainly in Kurdish areas, and villages all along the border were destroyed by Saddam Hussein's *Ba'athist* party soldiers, who suspected the villagers of being traitors to the Iraqi government, or loyal to Iran. Hussein was a dictator who fought against anyone who wasn't a *Ba'ath* supporter. During the disaster of the wars, our neighbouring countries supported different Kurdish armed movements, and different tribes aligned with them in return for food, supplies, shelter and protection. This led to different Kurdish factions fighting each other, and although the conflict between Iran and Iraq eventually stopped, their wars against the Kurds never did. The Iraqi border with Iran became porous, as Iranian Kurds (from the PDKI) brought supplies over the mountain to fight against Saddam, and other *Peshmerga* fighters from Iraq (from the Kurdish Democratic Party, known as the PDK) used the borders to fight the regime of Iran. Many of the Kurds living near the border were nationalists against the *Ba'ath* party and Saddam, but were also opposed to the Islamic regime of Iran. My family, like many in the region, was against them both. Thousands of Kurds fled from Iraq into Iran, but going back to Iran, as supporters and members of the PDKI, was not an option for us.

My family name, Palani, has long been associated with the PDKI, and still is. After living in Balkan camp near Sulaimaniya in northern Iraq, both my father and my mother were moved, with their families, by an NGO to the Al-Tash camp near the desert in Ramadi, in the centre of the country. Some of my father's family were moved south from Balkan to Halabja, and lived there from 1987 until the 1988 attacks.

On 16th March 1988 Saddam Hussein's forces dropped chemical bombs on the city of Halabja, killing thousands of civilians. More than 5,000 people were poisoned that day, and many more died as a result of their injuries in the months and years that followed. It is the greatest crime ever inflicted on our community, and remains the biggest gas attack ever launched against a civilian area. Halabja was not the only gas attack against members of my family, but it was the most personally devastating, as many of our immediate relatives died: thirty family members in all. My maternal grandmother lost her entire family. We have only one picture of my aunts who died, from when they were younger girls with my grandfather in Iran. We don't have any pictures of their children or family, so I often wonder when I see the famous images of the attacks if the bodies of the children I am looking at are the remains of my relatives. I will never know.

My mother had me quite young, but before me she had my three brothers and one of my sisters. My mother had all her babies in Ramadi: six in total. Two years before I was born, in 1991, things became more difficult for my family, as we had taken part in another failed uprising against Saddam Hussein. My father worked as a pharmacist, but like all *Peshmerga*, he helped the American soldiers when the Iran–Iraq war turned into the Gulf War in 1990.

Working with the Americans was a political pivot for my grandparents, as the Soviet Union had previously been our allies supporting the Mahabad Republic, and we were now aligning with US forces; but, as Kurds, we are not afraid of making strategic alliances against our enemies. As Kurds, we are targeted by the countries within whose false borders we live: Turkey, Syria, Iraq and Iran; and by their strategic backers. After Halabja, Saddam Hussein was our common enemy and we got help from the USA to depose him.

My father speaks five languages, having benefited from his education in Iran under the Shah, and worked with the USA to help the soldiers with logistics, translation and supplies in Iraq. When the Americans originally came to Ramadi they had not expected conditions to be as desolate as they were, and they were forced to leave again so that they could plan properly for a bigger operation. My father managed supply routes for them and spent some time working as a translator. He speaks with an American accent when he talks English, as many Kurds do. The

US soldiers would guard our camps so that Saddam's soldiers couldn't come in, and their combat medics would give basic treatments to those in dire need.

The Americans promised that a Kurdish region would be established in Iraq after Saddam fell, so naturally many Kurdish men joined up to secure this and to avenge our dead. But the Americans lost the Gulf War – they left in 1991 with Hussein still in power – and when they suddenly left Ramadi, our camps were attacked. We were on the retreating side and, as punishment for working with the Americans, we were again targeted by the regime. Around this time our camp in Ramadi suffered an attack, and my older brother Mariwan was killed due to the lack of medicine and treatment provided for our people from the hospital in Baghdad. Lots of our people died; from bad medicine, from no medicine, but mainly from the regime's attacks.

My brother was two years old when he died and was buried in the desert along with the others who were killed. Neither my mother nor father talks about him. The trauma of his bloody death lives on in both their hearts, and my mother places this event as the moment their marriage began to disintegrate. I'm not sure. I've only really seen my mother hysterical once in my life, and it was when one of my two surviving older brothers got sick. She screamed at my father and said that if another of her sons died, she would go with them and he would be left with us. Mariwan was named after a Kurdish city in Rojhelat, but in our family everyone called him Rambo, because he was very big when he was born, with white skin and black hair. There was one old TV in the camp, where we would watch American films huddled together, and *Rambo* was everyone's favourite show.

Mariwan was supposed to grow up to be a warrior, like our father and grandfather.

A few years after my brother died, on 22 February 1993, I was born. My mother said I arrived at first light on another freezing-cold day. I was named Hero Palani – a Kurdish name, but also after the Greek goddess Hera – by my father, but my beloved Christian uncle Jabbar changed my name to Joanna, which means 'beautiful' in Kurdish. I remember more from Ramadi than my siblings, but within our family there is endless debate over whether we actually remember events or just *think* we do, because we know the story behind the photograph. Old photographs are a particularly valuable commodity in my family: both my parents jealously guard pictures of their family and their childhoods in Iran, and then of ours in Iraq. There is a certain preciousness to our photographs; spread out as we are, and destroyed by such an array of enemies, these pictures are often the only evidence we have of our relatives and our past. In Kurdish culture we celebrate the group – the family, the community and the clan – instead of the individual, and the rules of the clan are the rules by which we live. The pictures of my family in Ramadi show us all huddled in a big tent. Inside, almost a whole wall of our tent is taken up with coloured blankets, and some of my earliest memories of Ramadi are playing on these blankets and looking up at the sky.

My father, uncle and I are the only ones who remember the Ramadi camp as it really was, for the rest of my family have these weirdly romantic memories of our lives there. I remember it as a dry and dirty place, without much food or water. I would accompany my older siblings and other relatives to dig for water in the sand. Because it's in the desert, Ramadi scorches in the summer and freezes during the winter. We would be sent to bed with gloves and hats on inside our tents, and if we complained of a chill we would be allowed to sleep in between my mother and father, along with my youngest sister, who in my mind was permanently attached to my mother's chest. I've never learned to sleep properly, and my memories of bedtime are of lying shivering in between my parents, or trying to find some relief from the oppressive heat. Many infants died from pneumonia and hypothermia in Kurdish camps around this time; it's hard to know how many, as we are not the kind of community the regime was interested in recording, and we would never trust them to keep count accurately anyway. Because of the lack of medicine, vaccines and healthy food, my siblings and I suffered from malnutrition. We had those big stomachs you see on television, where the swelling was caused by not having enough protein in our diet – a condition known as kwashiorkor.

I was too young to go to school, so I stayed with my mother and my baby sister as our older brothers and sister went for lessons. They had to walk to school from our tent in single file, with one standing in front of the other with a branch, so that if they came across a landmine, only one of them would be killed. When my brother and sister went to school, my mother would sit in the front of our tent and fix her hair and inspect her face, using a tiny pocket mirror that she would hold up to the light. She would always become very annoyed if we got dirty, and once we were washed we were expected to stay clean for as long as possible. Water was a precious commodity, so we weren't allowed to wash too frequently.

My older sister would collect sticks from ice-cream lollies from around the camp and we would transform them into dolls, and build them houses and furniture from the rubbish that we found in the sand. We had many cousins and family members across the camp, so we would sometimes spend the day or night with them in their tents or houses. Behind the tents the boys would play football, making a ball from different plastic bags fashioned together – the older boys managing to copy the stripes of a leather ball surprisingly well. The women built ovens to prepare the bread daily, and dug deep holes in the sand for water. Every night everyone would gather around the TV to watch the news. Although the camp had two entrances and exits, us Kurds shared with the Shia families, and we all lived together.

Saddam's soldiers were called 'the redheads' because of the berets they wore as they stomped around our camp. After the Americans left, they would come in whenever they felt like it, and my aunt would tell us kids to run and hide inside our tents. Our *Peshmerga* had no weapons in the camps, so we had no choice but to agree to whatever the soldiers demanded. They of course targeted our women, raping them with absolutely no consequences to themselves. In the Middle East, most people consider a girl able to have sex as an adult after she has had her first period. A 'woman' is normally a married person who has had sex, whereas a 'girl' has not had sex. The redheads would take any girl they wished, and they did so often. The girl was sometimes taken away from her family and never seen again – trafficked into prostitution or killed – or was returned to her family after the rape, so that the family would be destroyed by the shame. Either way, the girl's life was over. In a war created by men, the girls are sacrificed.

After the Americans had left, leaving the camp open to attack from Saddam, the military bases and medical hospitals all packed up and left; it was only the NGOs that remained. Suddenly everyone was trying to leave the camp, in case the redheads came back again. There was fear that the first bombardment was just a precursor to a second attack, and that they were planning to gas us alive. We had no gas masks of course, but my parents taught us how to cover our faces and ears with our clothing.

The United Nations helped my family apply for asylum to leave Ramadi, and suddenly, in 1996, we were told we were going to Denmark, as UN refugees. We got to leave more quickly than other families because of what had happened to Meriwan, but my aunt was not allowed to travel with us at the time. I remember three big buses coming to collect us and several other families who were going to Scandinavia. The women who were staying behind sobbed as we boarded the buses, and the crowd was so big that the bus driver got annoyed at everyone hugging each other through the open windows. My mother tells me that she held up me and my little sister at the back of the bus, so that my aunt could look at us one last time through the window, and then held me and cried into my coat until we arrived at the field where the plane was. She talks about our aunts a lot, and we remain close to them when we travel back to Kurdistan. Today I'm closer to my family in Kurdistan than to my immediate family here in Denmark.

On the plane I have vague memories of sitting beside the window and being high in the air, above our camp, and flying away from Iraq. There were many children running up and down the aisles, but my parents made us sit still in our seats and hold hands. We sat pinned down into our seats with big seatbelts across us, until I fell asleep looking out of the window.

The big signs saying 'UN' and 'WELCOME' let us know we had arrived safely in Copenhagen. I held my big sister's hand as we were leaving the plane with the other families, and my father held my little sister in his arms as she was sleeping. Everyone in Denmark was dressed very differently from us, and the women were wearing trousers and had these big mops of yellow hair, which I had seen on television in the camp, but never in real life. There was a group of NGO women at the airport, who met us and gave us food and water, and all of us children were given toys. They helped us with our luggage, which consisted mainly of blankets, our photographs of course and some special items of clothing belonging to my brother who had been killed.

Someone took a picture of us at the time, and in it my parents are wearing their traditional Kurdish clothes. My father is wearing his brown baggy *Peshmerga* trousers and the white leather shoes we make in the Kurdish mountains. He has a white shirt under his outfit and a long rope-like belt wrapped around his waist many times. My mother is wearing her Islamic headscarf, and although she looks very beautiful and maybe relieved, she is the only one in the picture who is not smiling. Growing up, I never understood why she wasn't smiling. Today, I think I might.

CHAPTER TWO

Growing Up Kurdish

I arrived in Denmark in 1996, when I was three years old. My first home in Denmark was a small apartment in Vrå, a very small city in northern Jutland, furnished for us by the government, who, at the time, helped refugees much more than they do now. It was the old 'Social Democrats' who were in charge at the time. I say 'old' because they were more leftist back then. As more people have immigrated to Denmark, every party has become less leftist and more central, and sometimes it feels like the left and the right are meeting in the middle in some strange way.

Our whole family had free Danish lessons, and a social worker called Jeanne assigned to us to help us settle. We all adored Jeanne and called her *Jiyan*, which is the Kurdish word for life, and she helped us navigate the unfamiliar territory of our new home. We were one of only two Kurdish families settled in the area at the time, and huge efforts were made to help us integrate. My mother and father were humbled and thankful finally to be able to provide a life for us. Everything was totally different. My mother, who had learned how to cook as a child from her mother, with very few ingredients, had to completely relearn how to work the stove and the oven and the gas cooker in our indoor kitchen. She attended special classes for ethnic-minority women like her, to learn how to cook Danish food. These classes were called 'integration' classes, but I think part of her resented them for being so patronizing, as she would call them 'indoctrination' classes behind Jeanne's back.

My mother was always concerned that we would be brainwashed by the Danes, and that they were on some mission to make us forget who we were and where we are from. Being in Europe was a blessing for us, but we were never really allowed to leave Kurdistan behind. The cultures, practices and ways of behaviour travelled with us, and manifested most obviously in how my sisters and I were expected to behave. My mother has always been slightly scandalized by Danish women. She was shocked at how involved women are in all aspects of society, and initially slightly aghast at the kinds of activities that Danish girls take part in. She was always screaming at Jeanne that we weren't allowed to climb trees or take part in anything too physical. 'She could fall and lose her virginity!' was my mother's most anguished cry for us.

My virginity was never mine; it belonged to my family and it was more important to them than my health and well-being. Like many Muslim immigrant girls across Europe, I lived a slightly parallel life: the rights of a young European woman, but the rules of my conservative family. Everything was what we call *ayib*, meaning shameful; or *haram*, which means not allowed by the Quran. Our god, Xua, was permanently watching me for signs of disobedience. My whole family would go to hell if either me or my sisters displeased Xua by our loose Danish behaviour, my mother would always warn us. As a Kurdish wife and mother brought up in this tribal way, she was the enforcer of the invisible rules that governed us, as girls and young women. My brothers were also expected to enforce these invisible rules of honour. It was their job to 'protect' us, as girls in their family, from showing off, talking with boys, dancing: doing anything that could bring *ayib* on our family.

For as long as I can remember, I was not allowed to play with boys, even at the kindergarten I attended with my older sister and brothers. 'It's your CUL-ture,' my kindergarten teacher would sing-song to me, when I asked why. Despite their very basic command of the Danish language, my parents had ensured that all of my educators were aware of the special rules my sisters and I had to abide by in school, and we were policed accordingly. So for me the word 'culture' came to represent rules and regulations imposed upon me that made me different from my classmates. I was already so different from the others in my class: I looked and felt very different, with my dark hair and swarthy skin, and I spoke differently of course, because I was still picking up the language. We didn't speak Danish as a family, and it was rare for me and my sisters to spend time outside our family.

When we painted in class, my friends would draw me with huge eyebrows and a big mop of hair, like a monkey. I don't think they were necessarily being cruel; I think I was a shock to them. It was just kids being kids, but that doesn't mean it didn't hurt me. Feeling so different and not understanding why was a frustrating experience, and my teachers, thinking they were being helpful by imposing the rules of my home in class, often made things worse. I made some friends as I started to speak

Danish, two guys I played with in class called Line and Mathias, and we would make secret dens under the table. One day we were under the table painting a picture. The teacher, Hanne, got really mad when she found us and grabbed me so hard she left a purple bruise on my arm. 'You are not allowed to do that,' she snapped at me and made me promise to tell my parents I had been misbehaving when I got home.

I responded with what I think is my first-ever lie: promising to tell my parents what I had done, when I knew I wouldn't dare, because I would be beaten. Perhaps she could tell I was lying, as this didn't seem to satisfy Hanne, so she called my parents up to the school. What had annoyed her and what would annoy my parents were actually worlds apart and showed how clueless most of my teachers were to this parallel life I was living: Danish rights and freedoms, but Kurdish laws and culture. When my parents arrived at the school, no one could find me, as I was so scared I hid from them in a bush, shaking and crying. Being caught with a boy under a table was something I knew would be severely punished, so I hid like a scared dog in our play area outside.

One of the other kindergarten teachers, a kind man called Mads, found me. He gently coaxed me out of the hedge and brought me to my family. When I looked into my father's eyes, I knew exactly what I was going home to. Sitting in the back of his green Nissan with my brothers on either side of me, it started before we even arrived. 'All of you girls will have white sheets on your wedding night, do you hear me?' He spoke through gritted teeth, and allowed my brothers to pull my hair to make me listen better. 'All of you girls will have white sheets.' What he meant was that we would be virgins – the sheets would be stained with blood.

My brother said it more openly: 'You hooker – if there isn't blood on your sheet on your wedding night, we will kill you.' I cried and asked for forgiveness and promised him I was still a virgin, but because I wasn't entirely sure what a virgin was, or what I had done, I began to fret and worry for the future. Maybe I had shamed our family for ever? My mother slapped me across the face when I got home, and told me to think of everyone in Kurdistan that I was hurting and disrespecting by behaving in this way. I was beaten up and locked downstairs in our basement – the two punishments that became my most frequent ones as a young child.

Before I really understood what my virginity was, I knew how important it was. Boys were potential thieves of this virginity, and if my virginity was stolen – if I didn't bleed on my wedding night – my father and brothers would have to kill me. It was that simple; this was their threat and, at the time, I had no reason to disbelieve it. This is what we call honour in our culture, and it's the most important thing for every Middle Eastern family I know. The girls of the family must have a clean reputation, and if they don't then the whole family will be shamed.

A few days later I was allowed back to kindergarten. I couldn't work out why Hanne didn't like me, and why she had called my parents. Though she might have been trying to be sensitive to my background, and the values my parents brought with them from Iraq, she betrayed me by telling my parents. I don't think she could have imagined their reaction to this affront to my honour, and therefore to theirs. I was beaten badly, in a way that was maybe normal for children to be beaten in the camps in Ramadi, but which would have shocked my teacher, I am sure.

It was the first time I realized that my teachers were not on my side – a lesson I sadly had to learn several more times over the next decade. Denmark is now fairly multicultural, or at least Copenhagen is, but back then it felt like we had arrived from a different planet. In the beginning, my family struggled to integrate us into Danish society, as our culture was so Kurdish at home. Growing up, I thought it was the cultural divide that caused this chasm, but now I believe it was more to do with their traumatic experience of war and death. My town of Vrå, and later Frederikshavn after we moved, was very homogenous back then – we couldn't walk down the street without at least one person pointing and staring – and feeling so different left us alienated in ways I couldn't quite grasp as a child.

My kindergarten teacher Hanne would never really let me forget I was special, and that I had to play by different rules. Those first years of school were probably the worst, in terms of policing me; thinking back now, it seems that Hanne just hated us Muslim girls. She didn't like my little sister, who followed me into our class the year afterwards, and seemed to relish our difference in a way that I would learn later was unusual. I had some difficulties hearing the differences between how certain Danish words end and instead of being helped to overcome this, I felt shamed by what I thought was my stupidity. Lots of Danes struggle with these kind of vocabulary problems but I was always made to feel like I couldn't get any better because I wasn't a Dane. I was different, and so was my culture and that was just how it was going to be for me.

Sometimes the fights I had with my family meant that I was kept out of school until my bruises healed. Taking me out of school was a way to punish me; like being grounded in the personal prison that my family home had become. As well as the beatings, one punishment my father meted out, when we first arrived from Iraq, was to hold my hand on the stove for a few seconds when I could not sleep. This was common practice at the camps in Ramadi – and we saw many children being punished like this when we were there – so it wasn't until we found out that others didn't get punished like this that we realized it was wrong.

One night my brother and I couldn't sleep, so my father held our hands over the stove to burn them; he normally did it lightly, but this time he held my hand down, and my palm scalded into ugly blisters. My mother had to bandage me up with special cream to stop an infection. I was eight at the time, and no one in school asked me in any great detail what had happened to my hand. Those who made cursory enquiries were given an improbable tale about playing a game that went wrong. It was confusing at that young age to feel somehow ashamed of myself and of my parents at the same time. I started to lie to friends about how good my family life was, and how close we were. As a Kurd, family is everything, so for me to admit that mine was chaotic and scary would have been the most shameful of all the many shameful things I did.

It's hard to evaluate how well my parents settled in Denmark – that's their story, not mine. They attended Kurdish society clubs and community centres. These clubs exist all over Europe, and there is normally a youth group attached, for those under eighteen. The youth group I was part of as a child was the PDKI youth wing, called *Lawan*. We would learn about Kurdish culture and meet other Kurdish children. We were encouraged to speak Kurdish, but often we were from different parts of Kurdistan and spoke different dialects, so when the adults weren't around we would talk mainly in Danish.

My father always warned us about Iranians, Turks and Arabs and what they had done to our people. He didn't really want us to learn Danish, as he wanted us to keep our mother tongue. 'A nation's language is the strongest weapon for their identity,' he would say to us, but obviously we all had to learn Danish. He speaks many languages himself, so I think it was more that he was concerned Kurdish wouldn't be our first language.

My father had his medical certificate from Tehran rejected by the local authorities and was unable to practise as a pharmacist. It was a bitter blow, as I think it affected how he saw himself. 'They accept the education and the training I have there. It's clear to see. So why can't they accept it?' he would ask himself. No one in Denmark seemed interested in his certificates, yet they were his pride and joy.

It was very painful for him to have to give up his profession, as he had assumed that it was his skills as a pharmacist that had formed part of why we were accepted into Europe in the first place – he was one of the few with a professional qualification working in the camps in Ramadi. In 2001 the Social Democrats lost the election, the government changed and the benefits we lived on were suddenly cut. Money was very tight, even with my father working two jobs as a waiter and a cleaner, so my mother worked outside the home as well – becoming the first woman in her family to do so. She worked in a launderette, cleaning sheets for hospitals and old people's homes, from 5 a.m. until 7 p.m.

From the age of eleven my oldest brother worked in a pizzeria to bring in money for the family, which is very normal in a Kurdish family, and my older sister helped my mother out a lot at home. They were typically good Kurdish children, while my second-eldest brother and my younger sister and I were more 'Danish', which I'm hoping you will have gathered by now wasn't a compliment in our home. To ensure we never got too Danish, we would go for long holidays home to Kurdistan every year, to stay with my extended family near the mountains. We stayed mainly in with my maternal grandfather, whom we call *Bawa*.

My mother's father would tell us stories about his life in Rojhelat – our eastern Kurdistan, their western Iran. He has many names, as he is still wanted in Iran for being a member of the PDK, for fighting the regime of the Shah and Sayyid Ruhollah Mūsavi Khomeini. He has been sentenced to death *in absentia* by an Iranian court, along with many other PDK soldiers, and is known for being a master tactician. We would sit around the fire in our courtyard at night eating pomegranates, and he would tell us stories from his time as *Peshmerga* captain for Mala Mustafa Barzani, the former Kurdish president from Bashur, who was also a general for the PDK in Rojhelat in the old days. My *Bawa* would explain the different tactics of our enemies in Iran, Iraq, Turkey and all over the world and how they work together. He is about eighty now and is the one member of the family I really listen to and honour.

Kurdistan was so different from Denmark and, weirdly, the restrictions placed upon me in Europe as a woman didn't seem to apply there. For my mother, though, it was much worse when she went 'home' to her family. Our family in Kurdistan was tough on her, as it's always the mother's responsibility to keep the family Islamic and Kurdish: all the shame lands on her. My father, on the other hand, was free to do whatever he wanted and to become as Western as he wished. According to their mad logic, that would be my mother's fault. My mum still lives under her strict Islamic rules in Denmark, yet no rules apply to my father. Women in Ramadi have stopped wearing the full headscarf and the large loose clothes, but my mother has not.

My uncles would take us hunting for wild pigs and the big rabbits we have in the Kurdish mountains – huge wild animals that look nothing like the tiny pets we keep in Europe. I cried the first time my uncle shot a little deer. I thought he had shot Bambi, and I remember the deer's eyes looking up at me as its pupils dilated. My cousins laughed at me for being upset, and I was careful not to stay upset for too long, in case I was sent back to the house to prepare the meals with my older sister, who seemed to love nothing more than coming all the way to Kurdistan to learn how to cook. She could make my mother so happy just by wanting to learn how to cook our traditional meals. When I demanded to go out with my uncles and cousins into the mountains, my mother would implore me to learn from my sister's example.

Our mountains in Kurdistan are stunning and are the location of my happiest childhood memories. The air is so clean and you can drink the water from the mountain streams. There are waterfalls and strong current pools that form at the bottom of different craters. As Kurds, we say we have no friends but the mountains, and what we mean by that is that we are one with them. We rely on them and believe them to be holy and sacred places. Kurdish mountains feature in both the Quran and the Bible: Mount Ararat is also known as Noah's Ark, and Zagros is our longest mountain range. It starts in Rojhelat (Iran) in the east and goes all the way to Bakur (Turkey) in the west. These are our mountains and they are our home. Halgurd is the tallest peak and rises more than 10,000 feet from the ground. We can live there, high up near the snow, in ways that others cannot, because it is not who they are. These mountain Kurds and my family taught me how to camp, how to make my own knife and how to make a fire. At night we would eat the animals we had shot that day – and so every day we had to make sure we caught something. We camped in the forest under the stars. I didn't learn to shoot in Kurdistan back then, but I learned a lot about hunting, and about the importance of making every shot count.

I was nine when I first picked up a loaded gun, at a competition in Finland. We were driving back from visiting my cousins up in the north of the country and came across a shooting competition taking place at one of the ranges. My father wanted to get out and have a look around for some things, so we walked about and had a picnic, and he bought some items at the market. My brothers and I noticed that there were children taking part in the competition with their parents. I couldn't believe it – despite pleading in Kurdistan, I was only ever allowed to carry the hunting gear or the ammunition. I was never allowed to shoot. I begged my father to let me have a go, so eventually he allowed my older brothers and me to take turns.

I had to make three shots, from three different positions. The other children were really good, and there was a girl around my age who was particularly adept at shooting from the prone position. The instructor told me what to do and I spent some time watching my brothers, who went before me. Insisting that I could hold the rifle myself, I held my eye too close to the scope when I fired. When the bullet released, the gun bounced back and hit me in the face, as I wasn't holding on tightly enough to avoid the blowback. The scope pushed into my eye, but I was so high from firing my shot I didn't even notice.

I was so small I had to fire in a sitting position, as I couldn't hold the gun properly standing up. Even sitting down it made my shoulder ache, but I loved it. I liked the power of the weapon and the fact that the power was not even within the weapon, but in the person behind it. I understood that it was up to me to become better, because the rifle could shoot, whether I was good or not. I found the girl of my own age and observed her as she concentrated and took her shot. She won her round of the competition and everyone was delighted for her. Even my father and older brothers were impressed.

When we got home from Finland, I begged my dad to let me go shooting again, to get better, and told him I wanted to follow in his footsteps. He bought me a rifle and began to let me go hunting with him. He didn't have a licence to hunt, but no one knew.

He was very patient with me, and slowly I learned. I really enjoyed those times we spent together, when he had time to show me how to hold the rifle, and how to operate it within the different conditions to ensure it worked as best it could. I'm a good listener, and I would listen in wonder as he explained all the different things you need to learn to help the shot: the wind speed, the temperature, even the time of day can affect the chances of hitting the target from a long distance. Slowly I learned which type of weapon was best for killing the different kinds of animal. I wasn't very good to start with, and I couldn't handle the rifle correctly as I was too small, but I listened.

It wasn't until I was thirteen that I managed my first deer-kill. And even though I had been working with my father for four years to achieve this kill, I didn't feel good about it when it finally happened. I was supposed to hit its heart, just beside the front legs. I had started by then to wonder if I could be a fighter, and instead of going for its heart, I tried to hit it between the eyes. I was lucky, but my father was annoyed as it took longer for the animal to die. He asked me why. 'That's what I'm training for,' I replied. He just laughed at me and didn't say anything, but I think he was proud.

In Kurdistan, that summer after I killed the deer, I went to the mountains to one of the survival training camps for Kurdish youth run by a group of *Peshmerga* and learned to slaughter a cow with a knife. Killing a deer with a gun was nothing compared to having to stab a cow. I was upset after I killed my first deer; after killing the cow, I felt like a murderer. It was totally different from shooting – completely brutal.

The *Peshmerga* youth camp consisted of three weeks of survival training in the mountains. We learned how to be junior guerrillas, how not to leave any traces of yourself or your presence. I wasn't allowed my phone, so just being away from my family with no contact for three weeks was a new experience. I had a bag with blankets, a filter for water, a lighter, a rope, a pen and paper and small snacks like sesame seeds. It was my idea to do these courses, as I wanted to be like my father and grandfather, a *Peshmerga* fighter. The organization that ran these camps still runs them today, as a pre-training course for Iranian *Peshmerga* fighters who are loyal to the PDKI. You start when you are a child with survival training, and then when you are old enough and have enough knowledge of general survival training, they will train you with rifles.

During those three weeks I learned how to use a knife and how to slaughter an animal, then skin it and barbecue it over the campfire, as I had seen before. I was never taught how to hurt; I was only taught to kill. There are no bomb-making clubs for kids, of course; they come later. The youth camps are near the Iranian border; one part of the mountain is in Iraq and one part in Syria. Kurdish kids like me from Europe, but also kids from all over Kurdistan, go and do this every summer. On my first camp there were about six of us, and I was the only girl from Europe, but of course I wasn't the only girl doing the training. Girls fight in Kurdistan. We have to.

The camps were also an opportunity for us to learn and converse in Kurdish, and at night we would sit around the fire and sing songs, or listen to stories about the Kurdish fighters and their brave battles against our many enemies. I didn't really understand what I was hearing, but I listened and tried to absorb as much as I could, and it was much better than being with my family.

Learning about the women fighters, and seeing the other girls on my course, allowed me to connect my struggle with my family in Denmark to the wider struggle that Kurdish women face. We fight enemies all over our region, but also the inequalities within our communities. The honour of being a fighter seemed to be the greatest honour a Kurdish woman could achieve. I had just become a teenager when I went to my first camp, and I had just had my first period. I wasn't a child any more. When I came back three weeks later I considered myself a different person: a grown-up, capable of learning how to be a fighter, and determined to realize this dream. That's when my double life began.

CHAPTER THREE

Rights Before Rules

President Masoud Barzani, the president of the Iraqi Kurdistan region, was in combat as a thirteen-year-old, fighting alongside his father, Mala Mustafa Barzani. My father and his older brother were both already *Peshmerga* when they were thirteen, fighting next to their fathers, but when I was this age I was stuck in school in Jutland, following all sorts of different rules.

I wasn't getting on with my parents particularly well at this age, as I wanted to be able to be like my friends, and wanted their support in this. I had rules at home, and rules at school. At school I loved learning about science, religion, social studies and politics, and in my early teen years I went to dance class and became a cheerleader. I always liked dancing, as I felt free whenever I danced.

My family was against me dancing and cheerleading, and refused to come and see any of my shows. My father once showed up after we had just finished a cheerleading performance, along with this Danish lady friend that he had started some kind of relationship with, despite still being married to my mother. I was so happy to see him, so I ran up to him like the other girls did to their parents who came every week. Instead of grabbing me in his arms and hugging me, he pushed me away and said I had to stop dancing as my behaviour was bringing shame on the family. Then he and his girlfriend left. I told my dance teacher I would have to stop, but I didn't want to quit immediately.

The only place I could find peace was at school and through cheerleading. It was such a great feeling to use my body to settle my mind. I would jump around with the girls and I could release what I didn't have the words to express. In those moments, I was on top of the world, and I felt free to be Joanna. We had so much fun in my team. We were all young girls, but we thought we were so sophisticated in our uniforms. I formed deep friendships with my cheerleading friends – my first 'proper' friends outside of our family that I associated with. They made me feel liberated. I wasn't told what to do, and I didn't have to serve anyone. My thoughts were allowed to be heard and my feelings weren't a sin. They liked my clothes, and how I looked. I wasn't shouted at for laughing, or being too loud: we were all loud, we were having fun together.

My family had been against my cheerleading from the start, but initially they had to accept it. It was only when my father and brothers started blaming my mother for my dishonour that I decided to stop. It wasn't worth the drama or the huge family rows that would happen after practice.

I couldn't understand how different my family's expectations for me were compared to the expectations of my teachers, or the dreams I had for myself. My life as a teenager was about rules, and my slow realization of my rights. As a Middle Eastern girl, I was being given fewer and fewer rights and more and more rules, the older I got. My behaviour was constantly monitored, and I was expected to be many things – shy, quiet, subservient – that I had no interest in being.

Dancing and cheerleading were two of my first cultural acts of rebellion and independence against my parents, although I don't think I was aware of it at the time. As a Muslim girl, it was seen as dishonourable to be jumping around to music while everyone watched. I didn't want to disappoint my family, especially my mother; I just wanted to dance. Cheerleading might look beautiful, but it is tough work and you have to be strong, fast and fit.

My older brothers and I were fighting a lot at this time, and they would attempt to use their strength against me, but training made me stronger. Before cheerleading, I already enjoying running and, after my brothers beat me up at home, I would go on long walks, and sometime long runs. When I was first training to get onto the squad, these runs and my training became more intense; I would sprint up hills and perform hundreds of press-ups every day, until I began to notice muscles popping out of my arms and legs. One day my older brother and I were fighting and he pulled me by the hair into a choke-hold grip, but I managed to get away. It was the first time he had not been able to overwhelm me physically and, in my mind at least, it heralded a new stage in our relationship.

Being able to fight him made me more determined to get stronger for my own sake. My mother would defend me from my brother sometimes, but she would also say that I needed to stop dreaming and learn what was needed to become a wife and mother, like other Kurdish girls. That was my destiny,

she said, and I would argue with her by asking her questions
that she couldn't really answer. 'What is a woman? What is a
Kurdish woman?' I would ask. 'What does that actually mean?'
As it was explained to me, a woman from Kurdistan was not
entitled to dream of her own destiny. My destiny was cut out
for me by my parents: I would cook, clean, organize and take
care of my brothers, so that one day I would be capable of
cooking, cleaning, organizing and caring for whoever would
be my husband. I realized how, in the Danish world, men and
women were more equal, and that only primitive societies turned
their women into servants – but it was hard to recognize my
community as primitive or being at any kind of fault. It was a
constant collision of viewpoints.

When I was fourteen and in seventh grade, we moved to Aalborg,
a bigger city in the north of Denmark. Aalborg was where I first
started living my double, or even triple, life. I had to behave a
certain way at home, and another way in school with the classmates
I was trying to turn into friends, and I also started becoming more
seriously interested in Kurdish identity politics.

As Kurds, we are born completely enmeshed in our culture,
our stories, the memories of our dead, and the injustices we have
suffered in the past and continue to suffer. I first learned about
the female fighters of the Kurdish movement in the songs of
our martyrs that my mother would sing to me as a baby – and
we would sing them at the various cultural evenings and family
gatherings that we attended in Denmark and Kurdistan. Having
done mountain survival training as a young teenager, I went
on a few more of these courses in Kurdistan over the next few

years. I started becoming especially interested in female fighters around this time, and in understanding the complexities of fighting for freedom in the context of human rights and justice.

I had increased respect for my father and grandfather, for their resistance against the Islamic regime of Iran and Saddam, even if I was finding my father's behaviour at home hard to handle. The more I learned, the more I became determined to follow in their footsteps, but also to fight for women's rights in my community, because that was certainly not something we had achieved. I began to read more about armed movements and women's struggles around the world. I never dared to say it out loud back then: that I wanted to become a female fighter.

I started becoming more engaged with various human-rights groups in Aalborg and beyond, and I spent a long time trying to figure out where I would fit in. Sometimes these rights groups work together and sometimes they don't, so I took my time to learn about the different groups and how they were active in Europe, but also about those linked to the Middle East. Some had different policies when it came to women, and some had a history of famous female fighters, whose stories I devoured as much as I could.

I became more active within the Kurdish youth movements that I had been attending through *Lawan*, and more interested in learning about Iran, Iraq, Syria and Turkey in general, and their relationship to our Kurdish issue. At school I was learning a lot in our society classes about politics, geo-policy and conflicts around the world, particularly in the Middle East – my part of the world. I wouldn't believe the textbooks sometimes, and argued fiercely against those who said that Turkey, for example, was a democratic and tolerant country. My experience had taught me differently. I believe that an educated mind is the best weapon a woman can have against men. I'm still learning, and I want my mind to be as highly educated as possible. A woman who knows her own mind can be a threat to many religions and ideologies, even those who praise women.

In Aalborg I started seriously dreaming about my future, as I was sure I wanted to use my life for something more than simply being a servant to a Kurdish man. My home situation became unbearable during this time, and I eventually moved in with my Christian uncle Jabbar for a few years.

Jabbar and his family lived near us, and I had become close to him as a younger teenager, as he was a lot more laid-back than my parents. He was very educated and would share his love of biology, geography and astronomy with us. He had a telescope, which he showed my cousin Shorash and me how to use. Jabbar worked as a waiter in a restaurant, so he had late shifts and would work until the early hours of the morning. I would wait for him to come home so he could tell me a story before going to bed at night, even though I had school the next morning.

I visited church a few times with Jabbar, and he would tell me about Adam and Eve and Jesus. I never fully believed in any religion, as I have always thought that the question of God's existence is beyond our limited knowledge as human beings, but I liked being educated further, and I liked asking questions about the morals on which the practice of religion is based. Being with my uncle's family was better, and I helped his wife take care of his kids, but this improvement was only to last a short time.

Having suffered from PTSD, from his time being persecuted in Iran, my beloved uncle didn't get the help he needed when he joined us in Denmark, and took his life by stabbing himself with a knife and cutting his own throat. I was the one to find him in the room with my baby cousins, but it was too late to rescue him. I alerted my aunt, who became hysterical and started screaming and tearing her hair out. I quickly took my cousins to their neighbours and ran back to my aunt, to get her away from my uncle and into their bedroom.

She screamed and cried as I tried to hug her and calm her. My cousin Shorash, who had a different biological mother from his siblings, was not home on that day, and when he returned we had to tell him what had happened. He was now an orphan, and the events of that day changed him for ever. After Jabbar died, I moved back in with my parents, but I spent as little time as possible at home.

Two weeks after he died, we had guests arrive from Kurdistan to mourn. Everyone dressed in black and the rooms were divided by gender, with my sisters and I serving everyone. After the guests left my uncle's house, I found my aunt crying in the kitchen alone. I approached her carefully and asked her in Sorani what was wrong. '*Chia mamozhin?*' I said.

She didn't respond, so I went back into the hall and found my mother also weeping to herself. My father was in the sitting room eating watermelon and bread and talking on the phone. I returned to the kitchen to get my mother a glass of water. My father was speaking to our relatives at home in Kurdistan about my uncle's children and his death. My aunt had been given a choice: accept becoming my father's second wife and keep her children, or find another husband but lose the children. The hand carrying the water that I had fetched for my mother started shaking as I understood what had occurred.

I returned to my mother and placed the glass I had been carrying in her hand. '*Daya, ama chia?*' I said softly – what's going on here?

She couldn't speak in her normal voice, she was so appalled. She whispered in a hoarse voice, cursing my aunt. 'All I have done for her. I have made her the woman she is now, and look what she does to me.' My aunt had travelled from Kurdistan to Denmark, and my mother had taken her under her wing, introduced her to the community and taught her how to live in Europe. They had loved each other as the sister-in-laws they were. 'She is going to take everything from me,' my mother choked, and buried her face in her scarf.

I patted her back as she rocked herself, to calm her breathing down. I realized I was still trembling, and I went over and looked at my father. With Jabbar dying, I had lost my true father figure; this entitled man could never be a father to me, if he couldn't be a good man to my mother.

The choice to lose your children is no choice at all, so of course the marriage was done. I hated my father for his decision and his hypocrisy, to suddenly impose this piousness on us. He, who had a Danish girlfriend, and who used the freedom of Europe to exploit the benefits for himself, but kept my mother in a Ramadi cage. Something happened to him when he returned my uncle's body for burial in Iran. He came back the picture of a middle-aged Islamic man, whereas before he had never been a big one for praying. It pushed me from his movement politically as well, as I looked for answers for his behaviour within the Kurdish movement and couldn't find many.

The movement for Kurdish freedom and democracy is very complex, and few who are not Kurds have any understanding of the array of different parties and their groups. Each group is normally from a particular location; you always know where you belong, and it's normally close to where you were born. Many thousands of Iranian Kurds fled into Europe – either directly from Iran or, like us, from Iraq after being caught up in the war. Before us, many thousands of Kurds had already fled from Turkey to Germany, France and Sweden.

Each different Kurdish region has a number of Kurdish parties that they brought with them to Europe, and many have formed councils and, at different times in our history, even parliaments in exile. There is no one party that all Kurdish people get behind; we are from geopolitical countries that speak different languages, use different Latin or Arabic scripts, and there are many divisions between the groups. Just as it is not uncommon to have different religions within one family, there can also be very different political alliances within families. Political alliances are more of a priority than religion for most of us.

Our internal battles, as Kurds, have long been exploited by the political countries that occupy our land; Iran, Iraq, Turkey and Syria have all used our soldiers against each other for their own political gain, as well as the USA and Russia. Each of the different Kurdish communities, from each different area, has a different political party attached to it, and attached to each party is the military wing. Some of these parties work together and have similar viewpoints or share the same ideology, but more often there is one wider rights agenda, and lots of political posturing as to how best to achieve these rights.

Lawan was the first Kurdish community group I was involved in that was linked to the Iranian *Peshmerga* fighters. *Lawan* is on the mid-left of the political spectrum, and believes in social democracy as it is practised in Scandinavia, so although the group is illegal in Iran and Turkey, it is perfectly legal in Denmark.

Lawan Peshmerga train female fighters, and some of these fighters are the best currently operating in the Middle East. They come from all over Kurdistan: Turkey, Syria, Iraq and Iran, because in these places our nationality is a crime and we are viewed as a threat. Though the party tries to use diplomacy as much as possible, Iranian *Peshmerga* fight across the four geographical locations of Kurdistan – Iran, Iraq, Turkey and Syria – which makes them unique. As well as having the best strategists and tacticians, Iranian Kurds are known their war-making skills. In Iran it's hard to know how many fighters are continuing their revolt against the Islamic regime, because there are a lot of what we call '*jas*', or traitors, so the specific number of fighters, and the details of exactly where they are in Iran, is kept secret. These groups receive help from former Soviet Union areas, which stems back to our connection during the Mahabad Republic that my grandfather fought for.

The Qandil mountains are one of the few areas where all the different groups have their survival and military camps, but even the mountains are divided and there are lots of conflicts between the different Kurdish groups. Ironically enough, it was after Saddam Hussein used his helicopter gunships against my family in Ramadi, after the end of the Gulf War, that a no-fly zone was declared over parts of Qandil, which made the area a haven for different armed groups, such as those fighting for democracy and justice. So maybe my big brother at least died for something.

These different Kurdish groups, though they want to liberate Kurdistan, are divided in their policies. Iraqi Kurdistan – what is officially called the KRG – has been the focus, as it is the only Kurdish parliamentary system that is operational, but President Masoud Barzani and his party, the Kurdistan Democratic Party (known as KDP or PDK), is not popular with all Kurds. He is believed to be the second-richest man in Iraq, while many barely have enough money to survive. The Kurdish resistance movements are often romanticized by the left-wing press in the West, but they fail sometimes to look into the way women are treated by the different leaders.

Barzani's wife is never seen in public, and he is a typical Kurdish man with a typical conservative view on the role of women and marriage. He has not fought for women's liberation in any specific way. The cities that are under his control have stricter rules than other cities. I don't consider any leader who doesn't support the liberation of women as an essential part of the struggle to be a true leader of the people. Our principles, from Mahabad to now, demand women's liberation. It's non-negotiable.

Back in Aalborg, while slowly learning about where I might best fit into the Kurdish movement, I started earning my own money by working at McDonald's at the weekends. I loved having money in my account, and would spend my money on books, clothes, so many shoes and make-up; but mainly this money gave me the opportunity to travel and meet other young people from different leftist movements across Europe. The key rallying point of these meetings was the concept of human rights, and challenging rules that infringe those rights. Rights before rules. It made me see that in my life, within my family, it was rules before rights. I tried to apply the learning I was doing in school and in these various political movements to my home environment, stressing my rights above my parents' and brothers' rules, and trying to prevent their infringement.

At the same time I had started sneaking out at night with my friends. We would get together and dress up like dolls; I would groom my hair and put fake tan on my skin – but luckily I didn't need as much as my pasty Danish friends. I slowly learned how to drink alcohol with my friends, and although today I'm not a big drinker, I found it would relax me. We would go to parties, and I started eating ginger-mint sweets when I came home in case my parents or older brothers inspected my breath. I was tired of the fights, and tired of my brothers. By this stage they were trying to take charge of my life, and I wasn't willing to allow this to happen. They didn't let me go to parties, and they wanted to approve all of my friends – even the new Kurdish ones I was making through learning about our movements. I started questioning my family and fighting back. And they started following me around.

I realized I wasn't the Kurdish girl my family wanted me to be, so I would rebel against them, but similarly my 'Danish' personality didn't seem to fit right, either. Although it was fun at times, I never really felt that comfortable dressed up like a doll and trying to look and dance like Britney Spears or Christina Aguilera. There didn't seem to be any middle ground.

During the week I would simply study and work. I decided I wanted to leave Denmark to get away from my family, so I worked really hard at school so that I could pass my exams quickly; in class I was quiet and motivated, unless I was debating. It was amazing to discover I had so much to say, and that people would listen to me. Staying in school and keeping my education was one thing I knew I could do, to avoid ending up like my family. I decided I wanted to try and train to be a nurse, hoping perhaps I could be a combat medic someday.

Learning about women's rights at school put me on a collision course at home of course, and also with others within the community, as it showed up the hypocrisy we lived with. Our policy, as Iranian Kurds and inside the PDKI, was to fight for women's equality, but the reality of the way our culture treats women – and the way I have been treated – completely belies this. The worst place in the world to be a woman is the Middle East. The worst places to be born as a woman are Afghanistan, Saudi Arabia and northern Iraq. Kurdish men do not treat women with respect; they do not give them the same rights they are born with, and Kurdish culture has allowed this to continue for generations.

The only area in Iraq where they still circumcise girls is the Kurdish area of Halabja, but within our community we are not supposed to talk about this, because it would be disloyal. FGM (female genital mutilation) is seen as being required by Islam, and as part of Kurdish tradition and identity. There are many Kurdish men who are Muslim conservatives, on the inside at least. Barzani is the case in point: he wears the traditional Kurdish clothes, but even if he looks like a Kurd from the outside, on the inside he is more of a capitalist than a nationalist.

Because of the conflicts with my family at this time, some of the teachers in my school helped me find alternative accommodation, and I moved into a home in Copenhagen for girls like me, who were fleeing their Muslim families. It was run by a woman called Anita. I really looked up to her – she was the first woman I had seen in the working world who was in charge. She owned the centre, she was really pretty and her boyfriend was hot (like, super-hot) and a lot younger than her. She was very strong, incredibly tall, well built and had a deep, authoritative accent. While living in the home I had different people 'assigned' to support me: a youth support worker; someone to help me with my homework; a liaison officer to help me stay in better contact with my family. But despite all these people working to support me, I still felt alone.

When the Arab Spring was erupting, I felt a particular pull to stand with the women in Iran who were taking off their scarfs and joining in the democratic protests. It made my heart soar to see this happening. I became hooked on social media, absorbing every protest, and we would talk about it in workshops and meetings. Unlike my friends in school, as I speak Arabic and a little bit of Persian, I heard the call to join the revolution. I understood what they were saying, in their mouths as well as their hearts. I could see their strength of will to live freely, to vote for their leaders and to share in the wealth of their resources. We have a saying in Kurdish: the strength of will is strong, even to move a mountain like a passing cloud. I could see their strength of will, and it inspired my own.

When the protests started in Syria in March 2011, I knew I wanted to go and take part. I thought I would go and help some of the groups I had been trying to support online, some of the ones fighting for Kurdistan and democracy; I could work as a journalist or a translator. In the Social Democratic Youth party in Copenhagen, I went to a meeting and we were all furious about what was happening in Syria. We debated how we could support these groups, and the others asked me what I thought we should do, so I said we should protest downtown. Some of the others were afraid of demonstrating, because the police had just been granted the power to use water cannons. Eventually we did the protest, but we got soaked and when we returned to our headquarters, the others were angry with me.

We were all pissed off at having been soaked, but as I was walking home, shivering from the cold, I stood watching the screens in a television shop and saw Syrian soldiers open fire with live ammunition on a protest in D'eraa – again. The protest was bigger than last time, and more protesters were getting hurt. I watched in awe as the people continued to chant and pushed forward against the soldiers' guns. Even though the televisions were showing different news channels, all of the pictures were of the protests and the killings. The slogans they were chanting – 'Peace and democracy for all' – were the same as the ones we were chanting in Copenhagen. My friends were so angry with the police for soaking us, but they had no idea that in other countries you could get killed for protesting. Compared to Syria, Denmark was Disneyland.

Without telling Anita, I decided to sign myself off as sick from my studies, which meant that I had three months when I didn't have to go to class, but I still got paid my benefits. Because of my situation, I had an independent allowance that I used for my expenses and, as a student in Denmark, you get paid for staying on and continuing your education. I decided to try to make it to Syria – and by signing myself off from school, I figured I could go and see what was happening and, if I had made a mistake, I would be back in time to re-enrol in school.

CHAPTER FOUR

Journey into Syria

Getting permission to join the revolution in Syria is not something it is possible to obtain right away. I didn't just decide one day to say goodbye to my family and friends and hop on a plane – as some of the articles later written about me have made out. I had to fight to get my place in the war, and the first battle was to convince those who knew the Kurdish groups there to let me go. I sought permission from a number of people, and was initially refused and passed along the line, and finally my request was ferried to a *cadra* called Cudi. I was told I could meet him at one of the Kurdish festivals in Copenhagen. *Cadras* like Cudi have a special place in our movement, as they are those who have pledged their entire lives to fight and, if necessary, die for our cause. Once a person has become a *cadra*, they can never leave the movement.

I immediately recognized Cudi as a speaker at rallies I had previously attended. I asked to talk to him privately, and then told him my plan quite simply – 'I want to be a part of the uprising in Syria' – and outlined my training and experience so far.

He listened very briefly, before setting out the reasons why it was unsuitable for me to go, and took the opportunity to share with me his knowledge of *Jabhat al-Nusra*, an *al-Qaeda*-affiliated group in Syria. I felt very honoured that he shared this military knowledge with me, as if I was already a fighter. Later I wondered if this was deliberate; he was treating me with the respect of a fighter, but making me fight him at this first hurdle, to see how much I actually wanted to leave.

I waited for a few seconds after he spoke, to show my respect and communicate that I had listened to his concerns, before standing up very tall, with my shoulders back, as we did in *Lawan* training camps during presentations, and making my case. 'I am doing these small things to help raise awareness of Syria, but I wish to go back and fight for my people,' I said, reminding him that I was an Iranian Kurd, born in Iraq. Everyone loves Kurdish female fighters – and there have been many girls from my region who have done well in our history.

I regret my outfit for this argument that I clearly wasn't winning. I was in festival clothes, which are stunningly ornate and colourful dresses, and was standing there in my fluorescent pink-and-gold mesh gown. He enquired in greater detail about my training, and I told him about the *Lawan Peshmerga* camps, my political activism, and detailed the political ideology lectures I had witnessed in Kurdistan and on our frequent trips home to visit my family. I spoke lovingly of my brave *Bawas*, and of how our tragic and difficult life in Ramadi had eventually led us to Denmark. He listened very carefully and was very respectful.

I begged him to find me some way to get to the front. I wasn't naive – or I didn't think I was, at the time – and didn't expect to be driven to the front and told to shoot. I volunteered to help with logistics or translations; I would do whatever was required of me, and just wanted to be there and to help. I said it could be a fact-finding and information-gathering trip: I could travel and make acquaintances and offer solidarity to the protesters, and find out how we in Denmark could best organize ourselves to assist what was, at the time, a democratic revolution against the thirty-year dynastic regime of the Assad family.

Cudi still wasn't convinced, and he looked me square in the eyes and told me so. As we continued to talk, I became more confident and open with him, and told him that I knew a few people who were already out in Syria. And I said that if he refused to help me, I would find someone who would. I knew that it was his job to refuse to send me, and my job as a young girl to prove my worth in combat as equal to that of a man.

The *cadra* wasn't convinced enough to send me. Because of the pink-and-gold outfit, or maybe because, at eighteen, I really was still very young (not for a Kurd, but perhaps he had been in Europe too long by this stage), he couldn't really look at me and see me as a fighter. As far as I was concerned, I might be in Europe, but I was still a Kurdish woman, and girls younger than me had fought and died for our freedom in battles throughout our history.

Cudi said he would think about it, would contact me again when he made his decision and asked me to leave. He never contacted me again – which I already knew as I left the room, almost tripping up on the black petticoat of my ridiculous dress. I was raging at myself for dressing like a doll while trying to fight like a man.

A few weeks later I decided to go to a Kurdish community centre in Copenhagen and try again. This time I wore plain green combat trousers and a khaki-coloured high-necked sweater; all of my skin was covered, so there would be no distractions for whoever I was meeting, and I thought I looked presentable and modest. I walked in and there was a crowd of men sitting around, who regarded me suspiciously. They were wearing traditional Kurdish clothing, yet instead of supporting the democratic revolution in Syria, they were sitting around Copenhagen smoking cigarettes and drinking tea.

Among the men was one older person called Ahmed who was very quiet, and I could tell by the subservient way the rest of the group treated him that he was in charge. I sat beside him and we talked.

'Can I speak freely here?' I asked.

'Continue, sister,' they urged me.

I told them I wanted to go to Aleppo, and if they thought I needed training, I would be happy to get it before going into combat. I volunteered to do policy work, propaganda work, to help Western journalists with our angle or provide them with translators. I just wanted to get close to the fight and assist them in some small way. 'I want to be part of this fight, and I want to be part of this resistance.'

They weren't happy with the idea of sending me over. I was young and they didn't know me directly. There had been talk of other girls from Scandinavia who had gone to see the revolution, but who couldn't cope with the shelling and were sent home again. Ahmed wasn't convinced, but he looked at me and said, 'My friend, my comrade, if you are ready to go there and make a difference, to people who need every help, then go there.' He suggested that the training I had done with *Lawan* would mean that I could be useful, but that I had to go and meet them in Erbil before they would decide if they would take me to Aleppo.

I knew then that I had been successful: Ahmed was sending me at least as far as Iraq to let the others decide. I skipped home and couldn't sleep that night. I didn't tell anyone, but started googling the cheapest way to get myself to Erbil, in northern Iraq. There was a flight in a few weeks' time, so I booked myself onto it and started to prepare, still not sure if I was actually going to go through with it, but at least pretending to myself that I was.

I arrived in Erbil's pristine marble airport with only a small bag with a few changes of clothes, some books and a few medicines. I was picked up by a man who called himself Kandil, who told me to get into a car with him.

He took me to a safe house near the Ali Mosque in the centre of the city. Stuck in traffic for two hours in the shadow of the mosque, I tried to take pictures that showed how the light was reflecting in the gold of the tower. Erbil was buzzing and I felt exhilarated. I'd been there loads of times before, but not like this.

The safe house was large and a sandstone colour on the outside, with a big garden out the front beside the road. Inside there were three other women and two men from different parts of Europe. We were all different nationalities and ages, but all of us shared a Kurdish or Arabic link, so we could communicate. That first night I cooked chicken and vegetables with two of the women – an older woman called Ezma and a quieter woman, probably in her thirties or forties, called Dilan. The next day I went out with Karan, the other woman, to the local shops and we talked a little about what we hoped to do in Aleppo. When I was alone I dropped in at the mosque, because we were so close and it was so beautiful, and prayed to stay safe. I might not believe exactly, but I figured it wasn't going to do any harm.

To pass through the border into Syria, we had to get our story straight, so I had some fake business cards produced in Erbil, saying that I was a translator. Barzani's *Peshmerga* are the official army in the KRG, but confusingly we still use this word more generally to mean 'fighter' in Kurdish, and there are various distinctions between the different political groups the army is connected to. They are either aligned with the KDP, which is Barzani's party, or with the other main party, known as the Patriotic Union of Kurdistan (PUK). Back then, when the border between Iraq and Syria was open, both the KDP and the PUK *Peshmerga* were more sympathetic in terms of letting people through. Even so, we all had to have some fake ID. I was a translator and the older women were the documentary team, so it fitted in well that I was their junior colleague. I had my real name on my ID, so I could use my passport and my story stuck. I realized after about ten minutes of talking to Ezma, Dilan and Karan that they were all fighters. I was so thrilled to meet them. They were kind, wise and hilariously funny. They had been in the mountains, I think, but they had also been working in Europe, so I could see they led these totally fascinating lives.

On the third day after dinner, we got in the cars together to begin the journey from Erbil across Iraq and into Syria. Back then you could simply drive over the border; there was no sneaking over the river at night, as the later international volunteers experienced. However, we still took precautions on the journey and travelled in a convoy of three. I didn't know it at the time, but we would be travelling first to Rabia, all the way over in western Syria, where we would meet others.

On the long car journey we swapped vehicles a few times, so we all got to know each other very well. We kept the music playing really loudly and wound down the windows and spent the trip joking and laughing. Everyone was excited to be on our way, and the drivers tried to race each other on the bigger motorways. I was delighted to be there, and pleasantly surprised that I had managed to wangle my way in. I could tell that the others were curious and impressed that I had made the journey to join them, as they were all a lot older than me.

We sang songs to pass the time, the Kurdish songs that I grew up singing. The girls also sang songs that I hadn't heard before – about the women fighters and the sacrifice of the women revolutionaries of our movement. One of the songs I knew a little, called '*Dilemim Zagros*', was about our longest mountain:

> *I do not care for you*
> *I'm going to the mountains.*
> *You did not kill me.*
> *My mother was burned*
> *My friends have gone,*
> *I'm going to our mountains*
> *Do not forget me,*
> *I've been with the hypocrites,*
> *But I will be successful.*

As we entered Halab I looked around at where I was and what I was doing and thought to myself: Yeah, this is it. I'm in the right place. We stopped for a food break and I decided to approach Ezma, the quiet, older woman whom I believed to be one of the commanders. I asked to talk to her privately. I was pleading with myself to stay calm and not to rush into any rash decisions, but the first thing out of my mouth when we were alone was: '*Hoskimim* – sister – how can I be like you?'

I wasn't embarrassed, even though I didn't think I had made my approach in a very respectful way. She looked me right in the eye, then shifted her gaze to my civilian outfit and slightly wrinkled her nose. 'Sister,' she said, 'you are on your way.'

I was wearing what I thought was a modest version of my normal European clothing, but Ezma was unimpressed to see so much of my flesh, and told me it wasn't appropriate for me to dress like this. Looking back today, I can't stop laughing. What was I thinking?

I squirmed a little and tried to listen, without being hurt, as the women explained that I needed to grow my eyebrows out and stop plucking them, as that was against the movement's policy. As fighters for *jineology* – the Kurdish policy of feminism and gender equality – they saw changing the body to follow fashion as one of the most powerful means of mind-control over women in capitalist countries, or within the 'system', as Karan later explained. They were kind and reassured me that I could get some different clothes once inside Aleppo. 'The journey you are on has just started,' Ezma said to me as she put her hand on my shoulder, 'but it's a long one, and you are just at the very beginning, so you will need to be patient.' I took her cryptic comments to mean she was telling me I had a lot to learn. I certainly did.

I became a bit emotional, and Ezma just laughed and invited me to ride in the car with her until the next stop. On the way they told me more about what they were doing, and why they were in Syria, and we talked about what kind of weapons they were trained in. One of the girls was trained in munitions – a position we call sabotage – and she explained that if I had any basic chemistry or science training, I could start the training process. 'Sabotage is the brains of the whole Kurdish liberation movement – that's why we women have to do it,' she joked. I was so humbled to be listening to them, and I asked loads of questions about their different lives in Europe versus their lives in the mountains.

They lectured me a little on my clothing, and warned me not to be too friendly with anyone in Syria. Ezma was especially serious about this. 'Have you been to Syria before?' she asked.

'No, but I am from Kurdistan – I am used to coping with the behaviour of men.' I laughed a little, embarrassed at how I had phrased the word 'used' in Kurdish.

'But are they used to you, Joanna? Are Syrian men used to you?' Karan teased. We talked about the political philosophy of women's rights in our movement – what we call *jineology* – as advocated by the Kurdish nationalist leader Abdullah Ocalan, and about how important this pivot was for the success of the entire movement.

'Without the repression of women, the repression of the entire society is not conceivable,' Dilan said, quoting Abdullah Ocalan directly. I fell in love with the spirit and the politics of these women during the course of that car journey. I decided I wanted to stay with them for the rest of my time at war: I felt safe. I knew they would teach me and accept me as one of their sisters. I had been in Syria for less than twenty-four hours, but I was ready to enlist.

CHAPTER FIVE

Aleppo Begins to Crumble

When our convoy began its approach into Aleppo, I was excited to be in the city of the ancient souks. We went through four different checkpoints, where our car was searched and we had our fake documents inspected. When I first presented my Danish passport I was met with a quizzical look from the officers, as if they were asking me, 'What are you doing here?' I answered them as best I could in Arabic, stuttering slightly as I went through my rehearsed story of being a translator for a documentary team.

Ezma, who I would later learn was one of the most senior female commanders in the movement, stepped in and took over, becoming chatty and friendly and playing her role as 'senior documentary producer'. By the time the second checkpoint came round, I kept my head down and avoided eye contact and stared out the window, wishing I spoke better Arabic with no accent, and feeling anxious and stressed. At home in Denmark we spoke Sorani Kurdish as a family, and I wished I had studied Arabic harder when I was preparing myself for this life within the war.

At the last checkpoint closest to the city we stopped at the side of a lay-by and I was put into another vehicle, this time travelling with a family, while the fighters continued to their prearranged destination. I was told they were going on a mission that I could not come on, but that I could meet up with them again. 'Be patient,' Ezma said as we hugged goodbye.

The family was Christian and spoke Arabic, and if we were stopped the cover story was that I was the new bride for their son, although I also took all my fake documents with me. I was really sad that the women had left without me and spent the journey looking glumly out of the window, feeling nervous about who this family were and where I was going. They took me to their home in Aziza in the south-west of Aleppo.

At the time the Kurdish groups were trying to create a stable alliance with other groups, such as the Christians who fight against *Jabat al-Nusra* and other armed radicals who put pressure on Assad's regime for a better domestic policy. Back in 2012 the uprising was still new; it was hard to compare the situations in different areas, as they were too complicated and varied from place to place. The alliances were very fragile when I was there; they were just beginning, and ultimately some of them collapsed. The democratic protests were inching towards war, but no one was really sure what would happen.

On the news at home it looked as if the whole city was united against the regime, so I had this image in my head of what it would be like, but when I got there this image shattered almost immediately. Aleppo wasn't a city united against Assad, it was a city crumbling into different mini-cities, with different alliances and different armed groups fighting for territory. Civilians were stuck in the middle, forced to take sides, or were already making plans to get out. For an outsider witnessing what the beginning was like, as I did, the fragmentation was very noticeable.

Once at the family's house in Aziza, I slept on a mattress that folded out onto the floor. The fluffy blanket I was given was covered in pictures of Disney princesses, and I would fold it up every morning and place it in the corner, close to where the weapons were kept – the building was a safe house for activists against armed religious groups as well as the regime, so there were weapons being stored there. The wife of the family kept herself fairly quiet and spent her time cooking food, serving us and cleaning her house. She apologized for the food, which was delicious, but after a few days I understood why: we had the same vegetables for every meal. The streets were slowly becoming more restricted; informal checkpoints manned by local volunteers were popping up all over the place and it was making food-shopping trickier.

The family was welcoming and kind, and helped me with some of the Assyrian Arabic dialects. I was informed by my contacts that I would be working as a runner and messenger between the Kurdish groups near Sher Musco, the Kurdish area, and other, mainly secular groups, while we still had the opportunity to prepare for the real storm. I tried to listen to what was happening as much as I could, as people came and went in the safe house, but my Arabic was far from perfect, and not speaking the same language as the people I was staying with made me a bit jumpy. I never really knew who was coming or going – all I had were vague instructions from people I hadn't actually met.

That winter we didn't see any large-scale attacks from Assad's side, but in February 2012 he bombed Aleppo twice, targeting

Jabat al-Nusra in Syria. There were rebels in the countryside around the city, and we all knew that Assad would not leave the destiny of the uprising in the hands of the people. Instead he started bombing Damascus and other cities, which even then some people were saying were staged attacks, in order to justify more bombings on the uprising when it finally occurred. Back then, the Kurdish areas were close to the military airbase south of Tishreen, which the regime would use to attack peaceful protesters – and there were huge protests going on against them – so it was a strategic priority for us to attack this position. My job, I was informed, was to gather information on the movements of the soldiers stationed around this location. I also had to ferry information and give some logistical support between the two groups, the Christians and the Kurds. This 'job' was not official, but was as per my wishes.

On the first day I wore a long, full burqa over my favourite navy-blue Nike trainers. The woman I was staying with helped me into the burqa, and I wore expensive-looking sunglasses and kept my earphones in. The plan was that I would stay in contact with the person directing me; they would check in if they needed something, and I would call them if I had any useful information. My first task was to get information from the soldiers around the checkpoint near the airport – logistical information that could be useful to plan an attack. There were a few shops and food stalls close to where the soldiers were stationed, so I would pretend to shop while trying to make conversation with them, which clearly wasn't going to be very hard for me. I knew I would have to create a bond with a soldier in order to get the information, and I was a little worried about how far I should go whenever flirtation crept into a conversation. I didn't know how much I was expected to do to get information, but I didn't ask too many questions and my contacts never directly requested anything of this nature.

With all the different protests, there was a certain buzzing energy in the city, but there were only specific times when it was safe to be out – or when the girl I was pretending to be would be allowed out by her family. In Aleppo, at the time, women would only go out during the day, and indeed many women in cities all over the Middle East would not dare to venture out after nightfall.

I went to the various markets close to the airbase and would slowly walk around, looking at the different labels on the dried foods, trying to read and understand them, which was actually quite difficult for me. In my bad Arabic, I would try to make conversation and flirt with the guards. It wasn't hard. I had a specific formula I would use, which worked every time. After spending some time selecting who might be the most susceptible soldier – normally someone close to my age – I would look at them over my sunglasses and smile.

In Aleppo this small action can reverberate very strongly. Next we would begin to talk, and normally the soldier would tell me I had beautiful eyes behind my glasses, and could he see them? After acting coy for a suitable length of time, I would oblige. We spoke in both Arabic and English, and they would try to guess where I was from. That first day the guard I spoke to was tall, with grey eyes and a kind smile. 'Are you Kurdish?' he asked.

'Yes. I am Kurdish, and I'm Christian from Europe as well,' I replied, and his eyes lit up.

Even though I was modestly dressed by the Christian family in Aziza, it might not have been obvious that I was Christian – I look Kurdish, but also a little Arabic, some say. I deliberately said I was Christian, because saying this on top of being European basically means you are easy, in the Middle East. I mean, sexually speaking.

Although Bashar al-Assad's government was officially secular, Syria is not a secular country, and there are many sectarian beliefs about each religion, which often manifest in the way their women are regarded. Christian girls have a reputation for being more willing to spread their legs, and I was inching the soldiers towards this possibility, but in an indirect way. The soldiers, I knew, wouldn't see me as much of a threat if I said I was Christian; they would just think I was a slut, or hope I was anyway. I would stay chatting to them about the contents of my shopping bag and let my glance linger longer than was appropriate.

The air was cool and crisp that first day and I could see a group of women throw their scarves over their faces deliberately, and shoot me the evil eye for my easy behaviour. It's quite a scandal for a girl, even if she is a loose Christian girl, to deliberately start up a conversation with a man in Syria. They were scornful, and I could feel the eyes of the younger women boring into my back when I turned.

One older woman was so enraged she completely stopped what she was doing to stare at me, and I admit that, at this point, I began to feel a little ashamed. 'I'm going now, but I'll be back again tomorrow, my sweet Danish flower,' my grey-eyed target said as he prepared to say goodbye.

I pretended to be busy checking a label on a tin of chickpeas I had been debating buying, and looked up, as if startled that I was to be left. 'What time will you be back tomorrow?' I asked.

'Four p.m. – come back to me then.'

I smiled my response and glanced down, as if the look of reproach from the older women had finally had an impact on me, and repeated the time into my microphone.

When I got home a few hours later I compiled the useful information I had managed to extract and sent it to my contact, who told me he was pleased with my work and that I should keep doing it. My job was to find out the different times the guard changed, when they changed and how often. It wasn't thrilling work, but I was happy to be in Aleppo, and to have some kind of intelligence-gathering role, even if it was small.

The road to the airport had a number of checkpoints on the way, and then one main centre guarding it. When not doing my fake shopping and flirting, I would walk completely covered up by my burqa and just watch the guards change. I measured how long on average they spent at the bathroom near the entrance, and what happened when one went to the bathroom. I noticed how many guards there were, what their rotational shift pattern was and how they were armed. Their ammunition was impressive, and the ones I met then were slightly nervous. It was always one of the younger, less serious soldiers I would speak to. The older ones viewed me with a mixture of suspicion and disgust. Perhaps they thought I was a prostitute. I didn't care. At night I went back to the family I was staying with and faithfully reported on my day's work to the man of the house, while his wife served us food.

The family living in the house were anxious about the war, and about the new alliances that were being formed – particularly the woman of the house; she was always either in the kitchen, as if this was the safe zone where she belonged, or sitting on the doorstep, looking around nervously. In some ways she reminded me of my own mother, but she was much younger, so I wasn't entirely sure why. Always ready to serve me and her husband, she didn't have a huge amount to say for herself and was different from any of the Christian women I had met in Denmark.

The house was always perfectly clean and she ran around after her son, who was about twenty years old. The family was being paid money to keep me, I was told, and they worked as smugglers to get out people who wanted to leave, and those who wanted to come and join the fight in. I think they were collecting money by smuggling so they themselves could leave and go to Europe. But because my Arabic wasn't great and they didn't speak English or Kurdish, we didn't talk much. Downstairs in their basement were quite a few weapons, so I wondered whether they were being paid to keep them there or whether the men of the house were part of a specific militia at the time. This is what was confusing at that moment: practically every street was forming its own militia. Ordinary men and some (mainly Kurdish) women were arming and preparing to fight the regime.

Different groups congregated according to neighbourhood, with different neighbourhoods being divided along religious or ethnic lines. It's hard to describe how divided most Middle Eastern cities are; everybody knows almost immediately what everyone else is: there is always some indicator of a person's faith or position, and often both are prominently displayed. It felt like all the communities in Aleppo at that time were turning on each other; minor fights about supplies would transform into battles, as if someone had just lit a match, and the people just wanted to burn down their whole city, street by street.

Slowly areas were barricading themselves in for protection, and although you could enter an area if you wanted to visit a particular shop or bakery, you couldn't ignore the masked armed men who politely let you through. After nap-time in the early afternoon most of the women would go shopping, and it was during this time that I would venture out alone. The kids would be out playing and the bakeries would be open, but fear and tension were there. Everyone was suspicious of each other, and especially of outsiders like me. I couldn't go out, even in the burqa, after dark. It would have been inviting trouble, and I figured I was taking enough risks already. So in the evenings I sat at home with the family and talked to them about their life.

The walls of the city were slowly becoming covered with graffiti, as the different wings of the revolution took hold. One day I came out of the mosque and noticed some new graffiti: 'Allah is not above me, he exists only if I believe in him.' This took me aback – the Middle East renouncing religion? I never thought it could be possible. I kept reading and rereading the graffiti, to make sure I understood it correctly. The secular revolution was finally coming.

I did my information-gathering/flirting thing for a few days, while it was safe, but it became slightly harder as we started planning protests near the airport so that we could infiltrate the crowds, and the regime put more guards on duty and on different rotations. I was only allowed to use words to gain information, and words are not enough in combat. Also I couldn't really see where the information I was passing was going.

To be honest, I was out of my depth, and I wasn't sure how useful I was being. The conversations with the soldiers weren't the kind you could keep on having every day, or they would start to expect more. On the fourth day of my information-gathering work I ran into the grey-eyed soldier from the first day again, and I had to delicately get myself out of his clutches. I decided that enough was enough. I called my contact in Sher Musco and told him he needed to find me something else to do. The work was boring, I told him, and I didn't really see its value. He tried to reassure me: 'You have just arrived. Your role is very useful to us.' But unless I was actually going to go beyond words with these men, which I had no intention of doing, there wasn't much more I could find out.

My system had worked for a few days, but perhaps because I had been so flirty initially, sexual requests began to be made, which I couldn't consider. Maybe my contact didn't know what to do with me. I had ferried some messages between the Kurdish and Christian groups near the airport, so they now decided to move me to an area called Visa in Aleppo to continue this work, this time closer to what was then becoming a more violent frontline.

I told the commander who moved me that I wanted to get involved in the fight. Although a few of the *hevals* knew that I was just about to turn nineteen at the time, my relatively young age wouldn't have caused anyone any alarm. Many girls in Syria and Iraq are already married and have babies by that ripe old age – as my mother has frequently reminded me. I was worried about doing this honeytrap information-gathering line of work, as women who do this in the Middle East are not respected, even by their own sides. I learned the Assyrian word for 'spy', as I kept hearing it a lot. Tensions and suspicions ran high, as alliances that were agreed one day were broken the next.

*

The man of the family drove me to my next safe house in Al-Aziza, where I was due to work in logistics and messaging. I was picked up by an Arab guy I didn't know, who travelled with an AK-47 in the front seat beside him. Great, I thought, I'm going to be killed for leaving my nice safe job, because these strangers I am trying to help think I am a spy.

We couldn't really communicate because we didn't speak the same language, and he scared me, so I didn't try too hard. He wasn't wearing a uniform, nor was there any insignia in the car to give me any more information. There were no Kurdish flags anywhere, and no sign of the green, yellow and red colours supporters often decorate their cars with. As he drove me through the unfamiliar city, I panicked more and more, and even though I was cold, I started sweating through my clothes.

I called *cadra* Cudi back in Copenhagen, to tell him where I was, so that if anything happened to me, he would know the last place where I had been. I was really nervous for the whole journey, but distracted myself by trying to take in the city and read the graffiti. Aleppo was very beautiful back then, not the city of rubble the war has now reduced it to. Images of revolutionary heroes like Che Guevara and Nelson Mandela were stencilled on some of the buildings, and sectarian name-calling was painted across many of the walls – at roundabouts and junctions, or near the entrances to different areas. It was exciting to see that the faces of the people whose posters hung on my walls in Aalborg had made it to Syria with me.

The car we were travelling in was old and noisy. I wasn't expecting a limousine transfer, but the state of the cars I had seen so far in Syria was pretty bad. In Iraq we have some nice vehicles, but in

Syria the Kurds have not done well under Assad's government. My impression of society was that it was politically contradictory: in some ways very left wing – energy and cooking supplies were extremely cheap – but also very Islamic, in a conservative sense. Assad is an Alawite, and the Christians supported him because the Alawites are a minority within the Shia Muslims; some Alawites don't even consider themselves to be Muslim. In those early days of the conflict, however, this was not clear; certain Christian groups worked with us, as well as with the other rebel groups who were beginning to establish themselves.

Because of the different checkpoints – some set up by the government and some new local ones – the journey to Al-Aziza took much longer than it should have, and we travelled all the way to the south-eastern part of the city. Eventually my fear of my driver and his AK gave way to tiredness and I managed to sleep. Finally, after many hours of being in this car, we arrived in what can only be described as an empty clearing, surrounded by rubble and half-built houses. I rose, still half-asleep and disorientated.

As I began to wake up, it suddenly dawned on me what I had done and how naive I had been. In my mind, I had wanted to come to Syria to be part of the uprising and join the women who were taking part in changing their society. In reality, I was here in the middle of a wasteland, in a filthy, hot, dusty city with lots of Syrian men I didn't know. I didn't speak the language, I had very little money with me and I was completely reliant on the kindness of these strangers. It wasn't the smartest journey I had ever made, and I was beginning to feel like it might be time to go home.

I put my sneakers on the stones, to pull myself out of the car, and before I looked up I heard a shout towards me: '*Marhava, heval*', which means 'Hello, my friend' or 'comrade' – but it's a greeting that is reserved as a sign of mutual respect for fighters, which I was not.

Shocked to be referred to as a '*heval*' for the first time, I looked around to see who was speaking to me and was met by a young guy who introduced himself as Lewant, which means 'marine' in Kurdish. Lewant was already one of the most famous fighters of the revolution in Syria. It was the first time I saw a Kurdish fighter in real life – a young man, not like the old men my father fought with. He was incredibly handsome, with a strong muscular body like a film star's and a bright, open face. He looked at me, smiled and said, 'So you are the new *heval* who is going to be here with us?'

I looked at him straight. 'Are you saying I'm a *heval*? I'm pretty sure I didn't say I was signing up to be a *cadra* – and so far this trip has consisted of lots of things I didn't sign up for.'

I gestured to the driver, and explained the length of our shared journey and the few words we had in common. Lewant paid the man, then gestured for me to come to his car to meet some of the others.

'Let me show you our weapons, *heval*,' he said, smiling again, and I found myself smiling back. Finally, some weapons, I thought, and raced over to see. I tried to remember the advice of Ezma and not talk too much, but being around Lewant made me nervous and excited, so sometimes I couldn't quite help it. He was the de facto commander of his battalion and he assumed a natural authority over the other fighters, who were friendly, but mainly spoke Arabic.

Lewant brought me to their safe house and did an exaggeratedly friendly tour – pretending he was showing me around my 'holiday home'. He was so funny and adorable. The place was small, dusty and dirty. They found me a corner to sleep in alone, downstairs near the kitchen, which had an oven that didn't work and smelled of gas. I was the only woman there, so it would have been inappropriate to share sleeping arrangements with the guys.

After my quick tour, we went back to the weapons in his car, and Lewant asked me which guns I had experience of. Not wanting to reveal that my experience was limited to target practice, hunting and survival-camp training in the mountains, I carefully fingered some of the weapons and asked him to give me his thoughts on each of them. In the end I went for the safest: a fake AK, probably Russian-made, which Lewant assured me was a reliable shooter.

Three of us got into one car, and we went to another house to pick up some other guys, who were clearly *cadras* from Turkey. No one had any kind of official uniform; the guys wore white T-shirts, and I was wearing green khakis and a high-necked polo shirt – loose comfortable clothing that I had purchased while doing my information-gathering in Tishreen.

I sat in the back of the white pickup truck and listened as Lewant talked quietly but authoritatively to one of the others in Arabic. I didn't catch everything they were saying, but it became clear, once I was in the car, that we were on our way to a street battle and that was why we had the weapons; we were going to be using them in just a few moments.

'Hey, hey, what's going on?' I asked as calmly as I could. I had said I wanted a fight, but I had no idea what was happening.

'What do you mean what's going on?' Lewant replied. 'A revolution!' And he smiled again, taking his eyes off the road to look me directly in the eye. 'You know how to handle a weapon, don't you? That's what we were told.' I just looked at him and stayed silent as he continued, 'We are going to pick up some more people, and then we are going to help a battle that's going on now.'

Shocked and embarrassed that the level of eye contact he wanted to maintain with me could have killed us all before we reached any battle, I looked out the window, then turned to the other guys we were travelling with. 'So, where exactly is it that we are going?' I enquired in a low voice, trying to sound authoritative.

Although my question wasn't directed to Lewant, he responded before the Arabic guys had a chance to speak: 'We are going where we have to go, *heval*. Just where we have to go.'

He sped through the streets of Aleppo and picked up two more men, who crowded into the car. I could tell the area was still Christian, because in the square there was a statue of a woman in white and blue – the Virgin Mary, I presume – and there are no Muslim statues of women. The protesters we were trying to link up with had already moved on; nor were there any government soldiers. Everything was quiet and seemed closed. It was dusk now, and the early-evening call to prayer could be heard faintly from across the city.

The Syrian Arab guys offered me some of their cigarettes, as they called their friends and found out where we were going next. Although not unheard of within our Kurdish movement of course, seeing a woman with a gun is still a very unusual sight for most Syrians and I was conscious that I was attracting a lot of attention. Not wanting to be on the streets uncovered, for any longer than I needed to be, I asked Lewant if it was okay if I went into a yellow church in the centre of the square.

'Wait, I will come with you,' he shouted over, so with our weapons hanging off our shoulders we went inside. It was empty as we sat side by side on the pew. We each prayed in slightly different ways; I was kneeling with my right knee on the floor, as my uncle had taught me Christians in Iran do, while Lewant knelt more as if he was on a prayer mat in a mosque – low down and leaning back on his heels.

'Are you Christian?' he whispered, though we couldn't see the priest anywhere.

'Not really – my uncle was Christian, so I have a lot of respect for the faith, but I am Muslim, or I was anyway…' I trailed off, in case he was offended. I had no idea what religion he was, but I suspected religion was not as important as politics to him. We had a deep conversation about Lewant's life and experience; he was a Syrian Kurd, but not from Aleppo, and he was impressed that I had come from so far to join the revolution.

Some other people came into the church, so we both went silent and started to pray. I prayed to my uncle to watch over me on this trip, and for the safety of the family I had been staying with. When I looked over to where Lewant was praying, he seemed emotional, so I moved towards him. 'What's wrong, *heval?*' I asked quietly.

'This war, Joanna. We humans are dirty. We destroy things,' he said to me.

'We don't destroy – we are trying to build something new,' I said, not really sure why he was suddenly so upset.

'Look around, Joanna, there's no flowers in this church – and we just brought our guns in.'

I didn't know what to say, so I moved closer to him and stayed quiet. After a long time, I asked him softly, 'Are you okay now, *heval*?' He didn't respond, and we just sat in silence together for a long time.

This was the first time I saw a Kurdish man so emotional and upset. Lewant didn't look me in the eye when he cried, and I wasn't sure what had happened to him in the days before. I liked that he seemed to trust me, and how open he was with me, so soon after meeting me. We left the church, climbed back into the car and returned to the safe house, shedding a few of our comrades on the way. I busied myself trying to be useful, and set about attempting to get the oven to work in the kitchen where I had been assigned to sleep.

Lewant and I continued our conversation from the church much later that night, when we shared guard duty on the top of our building throughout the night. The building was higher than those around us, and in the distance you could hear the firing of guns from different areas nearby. Lewant talked about his childhood, what it was like to grow up Kurdish under the Assad regime and his reasons for joining the fight, explaining that his family, like many Kurdish men, had been in the army. He explained how Assad's father, Hafez, previously allowed those who trained in the military academies of the PKK in the mountains to join the Syrian army as a soldier. 'Everything changed for many of us after Turkey intervened,' he said. Turkey threatened to invade Syria if Assad continued to allow the PKK to have training camps inside Syria, he explained, or allowed them to join the military in this way. This change of law stole the career opportunities of thousands of men, and was part of a number of new measures brought in by the regime against their Kurdish population.

'I didn't choose who I am, but who I am is illegal,' he said, as we smoked together at the top of the building. 'My crime,' he continued 'is just who I am.' We drank tea and talked together late into the night. As he opened up about his personal experience of the regime's oppression, I became more and more sure of my decision to come to Aleppo. I was expecting him, as leader of the group, to test me more on what my intentions were – particularly as there were already rumours that I was a spy, but Lewant kept his questions very muted, and instead seemed to want to discuss the wider Kurdish issue and the political manoeuvring that the movement needed to make on the international stage.

After a few days it was confirmed I could stay with this group and could take part in battles, and I was officially assigned the gun I had already been using. Some instructions were also given on what we should wear: red and black, to look more like a fighting force, as other groups in the city slowly began to dress their part, too. I took lots of advice from the others on the weapons, who took some convincing that a European girl had adequate weapon-handling knowledge. I took their teasing lightly and let them laugh, partly because I was nervous about how my skills would compare to theirs, and partly because words don't mean much in combat – they would see me in action when we were in battle.

We didn't get summoned to any battles around Al-Aziza those first days – or if we were called, when we got there it would turn out to be a false alarm. It was mainly locals fighting

Assad's soldiers, or more commonly locals fighting between themselves. On my third day in the house I was still trying to fix the oven, after getting some new gas and tubing, when a cry echoed throughout the building: 'Get your weapon and get into the car. It's happening. Uniforms – or dark clothing at least.'

I scrambled into the car and asked what was happening: 'Where are we going? Who are we fighting? How many groups are there? Is it going to be another local battle over turf, or is it against the regime?'

'No questions. Just prepare,' was the reply.

I turned to Lewant beside me, frustrated. He seemed to be able to read my thoughts because, before I said anything, he started a whole speech: 'It doesn't matter where we are going. It doesn't matter where we are fighting, as long as we are fighting.'

It occurred to me that these guys – with the exception of Lewant – were crazy and always squaring for a fight. I saw myself dying, after coming all the way to Aleppo, over some silly argument about the price of bread. As we sped through the deserted streets I tried to fashion a red headband around my hair, and buttoned my black shirt up as high as it would go.

We got to the square and I saw we were near a shopping mall, so I thought perhaps there had been some fight over the price of food. At that time in the city – as I have seen elsewhere in Iraq and Iran – the price of food could depend very much on who was buying it, particularly during times where there were shortages. If you were Christian buying from a Christian, you would pay a totally different price from someone who was a Sunni Muslim.

We got out of the car and went towards the fight, but this time for once it was a real battle between soldiers of the regime – who were Christian in this area – and the Sunni Muslims who had been injured in the democracy protests earlier in the week, when live rounds had been fired. Several of their relatives had been injured and were being treated in hospital, but the soldiers and police had been going into the hospitals to find those injured in the protests and make them disappear.

When we arrived, the argument stopped as everyone saw our weapons. 'Who are you?' one of the Sunni men asked.

Lewant spoke first, explaining that we were international Kurdish fighters and had come to support them in their revolution against Assad. 'You tell us the problem and we will help, and then we will leave these areas to your control,' he said.

As the details of what was happening were being explained to Lewant, a shot rang out and hit the wall behind us. The soldiers from the regime had seen us and were ready, so we each ran to a position and started to fire. I went with Lewant and we used the front engine-part of one of pickup trucks for cover as we responded. It was completely chaotic and I just tried to remain calm, stay down and remember my training from *Lawan*. The reason we used the front of the pickup truck to hide behind was because we were in a square – it was wide-open space and there was not much protection. Unlike what you see in Hollywood films, cars are not a good place to be, if someone is shooting at you bullets can go straight through. If you shelter behind the front of the car where the engine is, you have more of a chance, because of how complicated its mechanics are.

The regime soldiers were firing to disperse the crowd, as opposed to actually trying to target any of us – at that point the regime was responding with brutal force, but there were no real tactics; it was just kill people in crowds. Later, brutalized by the long war they had been fighting, they would become much more proficient at taking out our men, but at that point it was all quite haphazard. I fired a few shots from my AK and didn't embarrass myself in front of Lewant. Firing my first shots in Aleppo didn't make me feel stronger, but I had now directly joined the uprising. Next to me there were Syrians and Kurdish Syrians shooting. The regime was with one local group, and we were supporting the others. I was the only woman in these clashes, and I was treated like an equal while the shooting was taking place.

The actual fight did not last very long, but we used it as an opportunity to reach out to the locals; to gain their trust and reassure them that we didn't want to take over their area, but wanted to support the revolution and join their cause with our own.

It didn't really end – it just grew gradually quieter as the soldiers stopped firing, so we stopped firing too. When we got back to the car, the guys were asking me if I was okay, because I was new to it all; at that point I didn't really belong to anyone – I was just there out of solidarity, I was there to join their revolution and support their democratic ambitions, and they seemed to appreciate that. They were kind to me, more because I was new than because I was a girl. We went back to the house feeling jubilant, and ate bread and cheese together and drank sweet fruit tea. I crawled to my bed near the kitchen in the early hours, thrilled by the day's events and a little scared by how quickly it had all kicked off.

Over the next few days Lewant became busier as others joined our group, but it was all very fluid. Many of our group weren't from Aleppo, and we wanted to work with the local groups to support their fight for democracy. It's delicate, however, to come to an area with weapons and try to make friends, but that was exactly what we were doing. Some of the Syrian Arabs we were working with would be fighting for us one day, and the next day they would be gone from our ranks and would show up in one of the Islamic militia groups.

We were suspicious of the different factions growing around us and we wanted to unite the anti-Assad forces into one army: ours. But Aleppo was a bitterly divided city and Assad had ensured that only his cronies, the Alawites, had control. Everyone excluded and targeted by this group fought for the remaining scraps, and they relied on their own communities, clans and families to provide for them. This is how trust runs in this kind of situation; even though everyone was turning against Assad, it was hard to get communities to unite. We knew *Al-Qaeda* were going to try to use the revolution as well, so there were a lot of suspicions between the Arabic groups we were working with. We were suspicious of them and they were suspicious of each other. Men and money were flowing through Turkey to join this war, and we knew never to trust any group that had anything to do with that despicable place. *Al-Qaeda*'s Syrian branch *Jabat-al-Nusra* hadn't really started to be active in Aleppo when I was there – instead it was smaller Islamic groups, based on family tribes that were acting as an extreme kind of neighbourhood-watch patrol against the regime.

Aleppo is where the Syrian war really began, and the complications I witnessed there in the early days explain to some degree why the conflict is so intractable. Every community in Syria may hate the others, but they all love Aleppo. It doesn't matter if you win the four big cities of Syria, if you don't win Aleppo. It's like the beautiful virgin of Syria, and if Aleppo falls, so will all the others. Back then, Aleppo was called the heart and honour of Syria, and these men were killing each other because no one wanted to share her.

I continued to speak to my main contact most days, and they would inform me of what I was doing, who my commander was or what I was working on. Although I respected and admired Lewant, I didn't have the same relationship with the other fighters in the house, who regarded me with a mixture of disdain and suspicion.

No one seemed to understand why I was there or what I was trying to achieve, nor were they used to including a woman in military or logistics planning. Sometimes when I would walk into a room during a meeting, they would stop talking until I left. I was informed at the very last minute where battles were taking place, and often I wasn't informed at all. Being there, but not being officially part of the group, was isolating; my contacts would let me know that I would be in the house by myself that evening, so to lock up; or they would tell me that the people who had been staying with me last night, who I was preparing food for, were now dead, so I didn't need to prepare them anything.

As the fights got bigger and the factions started splitting, another larger battle started raging in northern Syria in Serê Kaniyê (also called Ras al-Ayn), and Lewant was told he would be moving to fight in that battle. I wasn't being moved to any battle, as officially I was still there by myself – I was in this weird informal/volunteer role, so I didn't have to report to anyone specific, like a commander.

I had been following the uprising obsessively for the previous six months, but now that I was here, it was morphing into something much bigger, so there was this sense that we needed to regroup and prepare. I learned quite quickly in Aleppo that I didn't see things clearly just by reading the news; the situation on the ground was much more chaotic, confusing and complicated than it seemed on television or online. I decided that I should leave Aleppo. I wanted to go to Serê Kaniyê with Lewant, but was told this was too much of a risk. It was gearing up to be a major fight, and I was still officially a translator from Europe, with minimal experience and only average Arabic and Kermanji. I was told I needed to get some training if I wanted to join the Serê Kaniyê battle. My choice was either to leave the city and go to the mountains for training, or to leave the city and go back to Europe and report what I had witnessed, to the Kurdish groups I belonged to in Copenhagen but also hopefully to the wider European community, in order to build awareness.

I didn't have a lot of time to think about my decision; a car was coming to pick me up and I was offered a lift out of Aleppo and into our area of Rojava in northern Syria. From there I could decide if I wanted to stay for a while or go back to Europe. Sitting on my mattress in the kitchen near the oven, which I never actually managed to get working the whole time I was there, I went over my options in my head. Lewant was leaving, and I wasn't close to anyone else in the house, so I decided to take this lift out. I didn't want to stay in the house alone and it seemed like there was a clearing-out process going on.

The car picked me up from the house in Al-Aziza and we travelled past some of the same checkpoints I had seen on my way in. The cars split up and we were each put into different vehicles, and I noticed that the soldiers manning the checkpoints had changed. Instead of soldiers of the regime, it was now masked militias from the neighbourhood groups who were in control.

After one of the checkpoints, nearer Rojava, I was put into a car full of men who were all Kurdish fighters. They were hyper, shouting and dancing and laughing in a way I would come to recognize as the way fighters behave after surviving a battle. Blasting the radio up, they all sang along at the top of their voices and danced around in the back of the truck. I laughed and sang with them – some of them were on the way to the Serê Kaniyê battle, so I tried to glean as much information as I could. Part of me was trying to figure out how I could stay near Lewant, as no one would send me to where he was.

On the way back into Rojava I met a commander called *heval* Kane, and told her about my experience in Europe and about the three weeks I had spent in Aleppo. She invited me to train under her and accompany her around the different academies that were beginning to be set up across the Rojava area. This woman is one of the most senior women in our movement, and we call her '*Apo*'s daughter' as a sign of respect, or 'the mother of the party'. Today she is the commander of the whole area of Shingal. Belonging to her, in this tutelage position, would make it easy for me to travel around the area and meet the all-female battalions I would later go on to fight with.

All over the area people were organizing and protests were

taking place; the excitement of the democracy protests had spread and there was much debate about how best we could take advantage of the revolutionary spirit that had settled in the air all over the Middle East.

CHAPTER SIX

The Real Revolutionaries of Rojava

After Aleppo, I spent some time thinking about my options. The choice was to go back to Copenhagen and the women's refuge and continue my education and life there, or stay in Syria and join the women's army and become part of the movement officially. Our army is the armed wing of a much wider cultural and political campaign aimed at destroying patriarchy. We fight with weapons as others fight with ideas, and in order to understand our fight properly, we undergo quite a lot of ideological training. These were lessons I had yet to receive.

In the spring of 2011, way before I arrived in Syria, Kurds in Rojava founded the Self-Protection Unit of Rojava, the YPR. This group would eventually go on to become the People's Protection Units, the YPG, and young Kurds from all over the region started to join. Aleppo showed me that I needed better training and more of it, and around this time various academies started popping up in Rojava and in our mountain areas inside Iraq. The YPG opened doors for different groups to cooperate in new ways.

I was full of energy at the time, but I had so much to learn, particularly concerning the ideology of what the YPR were fighting for, because what I had learned in Copenhagen through the different Kurdish groups turned out to be quite superficial when applied in Syria. We fight for democratic confederalism, also sometimes called democratic autonomy, which operates as a kind of participatory self-rule that respects the cultural diversity of an area, while ensuring that no individual culture can dominate. It is the ideology of Abdullah Ocalan, whom we call *Apo*, who is the co-founder of our movement.

Instead of returning to Denmark to go to *gymnasium*, I decided to take some lessons on the roots of the movement at one of the training camps in Derek, in the *canton* or state of Qamislee. At the time I considered it like an unusually practical term abroad, not dissimilar to the one I intended to take in the USA, once I got to university. I had missed registration for the university term beginning in 2012 anyway, so this helped me make my decision to stay.

I was still a figure who raised some eyebrows within the group at this point, and my new friends would ask me hundreds of questions about growing up in Denmark, why I had come back to Kurdistan, and about my life growing up within 'the system'. Having experienced the gentle ribbing of my cousins and family while growing up, I knew not to take the teasing too seriously and I made some good friends.

One night in Derek I started to open up more about my time as a cheerleader in Denmark, describing what it actually involves and explaining how it was more than just dancing around and waving pompoms, when I was interrupted angrily by one of the others present. 'Your whole life is ruined, because you are a daughter of the system. You have been marked for life.' I stared at this person in silence, then around at the rest of the group, who quickly tried to move the conversation on. 'Marked for life' was a reference to so-called honour. I wasn't a virgin, so I was classed as a woman, instead of a girl.

I went outside to the yard by myself. An older female commander saw me sitting alone. 'Why are you out in the cold, instead of inside by the fire?' she asked gently, before settling her considerable frame down beside me. She had not been present during the conversation (I was relieved to hear), so I recounted it for her as she listened, patiently correcting my poor pronunciation and smiling at me through beautiful green eyes.

'Sister, I couldn't respond to him, because he is right: I am a woman,' I said. I was nineteen at the time and, like many other Danes of my age, I had lost my virginity. I hadn't expected its loss to be a source of mourning within our feminist, socialist revolution and I was confused and hurt by this reaction. This is not what we do in our movement – we don't discuss each other's past, especially not our past with the opposite sex. In terms of where I felt I belonged, on the wide spectrum of the different groups that make up the Kurdish movement, being in Aleppo and joining the democracy protests meant that I had moved away from the conservative, Muslim kind of groups, or those linked to the Iraqi *Peshmerga* associated with my family, and towards the more radical policies of Abdullah Ocalan and those who believe that women's freedom is the key to Kurdish freedom.

I explained to this commander that I was dismayed to find such a conservative attitude within the movement; I didn't understand it, and it reminded me of the painful wounds my family had inflicted on me, and the battles I had already fought in my past, which I had no wish to return to.

One of the younger girls in the group brought us out some tea, and I could see that this girl was trying to hang on to the commander's every word. I felt privileged to have a private audience with her, and I listened as intently as I could as she shared her reasons for giving up her life as a civilian and joining the women's movement. 'A woman is not defined in relation to a man. If a woman in your system was selling herself on the streets,' she said, 'I would still want you to fight for her rights before you let a man fight for yours.'

Many left-wing fighters in Kurdistan held this view that European women sell their bodies in different ways, by virtue of living in the West. By questioning the very definitions of the words our language uses to describe women and girls, she began to explain *jineology* to me.

This conversation finalized my decision, and I decided to take *jineology* training in one of the camps in Derek. It was due to last four and a half months. I wasn't worried about spending that long away from Denmark; I was more concerned that it was a long time to spend away from the frontline, and really I wanted to join the fight back in Aleppo and Serê Kaniyê and see Lewant again. But I knew there was no way I was getting back to the front without proper training, and without being a part of the group officially. Which was fine by me.

I also applied to take the special-forces training – the more practical weapons and combat-skills training that was being taught nearby. The training grounds were only a few miles away from each other, and several of the new volunteers who, like me, had some experience were taking both concurrently. Our academies are not signposted, because our ideological links with Ocalan make us a target for the Turkish republic.

What most people from outside Syria don't understand about the conflict is that Turkey hates us as Kurds even more than it hates Assad. We hate Turkey as well, for what it has done to us, but also for what it is doing to support our enemies. Turkey contributed to the rise of ISIS both indirectly, by keeping its borders open to the tens of thousands of foreign fighters who flowed into Syria, and directly, by providing them with arms and buying their looted oil. This posturing – by Turkey and by our political and military leaders – was why the war fractured so soon for us; as Kurds, we could not fight as part of the 'official' opposition army, the Free Syrian Army (FSA), because Turkey is part of this coalition.

The FSA, for its part, was too supportive of the Islamist groups that would eventually overrun it. Equally, we could not support Assad, as we recognized that the war came out of the people's desire for democracy, and so our way, as ever, is to tread a line between these two opposing forces. But honestly, I couldn't have predicted back then that the war would go on for so long, and I was a little nervous about spending such a long time training.

Once you get special-forces training – which we all call the A-team training card – you can ask to join any group within the movement, and the chances are you will be accepted. I went to make my case to the senior commanders, and was told I would be informed in due course whether I was successful. In the meantime I was accepted onto *jineology* training, so I said goodbye to my beloved commander Kane, who was returning to Europe.

Only women are allowed to do *jineology* training; men are forbidden from taking part or from teaching the classes – although they do learn about women's rights as part of their own ideology training. They don't have the right to have any say in any part of *jineology*, and even the highest male members do not have input into what we learn; it's decided by the female leaders of our movement, who have been working since the 1980s and 1990s, before I was born, attempting to realize women's rights in our region. When I was in Rojava, women were training for the formulation of the Women's Protection Units – the YPJ – and I am incredibly proud to have been trained in one of our earliest academies.

Like the YPG, the YPJ didn't just spontaneously emerge; there has always been a separate armed resistance movement. Back in 2012, when women and girls started joining, we numbered about 16,000 fighters; today we make up around 40,000 of the fighting force of the People's Protection movement – the YPG – which currently numbers about 60,000 fighters across both genders. In the West we are the subject of online fascination and sexism, but our importance cannot be overstated. We are the avant-garde of the frontline in Syria; we fight shoulder to shoulder with the men of the YPG, and are taught to go forward first. The success of the YPG, and of the Syrian Democratic Forces (SDF) coalition that defeated *Daesh*, is driven by our sacrifice, our training and our professionalism. The YPG is the main partner of the SDF, and in the YPJ we recognize that we are equal to the men, but also special and different from them.

I got a lift to the house I would be staying in while doing *jineology* training; it looked just like a normal home from the outside, while inside the rooms were full of girls my age who were due to join. I didn't know what to expect, and any illusions I had about it being similar to a study term abroad vanished that first morning. I was with some of the most badass warriors I would ever meet, and I had signed up for the revolution, so it was time to get involved.

There were three bedrooms and each housed about a dozen girls. We tend to operate with the natural light, to avoid attracting unnecessary attention, due to the Turkish threat against our movement. Wake-up time was 4.30 a.m., when we would get dressed, take our vest and our AK and line up, according to our units. Though I hadn't specifically asked, I was placed in the sabotage unit, meaning I would learn about explosives: how to build them and how to identify and dismantle them for parts. My heart fluttered a little as I thought that perhaps I had been skipped ahead a few classes as I had impressed my commander, but when I started the training I realized some of the other girls were also about my age.

The structure of the training was intended to teach us skills to keep us alive on the frontline, and skills useful to our group. If you wish to stay alive long enough to be useful, it's necessary to be able to dismantle the many mines that our country has been littered with. It's slightly easier for me, as a woman, to learn how to do sabotage than it is for a man, as my hands are smaller, so I can make and unmake intricate wire and munitions devices, but I didn't know this at the time. *Al-Qaeda* are excellent at using mines, and it was clear from the earliest days in Aleppo that they would be raising their ugly heads sooner or later.

We would all assemble in a line in the yard by exactly 4.45 a.m. – being late was not an option. Once we were in line, the commander would enter and shout, 'Good morning' – '*Roj baş*' – and we would all shout back as loud as we could, '*Roj baş*'. Then she would shout that she wanted *takmil* – meaning a report, or the briefing from all the different units. So the leader of each different unit would speak up.

'Unit: sabotage. We are eleven, this morning we are eleven.'

'Unit: civil defence. We are twelve, this morning we are eleven.'

The commander would then ask why there was a person missing, and in *jineology* training the leader would respond, 'She is on her holy day', meaning that she has her period. In mixed training camps or mixed battles, when you give *takmil* and a woman has her period, we would not say this, we would simply say she was 'sick', because we wouldn't want the others to know, though they may have guessed. Each unit would do the same thing: state the name of the unit, the number of people in that unit and the number attending training that particular day.

After *takmil* we would start the physical-exercise training: athletic work like running and interval training. I loved this part of the day and found it very easy, as I had done a lot of sport growing up, something that girls in the Middle East are not really encouraged to do. According to our leader, Abdullah Ocalan, a woman's body should be athletic and healthy. This early-morning session would last an hour, and later on in the day there would be a second session, normally involving the same kind of interval and running tasks, but with the additional weight of our weapons.

From 6 a.m. to 6.30 was free time; we would wash, or some would even go back to bed for a little snooze. Then 7 a.m. was breakfast and at 7.30 classes would begin. Every day a different person would be responsible for breakfast, and that person would have to get up earlier to prepare. The mornings were when the most difficult ideology classes would begin, when we were most alert.

The classes started quite simple: they focused on the reasons why girls should be educated in classrooms instead of in the home, and the first stages could be described as a 'deprogramming' from the brainwashing that Kurdish girls receive in our families, from before we can talk or form our own thoughts. We learned exactly how our bodies were different from men's – it might sound silly to say this, but learning about their own biology in detail was something many of the girls I was with had very little knowledge of. These lessons were a mixture of biology and sociology, starting from the basic premise that women are the creators of life, and not the other way about.

We learned a lot about language. I don't really like the word 'woman', as it relates historically as a prefix to the word 'man'. I prefer the word 'female', as it comes from 'feminine', which has its own distinct meaning: as we are completely distinct from men, we deserve to have an adequate word that reflects this.

There was a sisterhood among those taking *jineology* training, and this was of course encouraged – it was the kind of bond very few people get to experience. We would spend every hour of every day and night together: brushing our teeth and hair together, in class, eating, training, singing songs or sleeping. It wasn't like a slumber party or a sleepover; we didn't talk about our former lives, boys or our families too much. We talked about our dreams for the women's revolution; we ate, slept and dreamed the revolution.

Make-up is a tool of sexual slavery, so it's not like we would share eyeliner tips, but I did spend many hours plaiting my hair and having it plaited by the others. My hair is very big, wavy and curly, so the other girls liked playing with it. I love having my hair done, and I love my friends doing it for me – but to ask people in Denmark to do so creates an awkwardness that simply didn't exist among my friends in Rojava. On one occasion, when I was sick, my friends washed me; it was really intimate and there were no boundaries. We talked about what we were there to learn, how we would apply our learning on the frontline and how we intended to take the women's revolution to the whole of Kurdistan, and the whole of the Middle East.

Lunch break would be from 11.30 till 12 p.m. and a different person would be rotated in to prepare the meals each day. After lunch there was more practical training and further teaching, which went on until around 4.30 in the afternoon; and then around 5 p.m. we would eat dinner and relax before going to bed early, around sunset. Our lessons taught us about some of the particular sacrifices that we, as female fighters, have to make. These ranged from small details to big sacrifices: artificially removing hair is not allowed, and neither is having a lover, a family or a husband.

Barring the international volunteers, it's very rare for a Kurdish fighter to have had any relations with a man during their time in the group, and relations between the sexes are strictly prohibited. We were not to talk to the men or boys too much while on the frontline; our communication had to stay operational, and we were taught to maintain a cool distance at all times, with minimal eye contact. Learning these rules, I began to realize why I had been attracting so much male attention in Aleppo, and why my normal behaviour could invite sexual advances in some situations.

We are not permitted to brush our teeth in front of the men, or remove or loosen even the hottest clothing in the most stifling heat. Because we are women in uniform and we are leading this revolution for women's rights, we are sometimes seen as aggressive or anti-men or anti-love, but we are not. We fight for a new kind of man and a new kind of love, just as we are a new kind of woman. It's a very new thing in the region, so the onus is on us, we are told, to make sure that we do not cause any sexual misunderstandings. It's confusing and at times, honestly, I found it quite frustrating; we fight for equality for all women and to change the culture of oppression, yet we have to agree to operate within that same culture, so that we can maintain support and grow our numbers.

Families would not permit their daughters to join us if there was even the faintest rumour of any kind of sexual contact between men and women as we fight together; it would be seen as dishonourable, not just for the girl who joined, but for the whole family. As it is now, we are viewed by our culture as the most honourable women, with more freedom than other women and more experience of what life is like as a man. The social-behaviour classes were the ones I found the most challenging, and I would constantly ask my trainer to explain things that others in the class accepted without quarrel. I found it hard to walk the line between what we were fighting for and what we were fighting against.

'Joanna,' one of my favourite trainers, Aya, said on one of the first days in *jineology* training, 'why are you wearing those clothes? Aren't you cold?'

Embarrassed to be called out so early on, I answered in my still-faltering Kermanji mixed with Arabic that I wasn't; I was roasting compared to how I would be in January in Denmark, and I liked to have the air around my skin.

'No, wrong,' Aya replied flatly. 'It is cold. You have just become used to this kind of sexually objectifying behaviour; you do it unconsciously.' Not knowing what to say, I let her continue. 'We see how you are in Europe: you think you are liberated, but you are just slaves to a man's society.'

I was pretty shocked at how forward Aya was, and as she delivered this judgement on my clothes she smiled at me mischievously. This 'false feminism' theory of women in the West was one of her favourite lectures, and I would argue in defence of the freedoms that women have in Danish society, ones that I was not permitted to have by my Kurdish family.

I was really fond of Aya; she was smart and funny, and eventually we became quite close. She praised me for growing out my eyebrows, as instructed by the fighters I met on the way into Aleppo. 'You know what you need to do, Joanna. You know how it works, but there's a difference between knowing and practising what you know, and that's where you fall down.' We argued a lot, the two of us, but she taught me so much, and she made me understand the reasons for the rules, as well as the rules themselves. Her nickname for me was *zaroki kapitalist* – which means 'a child of capitalism' – not the best nickname to have within a socialist revolutionary armed group, and it seemed to stick in those early years. Aya was one of the first women fighters of the newly announced YPJ to be killed in 2012 and died only a few months after she had trained me. Many of my old commanders from this time, sadly, are no longer around.

In the camp, and on the frontline, our lives have equal value – equal to each other and equal to those of the men. What we in the YPJ had in common was our desire to escape the life afforded to women in our region: to marry whoever our family chose, to be a servant to that new family, to take whatever treatment our husbands wished to give us, to give birth and be a servant to our children.

Some of the trainers were girls who had been with the Kurdish movement since they were young, and others were around the same age as us students, which I found particularly inspiring. It was good to have a variety of trainers. They told us stories about how arguments could happen on the front, and how important it was to stick together as women, especially if we were being accused of something in battle by a man: not running fast enough, or delaying for critical moments that allowed an ambush. 'A woman is always another woman's lawyer,' I said to Aya as she explained it, and I liked the idea of seeing myself as a lawyer for other women.

One of the older women trainers whom I was most fond of, a Kermanji Kurd called Avesta, taught us a class on shame and our bodies. Avesta was a very strong woman, with long brown hair that was dyed with henna, which she would style into these beautiful elaborate plaits. She didn't like any of us smoking, or being lazy, and she would constantly tell us off, but we all loved her. She was old school, but she understood young minds. Unlike the other trainers, she asked us a lot of questions: about our homes, our family life and what we were allowed to watch on television. She asked us about the first time we felt guilty or ashamed about being a woman, and we all laughed and cried and shared our stories. I had expected the girls to talk about the first time they got their period, but everyone shared weirdly revealing anecdotes about their lives: being prevented from playing football; having to help their mothers in the kitchen while their brothers got to stay with the men; praying at the mosque and having to cover their hair, legs and shoulders. Always covering, always trying to be invisible. One girl was from a family where she had to wear an *abaya*, a full-length outer garment; she ran away to the mountains to escape being married to her older cousin, who already had a wife. It was amazing to realize how much I had in common with these girls, even though I had grown up so far away.

This trainer, Avesta, stood up in front of us and opened up her military jacket. Under her jacket she was wearing a green-and-black sports bra, and we all gasped as she lifted up her bra and asked us, 'Should I be ashamed of these? This is a part of me. Is it my fault my body has this? Is it my shame?' Everyone gaped at her open-mouthed, and a few of us looked around the room nervously, as we didn't want anyone to come in and misunderstand what was happening. She sat down, having pulled her bra back down, but her flesh was still exposed. She referred to Ocalan's words that a woman should never feel apologetic about her body due to society's pressures telling her that she should change her body to fit its specified ideal. We all sat aghast as she sat there with her breasts exposed. And she asked us, 'Why are you here?'

One of the older girls ventured timidly, 'Because we want to train.'

'No!' Avesta said. 'Why are you here on this planet? Who brought you into being? Was it your father who put his breast in your mouth? Was it him who gave you life?'

She stood up and continued, as we all watched silent and mesmerized, and as her breasts became visible again there was an audible gasp around the room. She started shouting and yelling and walking around, as we stared in shock. A few of the younger girls, I could tell, were so nervous they were trying not to cry. I just stared at her smiling slightly, disbelieving what I was seeing.

'It wasn't your father who took milk out of his breast and gave it to you. None of your fathers, none of the prophets and not even our leader is able to sustain life with their body. Yet we can look at their bodies, while our body is something to be ashamed of,' she continued. Back at the front of the room, she told us all to look at her. 'I have no shame of my body, because my body is capable of life. Why do we look up to men, when without women no one would be here? Why do women's bodies break to give life, and then they have no life of their own?' We stared at her as she crescendoed into her finish. 'It's not our shame, girls – it's theirs. They own the shame. We have no shame, girls, no shame.'

She fixed her top back and covered her breasts, then asked, quieter now, 'How many of you have a good story from before you joined us, about a man?' Everyone who wasn't already crying with shock at this point let their tears flow. No one in the room had a good story about a man. I didn't go into the full extent of my bad experiences: with my brother, my father or my boyfriends; but I listened as the others shared theirs. Avesta listened to everyone and let us cry. 'We will only be free when women's security becomes more important than men's feelings. No one will give us these rights; not even within our movement. This is why we take them, and you, as fighters, will claim them for all women. Remember, you are not just fighting

for yourself; you are fighting for every baby misfortunate enough
to be born a girl.'

Avesta took a special interest in me because I struggled with
the language, and she helped me learn Kermanji so that I could
communicate better with the other girls. She would sit patiently
with me in the evenings, teaching me how to weave little plastic
pearls into my headscarf to make the scarf look more beautiful.
She never called me by my codename, as the other trainers
did. She only ever called me Joanna, and I liked the way she
pronounced my name. She also taught me to open up a little
more with the other girls; to share things with them, so that they
would feel closer to me, and I could feel closer to them. 'Joanna,
you have come a long way to be with us, and you will go further
than you ever thought was possible.'

Another class taught by Avesta and *heval* Newpelda taught us
the history of women's oppression. Newpelda's name means 'new
buds', like the kind that grow on trees each spring. She lived in
France for ten years with her family when she was young, but
left to return to Kurdistan and become a commander when she
was only seventeen. I believe she is still alive, and would be about
thirty now. She is the tallest Kurdish girl I have ever met, with
beautiful white skin and small black eyes. She was one of the
commanders in charge of the special-forces training, which was
also taking place near Derek, and was a complete badass. She
was always positive and calm, and I tried my best to impress her
in class, because I knew she could get me onto the special-forces
training, which would give me a lot of opportunities.

Newpelda took an interest in me as a fellow European girl and
seemed to make an effort to apply the lessons to my experience

and knowledge of European history. Our classes included reports from Amnesty International, the United Nations and other groups that covered women's oppression across the system – in the Muslim world, but also within areas where women supposedly had equality. 'It doesn't matter if the organization is right wing or left wing,' Newpelda told us. 'It doesn't matter if you are in Afghanistan getting stones thrown at your head; if you are in Saudi Arabia being beheaded for falling in love with a boy; if you think you have your freedom as a Western girl, when really you don't,' she would tell us. All of the trainers loved to talk about the false consciousness of Western feminism – it was really one of their favourite topics. 'What matters is that men hate women,' Newpelda said. 'Some do it subtly, some do it obviously, but the culture of society all over the world rests on its hatred of females: that is why we are fighting to destroy this culture and remake it as a new one.'

I made my pledge to the movement around the time of my *jineology* training, with a group of girls just outside Derek. The pledge is a kind of promise to the movement: we call it the *soz* and you repeat it three times, after which you get a certificate, about the size of a small bank card.

I made the promise at the start of my training, as everyone did back then, and I was the first woman in the world to do so as a volunteer, I was told. I made it in Kermanji, like the others, and I didn't know exactly what I was saying, but I knew what it was about, of course. I promised to fight and die for *Seroketi*, the ideas of Abdullah Ocalan, for the women's revolution and for the Kurdish *sehids*, martyrs who had passed before. I discussed beforehand the terms with my commanders, including Kane, who had started me on this new journey. I explained to her that I didn't want to promise to stay in the mountains of Kurdistan for ever: I wanted to go back to Europe and spread the word of the women's revolution. I wanted to become one of the freedom fighters for the women's revolution and I was ready to give my life for it, but I wasn't ready to give up my freedom. The others I trained with would all have been pledging to give up the rest of their lives and stay in the mountains, and they would have become what we in the movement call *cadras*. Back then, there were no international volunteers who came to train and fight. Anyone who was part of the movement was a *cadra*, but my commander agreed that I could pledge to fight and die, without promising never to leave.

On the day of the pledge the sun was shining, and we got up early to clean and make ourselves look and feel as nice as possible. The other girls were giddy, but I was slightly more pensive, in case the senior commander who was officiating at the ceremony wouldn't allow me to pledge unless I agreed to become a full *cadra*, like the others. Senior commanders from all over the area joined us for the ceremony, including my commander Kane, and I burst with pride as she walked past me and winked at me on the way to her spot at the head of the ceremony.

I was standing, like the other girls, with my shoulders back, my head high, my chest puffed out under my uniform and my feet hip distance apart. Now that I was a fighter, I didn't stand as if I was trying to look like a Kardashian – the way women in the West are encouraged to stand: making my butt stick out. I had my rifle on my right-hand side, but it wasn't loaded. I was thrilled with myself. The senior commanders stood at the top of our yard, underneath the Kurdish flag, opposite where we were standing in several rows, each waiting our turn.

Aya was standing beside our trainers, and her commanders were standing beside Kane and the other senior fighters who had come over specially. There were only around thirty of us joining that day, but about a dozen YPJ commanders had come to welcome us. Lined up at the top of the yard was Avesta with another older woman, whom none of us knew directly, beside the table. Beside her was our senior training commander who called the *takmil* every morning, and her commander, who did some occasional lectures, but whom we didn't see every day. Behind Kane was *heval* Newpelda and other senior women from the movement. Our last day of doing the test to join is really when our commanders are tested by their commanders. Everyone is in a circle, and equal, and every part must work correctly, like the cogs inside a watch. On the table was a picture of Ocalan, a picture representing the *sehids* martyrs who had already died for Kurdish freedom, and a symbol of the women's movement.

I was near the back of the yard, which I was relieved about, and as we fell into line and yelled our hello to Kane and the other commanders, I felt my hands become sweaty on my Kalashnikov. I breathed deeply and practised the formation we had rehearsed, and when the ceremony started I began to relax, as the other girls made their promises and were congratulated and given their papers afterwards.

We went up in groups of three, so when each group went up our line would shuffle forward a bit. Having run through it several times in the days before, I knew what to do, and I knew my *soz* promise off by heart. The camera was running; pledges are filmed, so that you can't lie about them or deny them in the future, and they can be used against you if you do something that goes against the movement, so you must be careful.

When it was my turn, I was in the centre, with two girls I had trained with, Ariya and Sera, on either side. They were both Syrian girls, and I knew they were nervous, too. We ran up to the front, placed our AKs on the table and stood tall and proud, ready to begin. Before we did so, our promises were read out to each of us. As part of the promise, you write your own future: saying what skills or aspects of the movement you want to work in, and what skills you want to learn as a fighter.

When the time came for us to make the final part of the vows together, we stood with our hands on the table to our left side, with the flag flying in front of us. With my body facing the flag, I placed my left hand on the table and my right hand in a fist on my heart. My hand on the table was spread as much as possible, across the trinity of our movement: Abdullah Ocalan, the women's movement and the *sehids* martyrs. Then we each shook hands with all of the commanders and the other girls were given their papers. I wasn't given my papers, because I didn't promise to stay for ever. When our pledge was finished, the commanders and those watching – but not pledging – clapped. We took our Kalashnikovs, ran back to our place in the line and another group ran up to begin their pledge. You only have to make this promise once, as it's normally for life.

A few days after taking my pledge, *heval* Newpelda informed me that I had been given permission to attend special-forces training. I had passed some sort of invisible test, and I thanked

Newpelda repeatedly. She smiled and told me she would be able to give me a lift between the two training camps, as I hadn't quite finished *jineology* and she was teaching at both sites. A few of the other girls had also been accepted, so we would travel back and forth between the two camps together.

Compared to conditions on the special-forces A-team training, our existing cramped bedroom conditions were like staying in a five-star hotel. Don't get me wrong: this hotel wouldn't score even one star on TripAdvisor, but that is how it felt in comparison. Depending on the course structure for the week, I would be informed where I would be going. Normally special-forces training lasts six months and is a serious investment by the movement: four months of physical training in the camps, then eight weeks of ideology to finish. Doing this course enables you to become an independent fighter within the movement; in a normal battalion of fighters, this training means that you will be one of the more experienced and, as is increasingly the case now, there are some special-forces battalions – such as those who fought as part of the SDF in Raqqa – where everyone has to have undergone the training in order to be in the battalions on the frontline.

Our special forces are those that go to the very front and face the enemy, and it's vital that we, as YPJ fighters, are there. What some of the international volunteers have found difficult to understand, when they come and want to fight, is that most of our fighters have had many months and even years of training; not just in ideology, but in combat skills and light-armour guerrilla tactics. These are all forged in the mountains, and commanders can be initially reluctant to send international volunteers into the most difficult frontline work, as few international fighters have any kind of guerrilla training. The Kurds in Rojava in the beginning were Syrian – now they are more likely to be from other parts of Kurdistan, especially the Turkish part, Bakur. Most of the Syrian Kurds who joined in the beginning are dead. The average age for our fighters is between seventeen and twenty-two – it's not often you meet a YPJ fighter who is over thirty.

I am considered a Kurd by the movement, not an international volunteer, but some allowances have been made. Even some of the international volunteers who have been professional soldiers don't know our methods, although they may have a lot of combat experience. It's not like *jineology* training, where you can do it once and then you have it; you can do our training time and time again, and many elect to do so.

If the Turks knew about our training, they would certainly bomb us, so we keep the camps completely covered. All of the girls whom I pledged with, and who were selected for the training, were told individually where to go; there are no signs, and even once you are in the mountains, it can be hard to make out where you are going unless you know the right way. Getting into the different academies is not guaranteed; you have to ask the academy commanders for permission to go, and it was not easy to get selected. I was honoured to have the opportunity to attend the special-forces camp, and I knew that I had a lot to prove.

Instead of staying in houses, we camped in the mountains with absolutely no comforts throughout the winter and into the spring. We were instructed to keep our faces covered with scarves, so that only our eyes could be seen; we call this having our faces 'locked'. We were supposed to do this even when sleeping, though not everyone did. Training was mixed-gender and we slept protected by felled trees, high in the mountains near Derek. On my first night we slept with minimal cover under some tarpaulin and trees, despite it still being winter. I was worried I would freeze to death, so like some of the others, I stayed awake and walked around, looking for food and the best areas to make a more protected camp.

We love the mountains and have learned over many years to survive there with nothing, but this was the first time in all my training so far that I felt I had perhaps pushed myself to too much of an extreme; how little I knew back then about surviving when you have nothing. I trusted my commanders with my life, and it's a weird feeling to accept the reality of that trust, when you are sleeping exposed on the side of a mountain without knowing where the next meal is coming from. I could hear birds and some wild animals, so I knew deep down that none of us would starve. I thought of Lewant on the frontline, fighting Assad's soldiers, as I surveyed my own peaceful, stunning surroundings, and felt at once both guilty and determined. I kept my spirits high by repeating to myself that I would get through this and get back to the front. We all would.

I found that first week the hardest, though the actual tasks grew progressively tougher as training went on. Our first task was to build a new place for us to sleep. Working together, we decided to dig a big hole in the ground, which took us two days. We tunnelled in, using a small hole that we then covered up, and which formed our way in; and then when we were about six feet down, the hole became a lot bigger – almost large enough for us to stand up, and big enough for the twenty of us who were training to sleep in. Then, at the other end of the bigger underground hole, we tunnelled another hole out. We also made several air holes, so the dugout would stay ventilated. Keeping my face covered the whole time with my scarf, I listened to the discussions, gathered branches from dead trees and dug wherever I was told to.

Instead of relying on the teams of food and ammunition suppliers that we call 'logistics', we had to survive in the wild by hunting whatever we could find, getting by on very little food and limited water. The mountains around Derek are not as green as those between Iraq and Iran, so it's a more challenging environment, and the threat of drone strikes from Turkey can be critical. Going underground protected us from drone strikes and also allowed us to maintain heat, as the conditions were freezing. We huddled together at night for warmth and comfort, still fully dressed and with our faces covered with our scarves.

After we built our new 'home', the first few days were fitness training; we had to run up a hill with a large tyre on our backs, and we would build up every day, until we reached the top of the hill. It took us a full five days to get up in a time that satisfied our trainer who, like us, wore his face locked, which muffled his voice, but did not disguise the volume of his yelling. 'Dead. Dead. Dead,' he would yell. 'Too slow. Too slow. Lucky animals feasting on your fat bodies tonight,' he would laugh, as if he had said the funniest joke in the world. Finally we made it up the steep cliff-like hill overlooking the ravine in a time that seemed to satisfy him. He didn't say 'Well done' or anything as he wasn't exactly the type for positive feedback, but he was at least satisfied enough not to make further terrible jokes.

The day that we made it to the top within the time limit we were celebrating a little, encouraging the slower among our groups and helping them with their tyres when they reached the top, when he interrupted our self-congratulation: 'Now time to jump off.'

We looked at him and at each other, and then down the side of the hill, which was probably almost 500 feet high and almost vertical, and we point-blank refused. 'This is suicide,' Jihan, one of the girls from my ideology training, said loudly. The guys didn't say anything, but just shuffled about and waited for the commander to explain. He gave us a long speech on the importance of risk-taking, and measuring risk in situations that are out of your control.

'If you think you will die, then you will die. But if you survive, it will be because you will do anything to survive.' Even though our faces were all locked, I am sure he could read the unconvinced expressions in our eyes. He continued, undeterred, 'In war, I won't be here to tell you what to do, and sometimes your mind won't always work as well as it should, so you just have to be prepared to do anything to survive. If you are here in this spot and the enemy is coming, and the only thing you can do that might help you survive is to jump, because maybe then you will make it, then you have to try. If you end up in the hands of the enemy, you will be dead, in the most awful way.'

At this point he looked especially at us girls, who had naturally gravitated towards each other, as we glared at him. 'No one is going to help you in a war because you are a woman,' he said, 'equal rights in combat means the equal right to die.'

This guy is a psycho, I thought, and I am going to die on some stupid mountain in Syria nowhere near the frontline. Jihan muttered my exact thoughts under her breath, and a few of us murmured and grunted our agreement. Everyone was looking at each other, and some of the guys started slowly down the hill, holding each other's hands the way you see kindergarten kids travel during school trips, and slowly walking sideways down the side of the drop. They were taking these tiny pathetic, nervous steps, as us girls looked at each other, unconvinced.

Heval Cochin was about nineteen, but had been in the movement for a while. She was a really small, curvy girl with tight black curls that you could see out of the side of her scarf. She didn't hide her ambitions to be a commander; she loved to dominate and be in charge and was always trying to prove herself. She charged straight over the edge and started down; she let out a huge scream as she did so, and half-ran, half-rolled down the hill. The rest of us girls screamed and dived after her; we all ran down – trying not to roll like her, but much faster than the kindergarten crab-walk the boys were doing.

I was really close to *heval* Cochin when she dived, and I could hear her scream the whole way down: 'Fuck! I'm going to die! Fuck!' was all she said. When we all piled after her, I thought we would be finding a body, as she was flying down, hitting different rocks, stones and trees.

'She is mincemeat,' Jihan said. By the time we reached Cochin, close to the bottom, three or four frantic minutes had passed. All her fingers were broken, from trying to grab the side of the mountain, and she was covered in blood.

I wasn't the first to reach her, but I went over to her with the other girls and we totally surrounded her to see how badly injured she was. She was still conscious and she was laughing, almost hysterically now. 'She's in shock – it's the adrenaline,' someone said.

But thankfully Cochin's brain was still working and she replied, despite being covered in blood, 'No, no, that was amazing. I want to do it again.'

We looked at each other: 'That psycho didn't kill her, but he definitely killed her senses,' Jihan said.

We went back to class and did a debrief; those who were injured were bandaged up and we sat down with tea and our commander, and he gave us some feedback. There was one YPG guy who was badly injured because, as the commander explained, he had not fought for his life. 'If you throw a bag of potatoes off the mountain, it will hit every stone, every piece of rock and every tree on the way down.'

I looked around at the injured ones among us and felt really sorry for them. I had managed to get down with only a minor graze to my ankle and a few cuts to my hands. I did hit my head, though, which could have caused some damage that I was unaware of at the time, and I have wondered about this many times since, so the jury is still out on that one. This commander may have thought that us girls were inspired by his little pep talk at the top of the mountain, but actually we were thinking: Fuck this guy, he is trying to kill us. I jumped because Cochin jumped: as a YPJ fighter, we protect each other from harm. The commander was still talking, and as I looked round my friends out of the corner of my eye, I could see that I wasn't the only one to be unconvinced.

'In our army, we live in nature and we die in nature: therefore you must become like an animal – jumping down a mountain like a squirrel, not rolling down like a sack of potatoes,' he continued. A few of the YPG guys squirmed in their seats; even those who had taken the training before hadn't performed well in that task, and I knew they were feeling ashamed. Turning to us girls, the commander told us, 'One of you jumped and the others followed; so you were quicker, but that is not a sign that you were successful. The next time all of you must jump as one person; you don't need anyone to lead you, you are already one person inside.'

We were dismissed, and our training was over for the day. We retired really early and a few of us girls were driven back to the comfort of the *jineology* training on the other side of Derek. About a week later, Cochin and I were talking after ideology class, and she said that after her fall down the mountain she had some unfamiliar discharge in her underwear, which lasted several days. 'I know I can't get pregnant now,' she said quite solemnly, even though I knew she had made the full 'for ever' promise and had already pledged to give up that life. The sacrifice the YPJ fighters make is unique within our culture of female fighters. In the other Kurdish movements that I trained with, as a younger teenager, the women would get trained and their baby could stay with them. They would then go back home, and if they were attacked or there was a battle, they would have the right training to protect themselves and their kids. But within the YPJ, the possibilities of this kind of family life are taken away.

Special-forces training was a shock to the system, and I understood why *heval* Newpelda was so amused at how happy I was to be selected. We moved over a large area of land throughout our time there, and one of the exercises was based on maintaining water in our bodies when we had no food and only meagre fresh-water supplies. This was to teach us how to keep our temperature stable. After this exercise Captain Cliff Dive (as we had started to call him) taught us how to survive in an area where there were no wild animals to kill for food, by making us catch and eat a variety of insects. He made us eat everything: woodlice, beetles, slugs, even daddy-long-legs, which I hated the most, as there was hardly any meat on them and their legs were disgusting.

The highest members of our movement do not eat meat, or even fish, as we believe that the animals have their own purpose in life, and that each living creature can feel pain; and just because some animals kill others to survive, we as humans do not need to do this. We have more food than we need, without killing. So eating insects is extreme for us, and is not our normal way. Our commander would get us to collect them and then showed us how to eat them alive. All of us who were new to this training initially thought he was joking – surely there was no way we would ever be in a battle where there would be no food, and where logistics wouldn't be able to get through; but he wasn't. And we were wrong: in Kobani we ate anything to survive, and I was glad this commander had been so strict and had made us all try every kind of these disgusting insects. His training helped save my life, as he taught me that I could eat anything.

'Proteins are important in battle, and there is more protein in these insects than in the bread we are making for you. The only reason we make the bread is that is it very cheap, but if you want to survive in a battle then you need to get protein any way you can.'

He was quite calm and matter-of-fact about the whole thing. The worst of these animals were clown beetles: disgusting tiny beetles that live off animal shit, dead animals or decaying bodies. These are, in fact, the best source of protein, because they can digest the protein from the bodies they eat, he explained, and they can kill the bacteria in the decay. 'It's better that you eat a plate of these beetles than a chicken, here in Rojava: chickens can't kill the bacteria from the dead they eat – these creatures can.' I am glad he taught us this lesson, but it was a disgusting evening meal. None of us got sick, though, which surprised me, probably because we hadn't eaten for the previous few days. Our bodies were craving protein, so they accepted the flesh-eating beetles.

There were times when it felt like the commanders were trying to give us rather shorter lives. Our final physical test was one that I had heard about from rumours before I entered the training – one that those who had gone before had warned us about. We had to light a fire, and attach a wire frame to the fire to make a shape that we could crawl through, holding a large boulder in our arms. If we dropped the boulder, the fire would spread and burn our bodies, so of course no one did. The boys went first, as we sat around watching nervously. The wire frame that held the flames was big enough to crawl through comfortably – so without the boulder it would be fine, but the purpose of the exercise was to improve our upper-body strength, while moving with our lower bodies.

One slip of the fingers and the boulder would go down, which would trip the frame containing the flames. 'Boys, will you make us a nice BBQ finger to eat tonight?' Captain Cliff Dive teased. We laughed nervously, and watched as the boys successfully made their way through the wire. 'Shall I tickle under their arms, girls?' he asked us. No one responded, as we were all watching their technique.

Next it was our turn. Cochin went first, of course, and despite her curvy frame got through fine. Our boulders were as heavy as the men's – just as our weapons are. We gathered round, encouraging each other by shouting and waving each girl through. Cochin, Jihan and three other girls, whose names I didn't know, all went through fine. I was sixth in line, and when it was my turn I lay down on the ground and focused my attention on the other side of the flames. The boulder was heavy – as heavy as a person – and I half-held it, half-rolled it into position behind the wire. Lying as flat as I could to the floor, with the boulder in my arms, I crawled forward. Taking a deep breath as I looked ahead, I grabbed the boulder tight to my chest and face – so tight I grazed my chin, though I didn't notice it at the time.

As the heat from the flames hit my face, I crawled through as fast as I could. Once my head was through, I was so relieved I almost stopped, but I could see the others yelling for me to continue: I wasn't out of danger yet. Still clutching the boulder, I used my elbows and knees to propel myself forward further still. A few seconds later, safely out of harm's way from the flames, I let the boulder go and collapsed on the ground, drenched with sweat. The whole task had lasted probably less than a minute, and the sweat on my face mixed with my tears of relief as I crawled over to the others.

Once you have this kind of training, there is no going back; you can't go back to the innocent person you were before. You have the skills now, so you are bound to do the right thing and fight.

I thought of this as I took my face-scarf off to help me breathe and lay on my back, looking at the sky, with my whole body convulsing as I tried to recover. I might not have been an official *cadra*, but I knew I had just entered a different league.

CHAPTER SEVEN

The Friendly Agents of the PET

After completing the physical classes of our special-forces training, and the *jineology* training that enabled me to join the YPJ officially, I decided to return to Europe for a while that summer, and this visit turned into longer than expected, so eventually I was able to continue my European education. Some of what I had learned in the camps had jarred with what I thought I knew before, and I wanted to know if the unsettled feelings I had about the ideology training – and my tendency to argue so much with my trainers – was due to some deficit in my understanding.

I knew I didn't want to pledge to stay in the mountains for ever, to give up my freedom or the lifestyle of Europe, but I did want to be part of this movement for the rest of my life. My vague plan was to get an education and see how else I might be able to contribute to the war in Syria and other war zones where females were left alone. I flew back to Copenhagen and asked Anita, who ran the women's refuge, if I could come back. I then enrolled in a nearby high school called CPH West.

Initially I was lonely back in the hostel, isolated in my thoughts, missing the girls and confused by this new plan. Without any family support and only sporadic telephone contact, I started making new friends in different political organizations, and becoming close to different movements that had settled in Christiania. Officially called Freetown Christiania, this is a self-proclaimed autonomous anarchist area of Copenhagen, home to about 1,000 people from all walks of life. It exists in this weird way with the city authorities, but is self-governing, with its own set of laws. It is also somewhere that marijuana is readily available.

Towards the end of 2013 I somehow turned from a regular user of marijuana to someone who relied on it. What had started as a bedtime treat turned into an expensive daytime pastime and an emotional crutch, and as I wasn't working at the time it became a huge drain on my finances. My family was living hundreds of miles away in Jutland, and we had very little contact. They didn't know I had been in Syria for almost nine months. They weren't giving me any kind of support whatsoever, and although I had many contacts in different groups in Christiania and school, I was missing close friends.

By this stage I had moved out of the shelter and into an apartment by myself in Norrebro. I was trying to obtain the qualifications I needed to study nursing, but was also figuring out where I belonged politically. I took a school loan to help me pay my bills, but I spent most of my money on marijuana. Whether I needed it to stay calm or not, the fact that I thought I did made me reliant upon it.

I decided to pluck up the courage to tell people about my plans to go and join the fight in Syria, and to share my thoughts

on arming women wherever they need protection. I told my family at the start of 2014 that I planned to go into battle with the YPG in Syria, and of my ambition to bring the philosophy of the armed women's movement to all of the Middle East. My family are Iraqi and mostly Iranian *Peshmerga*, whose politics are chauvinistic conservative Islam, and politically they are very far away from the YPG, though on the battlefield against *Daesh* these groups have worked together. By this stage my father was no longer living in the family home as he had moved in with my uncle's wife, so my brothers had assumed full control of our household. I hadn't lived at home for almost two years now, and I returned only sporadically to visit my mother. I didn't expect them to be happy with my plans, and I had prepared myself for their negative reaction. But I wasn't expecting the violence that I was met with. Being back at home and being beaten up made me feel like I was thirteen again, and entirely helpless. How can I stop *Daesh* from beating and capturing girls, I wondered, when I can't even stop my own brothers' violence against me?

My older brother laughed at me and taunted me: 'What the hell are you going to do in a war? Have you seen how small you are? And just a worthless girl!' We argued and he ended up slapping me across the face. He laughed as he did it and I didn't fight back – just as I had never dared to as a child. I stayed calm and looked into his eyes, and thought to myself: You are not half the man you think you are.

It was weird because I think he expected me to fight him back, or maybe he could tell that something in me had changed. No one in the family knew I had already been to Syria, or about the training I had completed there. They knew, of course, that I could shoot, and that I had been to the *Lawan* training camps, because they had taken me there, and they knew about my connections to the different Kurdish movements in Denmark, because in many cases it was my family who introduced me to them. But they weren't happy with the new connections I had managed to make for myself.

Back then, despite the smoking issues, I was making a new life for myself in Copenhagen, away from my family, and I felt good about myself in ways I hadn't ever felt as a younger child. I was very confident and had big dreams that I wasn't prepared to let my family destroy.

My older sister came to stay with me at the start of 2014, shortly after I had that final fight with my brother. Ostensibly she came to 'help' me with the troubles I was experiencing with sleeping and smoking, and with my finances. I didn't find her helpful at all, and we argued a lot. She would tell me that the reason our mother wasn't happy was because of the shame of having me as a daughter, living away by myself in Copenhagen, instead of the fact that my father had taken his brother's widow as a second wife. But I was no longer willing to accept the blame for our family problems.

It did strike me as weird that my sister felt this sudden concern for me; she had never stepped in to protect me at home throughout the time we were growing up. That's not to say I didn't appreciate her staying with me for those weeks – I did. Or at least I did until I discovered her real motive.

On the morning of 26th January 2014 I was lying in bed when the doorbell rang unexpectedly. It was a Sunday morning and we had no plans for the day. Before I could say how strange it was, my sister sprang up to answer it. I was immediately suspicious, as I know my sister is quite shy and it was unlike her to answer my door. There were two plainclothes police officers outside, a blonde woman and a man. My sister didn't seem confused or surprised by their arrival, and from the way she was monitoring my reaction I suspected that she had arranged this friendly little chat that we were about to have.

I couldn't believe it. My family – the same family who wouldn't allow me to play football, but who raised me to be a Kurdish woman of honour; the same family who forced me to learn Kurdish rebel songs before I knew the Danish alphabet, when I was four years old – had shopped me to the authorities. I stayed very calm and surveyed the people gathered in my room: my traitorous sister representing my family, and these two awkward Danish police.

'I would have tidied, if my family had told me you were coming,' I said, shooting a look at my sister, which she carefully ignored. They settled down and refused my offer of tea, coffee or water. I was very open with them when they asked me why I wanted to travel to Syria and go to war. 'I have nothing to hide. I intend to go to the Middle East and I have told my family, who have clearly told you,' I said to them.

They skirted around the issue of my family reporting me to the authorities, only saying things like 'Your older brother is concerned about you' and how my family was 'worried about me'. Luckily, my sister didn't have the barefaced shamelessness to look me in the eye when my brother was mentioned. That same older brother who beat me mercilessly as a child, and who had suddenly become overwhelmed with brotherly concern. As far as I could make out, he and my sister had got together and hatched this plan. Which was why my sister had been staying with me, of course. She had been sent to do the dirty work of the family, and she had played her part magnificently well.

I let what the officers were saying sink in: my family was concerned for me. That same family who would lock me in the basement and not feed me, for days on end, as a young teenager. The same family who let my brother abuse me, and then blamed me for his crimes when the truth finally came out.

I answered the questions the police put to me, talked about the YPJ and explained what their position was politically, because they appeared not to have heard of them.

'Do you know what would happen if you went to war?' the female officer asked me. She didn't wait for me to respond before launching into a litany of the terrible injuries that can befall a person in war. 'You could lose your arm, or your leg, your sight, your hearing,' she said, before pausing for dramatic effect. 'You could even die!' As if death was something that anyone could escape; as if freedom meant nothing, compared to survival. In the end we all just live a certain number of days, and it doesn't matter how large my numbers are. What matters is that I use those days wisely and worthily, even if that means a smaller number of days.

I almost found her concern for my safety quite touching, and I could see that her motives for visiting me were good. 'Yes, I know how to handle myself,' I said slowly.

I explained my political activism, and my particular solidarity with what the Kurds in Syria were facing. I explained our family's connection to Kurdistan, and our frequent trips there as a child and our many camping adventures, the mention of which made my sister squirm on her seat, which I enjoyed greatly. Then the police explained their work; they said they weren't police who arrest people, but were a specially trained group of officers who work with young people who they think might be in danger of going to war, or of doing something extreme – something like what I was planning to do. I explained to them that what I was planning to do wasn't extreme; I was fighting the subjugation of women in the Middle East and applying the values I had learned in my Danish education and belief system – values that my family had consistently punished me for – to Kurdistan.

I was open with them about my desire to join the war, and we discussed the different Islamist groups that were operating in the war, and Islamist extremism in general. I enjoyed seeing my sister's discomfort as we discussed the lack of basic rights experienced by many Muslim women living in the Middle East, but also within the diaspora communities, and how I wanted to fight this.

The war in Syria had by this point begun to overflow into Iraq, and massacres were taking place along the border areas between Iraq and Syria, as the group that was called ISIL at the time prepared to declare its statelet. We discussed the role of women in these kinds of societies and I told them about the YPJ, and they listened carefully. Neither of them seemed to have any idea about what was actually happening in Syria.

Back then there wasn't a mass of propaganda on social media as there is now. YouTube and Instagram were still relatively new and, barring a few pictures that I had taken privately and not shared, there was no evidence online that I had been in Rojava.

I was examining the police officers closely, to try and read their faces for signs that they knew I had been there.

They stayed in my flat for more than an hour, and as I was being so frank, it seemed as if they were being straight with me, which put them higher in my estimation than my own sister at the time. The male officer left his card and asked if he could contact me again. I said yes, reiterating that I had nothing to hide.

When they left, I turned to my sister, enraged. She ranted and raved about the harm I was doing and the stress I was putting Mum under. As far as she was concerned, I was mentally sick, addicted to marijuana, and I wanted to go to the Middle East to kill people. I couldn't believe that, after what had just happened, she was yelling at me. I was astonishingly calm, but it was as if a fuse had blown without the sparks. My family, who had been pushing me into becoming more 'Kurdish' my entire life, who had bullied and brainwashed me since I was a child about my role as a Kurd, as a Muslim, as a woman, had twisted the knife into my back like this, because I had made up my own mind about who I wanted to fight for. I had called the authorities against my family before – when I was forced to by my teachers – but I had always wanted help for all of us. And even then, my older sister had always forced me to withdraw my statements before any action was taken. I never once sought to put them in jail, even if I heard several of my teachers say that this would be a better place for them.

My sister was speaking at a hundred miles a minute, and I watched her as if seeing her for the first time. I didn't really know her, and she didn't really know me. She had been in my house for weeks – accompanying me to the doctor's to help get me sleeping pills, cooking together, buying food together – yet I had had no idea of her actual reason for being there. I was furious of course, but the early feelings were more of shock and betrayal. I couldn't speak, I could hardly breathe. I had been directly betrayed by my own family – the family I had lied and lied and lied to protect. And they dared to call me a bad Kurd. I was about to explode, and I needed to get away from her before I did something stupid.

I rushed out of my apartment, to go to Pusher Street and buy some marijuana. My sister tried to stop me, but I warned her, 'It's good for me to be calm now,' so she let me past. I got out of the apartment and tried to call my father. He didn't answer my calls, as he never answers my calls, so I called my mother, which was a huge mistake. She yelled at me, but mainly I yelled at her. 'How could you call the authorities on me? The same authorities you never allowed me to call as a child? All those of years being too Danish, and now I'm too Kurdish?'

Screaming at her, I let go of some of the rage inside me. She refused to listen, yelling back at me that I was mentally ill and a junkie. 'You are brainwashed and you are shameless,' she said to me, before hanging up the phone. I knew that if one of my brothers had decided to join the YPG, there would be no calling in of the authorities. Even though the YPG were fighting with their precious *Peshmerga* at the time, my mother couldn't see past the Ocalan connection; my family believed then, as they continue to believe now, that I was a fully signed-up member of the PKK.

I returned to my apartment and spoke to my sister about the family's reaction, and how things would have been totally different had it been one of our brothers joining. I called her out for betraying me, for the values of our fucked-up family, who only valued her slightly more highly than me because she was still a virgin. She was furious, as she had recently dropped out of university herself – to help me, she claimed.

'Help me!' I screamed at her at this point. 'Why, you haven't been my sister for twenty years. Where were you when I needed my big sister, huh? Where were you when I was screaming and crying down in our basement? Have you forgotten how you also blamed me back then? Where were you all the times I was in hospital? Where were you when I was the one getting beaten up for your chats with guys? Where was my big sister then? Huh? Where? Focus on your own life, and fuck off out of mine!' I almost spat the last words, and we were both crying.

Quieter now, I went on, 'Trust me, sister, we both know that your university education is more important to you than I am. You don't get to claim you are my big sister now, when you have so often said you simply don't wish to have any contact with me, and that you don't see me as your little sister. We have been living in the same family all of our lives, but you have hated me since I was born. Why? You dare to call yourself a sister now, when you don't even want to share our last name, because you are ashamed of me? You have blamed everything that is wrong in our dysfunctional family on me being "too Danish", but now you want to sell me out for being Kurdish? Shame on you!'

A week later the male officer wrote me a message. I didn't reply to it, but then he called me and I answered. He asked if he could meet me, and said that his police station was based very close to where I was staying. So we started seeing each other regularly, meeting for tea or coffee and cake in shops near my flat, or he would come over and we would talk at mine. I was going through a tough time, regarding the marijuana and the money situation, so it was nice to have someone to talk to about what was going on in my life.

Over the course of the next few months I became close to him, and he also maintained contact with my sister, with whom he developed what she called 'a friendship', although she didn't remain in touch with the female cop. I believed that he was trained as a police officer, but was working as a councillor and a mentor. It was only when he eventually testified against me in my court trial much later that I realized he worked for the Danish Intelligence Agency, the PET. We developed a complicated relationship. He talked incessantly about sex, or what men find attractive in a woman. He would say how much he missed having sex with his wife, or anyone, and would stare deep into my eyes as he spoke. I knew he was being inappropriate, but with my history and in my current circumstances, who was I going to complain to?

My sleeping problems hadn't improved, and I was getting stressed by the loan I had taken out, as I was spending it all on marijuana. His theory was that I had PTSD, like his wife, who was also from an Arabic background and had experienced violence in her home while growing up. He told me my family thought I had bipolar disorder and other serious psychological health problems. I knew these words were coming from my sister; no one else in my family knows what these terms mean. I didn't think I had PTSD. I think I was just lonely and miserable, and missing living in the shelter; I moved out before I was ready because being there had made me feel stronger than I actually turned out to be.

My intention, at the time, was to stop spending money on marijuana, and to get some rest in order to feel better – and to get my family off my back. Anyone who has suffered from difficulty sleeping knows how bad it can make you feel. I had heard of a certain drug called Seroquel that can help with sleeping problems, something I had already been to my doctor about. Together he and I went to a clinic in Copenhagen called OPUS that specializes in mental health in young people. It was a beautiful, welcoming place, and there I was finally prescribed Seroquel. In the USA they prescribe it for sleep problems, but in Denmark it is used for a number of mental-health problems. I didn't want to argue with the doctors at OPUS as I had done with my family, so I went along with his recommendation, and lied to the doctor to exaggerate my symptoms so that I would get the prescription. I looked up online the symptoms I needed to pretend I was suffering from, and repeated to the clinicians at OPUS what I had read. Seroquel is a strong drug, and it did help me in those initial weeks in particular. It also helped me gain weight, which was good, as I wanted to have more curves.

Because of the lies I was coached into telling, and the exaggerated symptoms I described, I am now banned from being prescribed this drug in Denmark by any doctor, regardless of whether or not they believe me. It was a stupid, reckless thing to do on my part, and I can't blame him entirely for it. I also thought it would be good for me to be diagnosed with some kind of disorder, so that I could get these pills for free, and therefore save more for my marijuana spend. I also thought that if I got into some sort of trouble later, the courts would be more lenient with me because of this diagnosis. I was completely wrong about this, and I have been severely punished for it now.

It took a long time to convince the doctor to give me the pills, and he hates me now as he got into trouble because of me. I said things like, 'Well, a sick person is the last to know they are sick' and tried to look convincing. The doctor eventually relented and he has been punished for this prescription. Despite the pressure I put on him, I'm not entirely sure why he elected to give me this powerful medication, except that for each patient you have registered in Denmark, the government gives you more money. The drugs didn't help me as much as I thought they would. They made it easier for me fall asleep, but I would wake up two hours later, thinking and feeling the same things.

I stopped taking the drugs about six weeks after starting them, when I began to read more about the side-effects, and they didn't seem to be having the magical effect I had naively thought they would. I kept going to the doctor and getting the pills, but I stored them in my room.

In March 2014, after my sister moved out, I met a guy called Jackson through a friend from the shelter. We started seeing each other, and early on in our relationship we decided to go on holiday together to Sharm El-Sheikh in Egypt. The problems didn't really begin until we were on our way back home to Denmark.

Jackson only told me the day before we were due to return that we would be flying through Istanbul, with a twelve-hour stopover in Ataturk Airport. This was the airport where my father was delayed when bringing my uncle's body back to Iran, and I was nervous about travelling through it. They had delayed my father because his religion was listed on his passport – in Iraq they list your religion as if it is a vital detail – and as he is a Sunni Muslim, whereas my uncle was Christian, the authorities wouldn't believe they were brothers. The other reason, of course, was my father's work in the region; he is known as a Kurdish activist against Iran, just as the Turks are against Iran. Jackson knew all about my travels to Aleppo and Rojava, and it was obvious to a Turk from the way I look that I am Kurdish. Turkey calls us Kurds 'mountain Turks' or, worse, 'gypsy Turks', so I wasn't delighted to be flying into this airport and I made my feelings known.

On the way to the airport we discussed what to do if anything happened, and I made Jackson promise to pretend he wasn't with me, in case they took him down too. If they looked through his phone and found pictures of me, he could pretend we had just met out in Sharm. In the queue to change planes for our connection, sure enough, I was taken out of line by the Turkish security police – the ones with the black scarves covering their faces.

The guards came at me from behind and, as I was taken out, I could hear Jackson kicking off. He started yelling and shouting, as if they were about to kill me in front of him. They said something in Turkish to him, and I yelled in Danish, 'Stop yelling – act cool or you will be where I am right now.'

I stayed as calm as possible as they took me away and placed me in a holding cell, still inside the airport. I had taken the precaution, as I was taught by my father, of taking an extra phone when I go to the Middle East, fully charged and with credit. It was one of the really small phones that flipped open, and I hid it in my sock underneath the arch of my foot. In the holding cell everyone was Armenian, African or Turkish, with brown eyes, and no one had pale skin. They were all being held for different reasons, but all were political. I knew I would have to share the phone, if I didn't want to lose it – or lose something worse – so I told everyone they could use it after I made my call.

I called the male officer in Denmark and told him where I was, and what I was doing. He immediately contacted consular assistance in Turkey, and gave them my number and the number of the Danish Foreign Ministry. He also, annoyingly, contacted my family, which I didn't appreciate, as I was over eighteen. The woman from the Danish Foreign Ministry called me almost immediately. I answered quietly, not wanting to draw attention to my phone, and explained to her that I was okay – so far. 'You have been accused of being in prison in Turkey before,' she said, but when I asked for what, she said she wasn't sure and was trying to find out.

'Is it true?' she asked.

'No, of course not!' I snapped.

'What are you doing in Turkey?' she asked, and I explained to her that I was on holiday, but when she asked if I was alone, I stupidly said yes, because I didn't want Jackson to get into any trouble. At the time I thought he wouldn't be able to cope, judging by his hysterical behaviour when I was taken out of the queue, but I should have better understood what she was doing, and not lied to cover for him. She signed off by promising to clear it up and said she would try her hardest to get me back on the plane.

Two anti-terror police, with black clothes and covered faces, collected me from the cell and took me to the security chief's office, where I was seated facing the chief. There was an interpreter there to help, as his English was so poor.

'Are you Joanna Palani?'

'Yes.'

'Are you visiting from Denmark?'

'Yes.'

'What are you doing in Turkey?'

'I've been on holiday, and needed to change my flight in this airport.'

'Have you been in Turkey before?'

'No, and I don't know why it might have seemed as if I have.'

He then presented some black-and-white pictures from a file, showing a military base outside the Kurdish capital city that we call Amed, but the Turks call Diyarbekir. The Kurdish capital city is situated inside Turkey. Beside Amed is a city called Bengul (Bingöl), which is very supportive of the PKK. In this city there is a military base, and the pictures showed a small girl with long, dark hair, light skin, a protruding nose and dark eyes – so any Kurdish girl really – entering the compound and then leaving. Shortly afterwards, apparently, there was an explosion. The images were stills taken from CCTV, and the quality was really bad; you couldn't see any distinguishing marks, such as the birthmarks that I have on my face.

'This is you.'

'No, sir. This picture is very bad quality and it's not me.'

'It's definitely you.'

'Sir, so you are saying I bombed a military bus on a military base in Turkey?'

'Yes.'

'How many people died, sir?'

'No one died.'

I looked at him again and said, 'So I came from Denmark to bomb an empty military bus? Right next to the Kurdish capital?'

And at the mention of the word 'Kurdish' he became furious. 'There's no such thing as the Kurdish capital city in Turkey.'

At that point I relaxed a little: they didn't know about me going to Aleppo or Rojava, but took me in simply because I'm Kurdish. I asked when the events happened, and explained carefully, as if I was speaking to a child, so that even he could understand, 'I can prove to you that I was in Denmark, through my phone calls, through picture records and through my school records.'

'You are lying. You are a member of the PKK and we have proof right here.'

He thumbed the picture as he said it. I was still calm; I wasn't who he was looking for, and I was sure I could prove it.

I was taken back to my cell and half an hour later I got a call from the woman at the Foreign Ministry. 'Joanna, we have made a deal with the authorities that you can go home, but you are never allowed back in Turkey again.' I said, of course, that I had nothing to do with Turkey, only Kurdistan. She got annoyed at me. 'Joanna, keep a lid on it. Don't mention Kurdistan or they will put you in jail for a long time. Not again. Don't go there.' Back then I was very stubborn, as I hadn't had many negative dealings with the authorities, so I began to argue, but she cut me off mid-sentence. 'Joanna, if you say you only want to be in Kurdistan, they will lock you up, and you will never see Denmark again.'

So I kept quiet, let the other people in the cell use my phone and waited to be released. Another hour passed, and I was beginning to wonder if there was some other problem, when I was taken back to the airport terminal, where Jackson was waiting for the next flight. They had kept me for about half a day; it was awful, but I couldn't help thinking of my cellmates, who had been there so much longer and under worse conditions.

I went to the gate and met up with Jackson. 'How did you get out?' he asked, rather breathlessly.

'By telling the truth. I am not a member of the PKK and I didn't blow up their stupid empty bus.' I asked him what he had been doing, and he hugged me and told me how afraid he had been for me.

'I went to the *shisha* bar and ate some cakes and had some beers,' he told me.

I went on Snapchat and saw that he had been sending videos of himself at the airport, looking as if he was on holiday alone. I couldn't believe it. I understood that he had to be careful with the authorities, but if my boyfriend had been taken away by Turkish security, I would have been calling the embassy and the Foreign Ministry; what if I hadn't had contacts like the male officer and the police in my secret phone? I would be like those other poor people in the cell. I was seriously unimpressed by Jackson, and after the few chilly evenings we had shared in Sharm, I knew the relationship wasn't going to develop into what I had hoped it might.

We stayed friends, and I am still in contact with him online. Jackson was the last person I was with before Kobani, which makes him stand out in the events of my life – for that reason, if no other.

CHAPTER EIGHT

The Martyrs of Kobani

When the battle of Kobani started in June 2014, I was living in Copenhagen, and the male officer had been taken off my case. He said this was because I hadn't shown any signs that I had changed my mind. I was still determined to go to the Middle East and fight, so he had been unsuccessful; but I think it was because his bosses suspected he was acting inappropriately towards me. Which he was, but I was more worried about what he was up to with my sister.

I didn't like it when he talked about his personal life, his love life or his sex life, and he did this a lot. He seemed to think that because his wife had a Middle Eastern background, he understood what women from our part of the world have to go through. I don't think he understood women from the Middle East at all, but I do believe he had enough knowledge about our culture to know that he could abuse young women from our region and never face the consequences. I have no idea what went on between him and my sister, but I suspect they were dating – or that's what she believed was happening, at least. My sister didn't share this information; she's a good Kurdish girl, so he could be certain that whatever the relationship was, she would never tell.

He did nothing to deter me from taking up arms to protect women's rights. Quite the opposite, in fact. He made me see how patriarchy can disguise itself so cleverly within the capitalist, democratic system and maintain a position of power. He made me more determined to fight the system that created men like him, and I take some comfort from the fact that he completely failed in his job, when it came to his work with me.

The decision to go to Kobani formed slowly in my head, and was the sum of a number of factors. I always find it difficult when anyone asks me why I went to join the war, and I have decided there is no easy answer – or at least not one that seems to satisfy. In some ways going to war was just natural for me, in the way that it is completely unnatural for others. When people ask me why I went, I always want to ask them, 'What made you stay behind and watch all this suffering on your television, and do absolutely nothing about it?' I really think that's the bigger question, actually.

Some people like to believe that I am a victim of my circumstances – that because of the unusual childhood I had, divided between Iraq and Denmark, there was an element of inevitability, but actually there was nothing inevitable about my decision to go. I was staking a claim to decide the direction of my own life, and my own path. I knew that this time I would be sent straight to the front, as the movement had already invested a lot of training in me, which they hadn't really got the benefit of yet.

When I first got home from Istanbul I spent weeks feeling outraged – to the extent that my bad sleeping patterns were even worse than usual. I had all this anger pulsing around me that would keep me awake, so I spent many nights having long conversations with friends in Kurdistan, who kept me updated on what was happening in the war. It sounded even worse than it looked on the news. *Daesh* were monsters. They were bad enough for even *al-Qaeda* to say they took things too far, so they represented a whole new level of extreme. *Daesh* beheaded civilians in Kobani, and then killed those trying to flee. They were master propagandists, broadcasting their grisly crimes in HD across every social-media platform I was on. I would stay glued to my computer watching the genocidal takeover by *Daesh* of both Syrian and Iraqi Kurdistan.

I was proud that I stayed calm when I was arrested in Turkey, but it was terrifying to finally experience the brutality that every Kurd, in some way, endures because of that despicable republic. After my return I went for long walks alone and went over what I had said, and how I could have reacted better, but I was aware of how lucky I was to have had my spare phone and have help from the Danish Foreign Ministry. I thought of the other people I had shared a cell with in Istanbul airport, some of whom were probably still there, and wondered what would become of them. Being released as quickly as I had been demonstrated the enormous privilege of my passport, but also infuriated me and made me feel complicit in the global order that kept Kurds – and the whole of the Middle East – in the mess that it all is today. Why are rights dependent on what passport you carry? All this swirled around my head as I walked along the canal paths in Christiania.

I also heard a voice telling me I had some issues to attend to in Denmark, before venturing back to Kurdistan and into what was now a growing and bloody war. *Daesh* were much stronger than anyone had anticipated, and we, as Kurds, were becoming more useful to those trying to get rid of them. The full threat they posed, not just to Kurdistan, Iraq and Syria but also to Europe and the rest of the world, was becoming more bloodily real. My previous frontline experience hadn't necessarily made me think the war was one that I could survive, although I had this bud of pride and self-belief inside me that allowed me to believe it was possible.

I was also wondering what to do about my family. Was I going to become one of those girls that forgot who they were and rejected the culture of their heritage? The kind of girl the community hates and the family is shamed by? The kind my mother, in particular, despises? It made me feel sick and I am still heartbroken by my mother's betrayal, or at the very least, her being part of my siblings plan against me – I wasn't ready then to believe it was her idea, and to be honest, I still don't think it was.

On social media every day I was seeing these pictures of what was happening in Syria, and I was beginning to hear about how the YPG and YPJ were mobilizing and growing, and of those who were coming down from the mountains to support them. I wanted to forget about my small life, and be part of a bigger ideological project, building the future for women like me all over the Middle East. In the YPJ, we say we fight for public justice over private happiness, but the two aren't mutually exclusive. For me, one can lead to the other.

Going to Kobani represented finally making the decision that my life was my own, to steer as I saw fit. I decided to go there after *Daesh* crossed into Iraq and were just outside Mosul. They were too close now. There are several towns and settlements outside Mosul on the way to Erbil, and I knew they would have to begin to mobilize against *Daesh* or flee. It was time to go and get rid of this evil.

When I was with the Kurdish groups in Aleppo in 2012 a note was sent by leader Abdullah Ocalan urging us to protect Şingal – the area more commonly known by its non-Kurdish name, Sinjar, in northern Iraq. He warned that Islamist movements would attack this area and take sex slaves, as previous Islamic Arab groups had done before. Now this was exactly what was happening, and I wondered how the movement felt about not having paid proper heed to Ocalan's warning.

I was inside the Kurdish cultural centre in Copenhagen, having come back to base after a protest in the centre of town, when we saw the first pictures coming from Şingal and heard the testimonies of the women. *Daesh* had delivered on the threat predicted right at the start of the uprising, and had launched an offensive against the Yazidi people in Şingal, massacring thousands of civilians and abducting women. Everyone went silent when the news showed the images of the Yazidi community stranded and starving on Mount Şingal, and we heard how the KDP *Peshmerga* had abandoned them, leaving their positions and running away in order to unsuccessfully defend Mosul. I became breathless and excused myself, as the images we see on Kurdish channels are a lot more graphic than those we see in Europe, and they had already found some of the mass graves.

The genocide of the Yazidis, and the attack on minorities all over Şingal, was an abomination that should never have happened. I cried to myself in the toilet after seeing the images, and when I returned to the room I saw that I was not the only person to be appalled. We stayed talking about what we were seeing on the television late into the night, but I was too shocked to speak much. Everyone was subdued as we debated the options in front of us, and one of the *hevals* asked our group what we could do directly to help. Everyone answered with their ideas, but I was the only one who didn't answer. I decided right there: it was time. Time for me to go and practise what I had been training for. Time to go and get rid of the so-called Islamic State and its caliphate.

Getting back to the war was, predictably, difficult, as there were only a small number of groups beginning to mobilize. There was no official route into Kobani, so everyone who wanted to join the battle had to smuggle themselves across the Turkish border. Wearing my favourite activist T-shirt, I took a plane to Erbil in the summer of 2014, where I was picked up at the airport and taken directly to a camp nearby, to wait for others who were coming in from the east. The camp was in the mountains – one of my favourites in Iraq, *Ciye Spi* or the White Mountain, which feels like it is located near the gates of heaven; the air is so clean and clear and crisp, you feel as if you are at the top of a hill in the middle of an ocean. No one smokes there, and it's very far away from any towns or villages. I was at the camp for a few days, sleeping in the tough terrain; it was hot during the day and cold at night, because we were so high up, so we sometimes slept in caves or just under the stars. I couldn't decide which I preferred, because I found them both quite a shock, having had almost two years of comfort in Copenhagen.

I had expected that I would be taken on a similar journey to the one into Aleppo, but these were proper mountain conditions, and I was greeted as a curiosity by the *hevals* this time. I had packed slightly haphazardly and had my fake Gucci make-up bag, which caused me to be teased mercilessly by the others, and I can't really blame them. What was I thinking, bringing a fake Gucci purse to a war where we were fighting a revolution against capitalism? Fortunately, they saw the funny side of it.

I'd brought some books with me, so I spent the first week reading and adjusting, and getting some basic refresher weapons and ideology training. Our camp in White Mountain is spread across different countries – Iraq, Syria and Turkey – and the woman in charge of my part was a woman called *heval* Sevin, who is a famous YPJ commander. Some of the best commanders in our movement are based there, and they were beginning to organize training for those going into Kobani. There were volunteers from all over the area, and everyone spoke my Sorani, or Iranian, Kurdish.

I helped out with the cooking and ate lots of delicious food, and slowly became good friends with the others. I listened a lot, as I had just come off the plane from basically two years of European life. I knew I had to prepare myself, and even though I asked to go to Kobani immediately, Sevin rejected my request: 'You are always trying to rush ahead, Joanna; you have to take your time slowly and adjust.' She said it with kindness in her eyes, though, and so I applied myself as well as I could, and waited for the others who were coming in from the east of Kurdistan.

There had been an appeal by *Apo* (Abdullah Ocalan) to defend Kobani, and there was this buzz to the camp; people were coming and going, and new volunteers were arriving from all over Kurdistan to stand and fight against *Daesh*. There were even a few international volunteers, but I don't think any of them made it to Kobani. Those I heard of came after the huge battle.

In order to cross into Syria from Iraq we would have to travel through the mountains in Turkey, and this was the part we were most nervous about, but I knew it would be good experience, so I was looking forward to the journey. I waited at the camp for about a fortnight, before we began the journey across the border. There was a big group of us – about thirty people in total crossing, and we did it at night, in single file, as this was a new route in, and we were one of the first groups to be brought into the city.

We had a special team to help us cross the mountains and arrive safely. Haroon was a YPG commander and a friend, who led our group and walked directly in front of me. After about an hour of crossing the mountain, he stopped suddenly and gestured for everyone to be silent and wait. We crouched close to the earth and waited, but nothing seemed to happen; there was just silence. After about twenty minutes I asked him what was going on. '*Heval*, why are we staying so long when there's nothing here, and we need to get past this bit of the mountain as quickly as possible, so we arrive in the Turkish part of the mountain by the right time.'

'*Heval*,' he replied, 'we cannot pass – can you not see he isn't moving?'

'Who isn't moving?' one of the *hevals* behind me asked, and Haroon pointed.

We all strained to look for the figure blocking our route, but all the time Haroon had been staring at a group of rocks and a funny-shaped bush, which might have looked a bit like a figure with a rifle, but wasn't. So now our group was split – half in Iraq and half already in Turkey. Those of us who were with *heval* Haroon were stuck in Iraq, far behind where we should have been. Everyone was annoyed at Haroon, but we laughed at how silly he had been, as we increased our speed so that we could pass into Turkey during the darkest hours of the night. I remember thinking I hope we all leave Kobani the same way we entered it – smiling and laughing – but most of those I went in with didn't make it out at all.

Before we left the mountain we sat around the fire, singing and clapping and enjoying ourselves – what we in the YPG call 'making morale'. As I think now of those I sat around the fire with in the mountains, I realize I am the only one left today. As we walked, we sang the same songs on the Iraqi part of the mountains, before entering the Turkish part, where we were quiet as we had to be very careful. Turkey considers all Kurdish groups to be legitimate targets, so there was no singing there.

The majority of us travelled without weapons, but there was a small group of about seven armed men who followed within hearing distance behind us. If we were caught by the *Peshmerga* in Iraq, we were told to put our hands in the air, but if we were caught by Turkish soldiers, then we would pretend that we were innocent kidnap victims. I was so impressed that these fighters were ready to give up their freedom – and maybe even their lives – just to get us across the border. I know that we all make sacrifices as Kurdish fighters, but to be ready to do so just for the purposes of transporting us was impressive.

The whole journey from the White Mountain into Kobani took about fourteen hours – nowadays it takes about half that time. We walked through the night and arrived the following morning in northern Kobani – what we call the *canton*, meaning the wider state rather than the city of Kobani.

I was assigned my unit and became part of *Tabur Berivan*, named after a famous PKK fighter who was killed by the Turks. I was put in one of our cars, along with some of the others who had arrived with me, and we went immediately towards the city.

The first *Daesh* soldier I saw in Kobani was dead at the side of the road. I saw his feet first, and there was a brief second when I didn't know what I was looking at. He was tied to another two corpses, and all three of the fighters were naked. When we kill *Daesh*, we remove their clothes to check them for explosives, and we take their weapons and personal belongings away for inspection. This allows us to get to know them better, so that we can understand their tactics. We are meticulous about investigating the details of their corpses, as so much of urban warfare is a mind-game, so anything that will help us – even small things – can be useful. I was on the way to meet my *tabur* commander, who was already inside the city, and I had a momentary daydream about some of my friends from the Christiania shelter and how they went on holiday to see the half-naked bodies of young men on the beach, while here I was, seeing them dead on the streets of a war zone that I had opted to join.

I was entirely silent when I saw the bodies; I am not someone who feels the need to articulate every thought I have. I often prefer to keep my thoughts to myself and listen carefully to the perspectives of others. That's part of the training, and I wanted to demonstrate that I had been learning in Europe; I wasn't just hanging around doing nothing and forgetting about my friends in the war.

I was listening to the driver, who had been there a few months already and was telling us about the latest attack, and our push back. We were going towards an area where we knew there had been a battle, so I was prepared to expect more corpses – and to be honest, I was hoping to see them. After a big defeat with many dead, you retreat, naturally, so going through an area with *Daesh* corpses meant the chances of encountering living fighters was slightly lower. Only slightly, though, because Kobani was a complete mess, and at the time I entered in that car it was already overrun with *Daesh* fighters. They had mobilized and moved in men from as far south as Raqqa; after being defeated in Kirkuk, they wanted to maintain Kobani, to prove how close they could get to Europe, touching on Turkey's border. Of course, had Turkey not been tacitly and actively supporting the group, they would never have made it so far.

I wasn't scared of the dead bodies when I was in the car, and I wasn't scared about going to battle; I didn't feel the same kind of fear or anxiety I would feel if I needed to smoke marijuana or was unable to sleep. I don't get scared of the sounds of war; I'm a Ramadi kid, and you can't fear what you have always known. I was mainly scared of doing something stupid that would make my commanders and my *hevals* believe I was lacking the training to be where I was – something stupid that might make me a liability within the group, a weak link that could endanger others.

We came to what was our unit's base, a big house, and were told we had to split into three groups and find new safe houses to obtain new firing positions, taking over from the *hevals* who had cleared *Daesh* from the streets we had passed through. I went with two guys from Turkey, *heval* Mehmet and *heval* Gökhan, and two YPJ fighters, *heval* Medya and *heval* Aria, who would go on to become my good friends. We were sent to find a safe house close to the front, as we were advancing forward from the area we had just passed, further south in the city, where *Daesh* were still present, to push them out and take back the city.

We chose a house that didn't look safe at all; it was a two-storey building, but one of the walls at the front was partially blown off, so looking at it from the street, it was a mess. Most of the houses in Kobani – as in most of the underdeveloped areas across northern Syria and Iraq – are built from a type of sandstone that disintegrates in explosions, which is why the cities that the YPG has taken back are now rubble.

On the third floor of the house there was a small roof yard that looked as if it had previously been used for washing and drying clothes; it was only half-built, but it gave us enough height to have a vantage point looking south. Because the house looked so insecure, we knew it wouldn't be a target too quickly. The bullets from the AKs could actually go through these kinds of walls, and by this stage we realized that *Daesh* knew this already. Our calculation was that they would assume we wouldn't be stupid enough to use a building of this kind. We constantly had to think of what they expected us to do, and do the opposite, to stay ahead.

Those first days we still had logistics, but only from suppliers inside Kobani; no outside suppliers were able to reach the city. This is why the blockade was more dangerous than the attacks; *Daesh*'s method, which almost worked, was to pummel the grounds with their amazing weaponry – mostly recovered from the dysfunctional Iraqi army and, to a lesser extent, from the KRG *Peshmerga*, who were being supplied by the Americans – and then starve us out. None of the units in Kobani received any official logistics from our central command. We were almost completely surrounded the entire time I was there.

So we found this very unsafe-looking safe house and looked for our final firing positions, or what we call 'spots'. Medya, our commander, was satisfied that we were covered and we went back to sleep in a bigger house, in the south centre of the city. This was our local headquarters and still had electricity (I think from the mains), whereas none of the frontline houses had any electricity – *Daesh* had cut it off, which is why we couldn't communicate with our friends in other parts of the city. This radio silence was also what prompted the furious campaigning by Kurdish communities all over Europe; they couldn't get hold of anyone, and rightfully feared the worst.

We bedded down for the night; myself with the other girls from the YPJ, while the guys had their own room. We might have been in hell, but God forbid there's any mixed-sex sleeping. Not that I slept much that night. I stayed awake and listened to the drill of the AKs nearby and to the sound of RPGs in the not-quite-distance.

First thing next morning, before sunrise, our little *tabur* was dispatched to the front, to find our unsafe house and see how far forward the others in the group were going. Normally we wouldn't have moved together as a group early in the morning – we would have waited until night – but the orders were to go forward immediately, as we didn't have much time. I was silent as we walked through the suspiciously quiet streets, and didn't joke with the others as we normally do on our way to the front. It sounds stupid, but in the YPG we relax and have a lot of fun even on the front, as we are very close to each other and try to laugh as much as possible. My head, however, was back in Copenhagen, or more precisely with my friends' holiday adventures with handsome, half-naked men.

I was trying to hide that I was ever-so-slightly freaking out about what I had actually done, and I was enjoying the sight of the sun rising when suddenly Medya, in front of me, was shot. I was behind her, so it was my job to return fire immediately, but I wasn't sure where the shooter was, so I dived to the ground to better hear the direction of the incoming fire. Two seconds earlier I had been too involved in my stupid thoughts to pay attention; I responded as quickly as I could, before crawling to the side of the road. At the time I thought it was a good spot, but afterwards one of the guys who was based closer to where the shots were coming from said he could see me lying on the ground as I responded.

I can't remember the name of the other girl who was with us that morning. I remember faces, but am not so good at names. She was from Iran, so I knew her. She was directly beside Medya when she was shot, so Medya was at her 11.30 position – which is almost directly in front – and because she could see this, the other girl immediately responded from her standing position, while Medya went down to protect herself. Seeing what this other girl was doing, I scrambled and we just fired at them, with both of us sort of standing over Medya. When I opened fire I was relieved to find I liked the rusty rifle I had been given the day before. My AK was a good gun, and the ammunition was .4-calibre; the end of the bullet in the full metal jacket is red, which means it makes more fire when it hits somewhere; it's not the type of bullet you shoot anyone in the head with, obviously, as their heads would explode.

When I was shooting, I honestly had no fucking idea what I was doing. I might have had a lot of training, but this was different, and I had yet to face this group. I'd prepared myself for being killed in a brutal way, as Islamic terrorists had shown on social media. Before I was in Kobani, I remember looking at a video of a decapitation: looking at the time it took to die, when the pain was greatest, and how to prepare for this kind of eventuality. It was important to do this, as the chances were, should this be my fate, that *Daesh* would film the process, so I needed to know how to die with honour. Their propaganda makes them seem scarier than they actually are in battle – they spread fear through their videos, and that is how most people know them. Actually seeing them in battle, as real humans who can die by real bullets, was kind of a relief. *Daesh* are just like us, but badly brainwashed or, as I like to say, brain-poisoned. I was concentrating so hard on keeping my hands still and not allowing them to sweat that elsewhere the sweat ran all over me – down my back and down my face, until my uniform was drenched.

Being behind Medya when she got shot, I saw and heard the bullet enter her flesh. Even though she was injured, while the other girl and I were shooting, Medya called the main house to tell them what had happened and to request help. Three cars full of men arrived within a few minutes, and a huge fight broke out: everyone was shooting in different directions, and I think *Daesh* had predicted that if they shot one of us, more of our fighters would appear.

When everyone suddenly turned up, I realized what kind of team I was fighting with: everyone had their faces 'locked', meaning they had all had special-forces training, and they were all guerrillas from the mountains. I had thought they were just (fairly) normal people like me. As the bullets rained back and forth, I fretted about who I was fighting with: no wonder we were taking such precautions inside Turkey.

Everyone wore red bands on their heads, or they had more discreet white bands. This means you have pledged to sacrifice yourself – and you will not allow anyone to sacrifice themselves for you. If you are wearing a white band, you go straight to the front. If it's a red band, you are responsible for the unit, so that's normally just the commanders. Both those who wear white and red are responsible for the mission.

You don't show the white band to others in the unit, and it's usually only the commanders who know who wears it. If you don't have anyone in the group who volunteers to wear the white band, then the commander will choose someone. If the person who is selected doesn't want to perform this role, they go to the commander and explain that they don't want it. If someone specifically wants to wear the white band, then they can request to do so. I always insist on wearing the white band, especially after Kobani.

Shit, I thought to myself, will I have to blow myself up? I was ready to, as well. But this time in Kobani I wasn't allowed to wear the white band. Many of the other girls did wear it; I saw them go and they never came back. But I was not permitted by the commanders to perform this role on that occasion. I think the reason they would not allow me to is because I am from Denmark.

Medya was okay. She lay on the ground, and even tried to take part in the shooting again. The guys were impressive shooters – even before they got out of the car, they knew exactly where the shooting was coming from. I quickly realized that the people I was fighting with had many years' experience in battle: this was not their first firefight. Eventually, after a few hours of shooting and diving, until I almost ran out of ammunition, everything quietened down; Medya was taken away to have her leg examined. I stayed on the front with the others until it sounded as if *Daesh* were preparing to leave the area. We had no supplies with us and slowly I was getting hungry and tired, so eventually we went back to our house.

As we were leaving, *Daesh* were yelling – we could hear them and they could hear us, we were that close to each other. It was one of those stalemate battle endings; the fight wasn't over, but it quietened down for a while, before it would pick up again later. I was still sweating, and one of the guys gave me a lift back to our other house, as the others continued going forward. We three girls had been further forward than any of the older men who turned up later. We went back to base and slept for a few hours again.

That was our first attack, and from then on it was pure mayhem. The days and ambushes have rolled into one, and thinking about it now is like watching a horror film where I star as some kind of un-killable zombie in the apocalypse. So many people died. Time slowed down when I lost my friends, but otherwise it was non-stop: firing, hiding, trying to stay alive.

Normally, in our movement, they don't tell us what is happening every day, or give us a plan; they inform us of what we are to do just beforehand, to keep things safer. In Kobani this meant it was constant chaos, combined with no food and no supplies. This is why it seems nightmarish now, when I think about it: suddenly I was in one place, then another, and I have difficulty remembering the steps in between. Back then it didn't help that my Kermanji Kurdish wasn't so good and I didn't speak Turkish – which most of the *hevals* spoke – so this added to my sense of confusion.

I was given an SVD sniper rifle in Kobani, on the understanding that I had taken the special-forces training, so I had some experience. I started to carry this SVD rifle around with me during our daytime push forward, to get used to holding it alongside the AK, and because I wanted to get in some kills. One morning, before we were due to head out to find another safe house, I was looking through the scope in my SVD and I found a house that, I thought, was a really good place to set up. We would find somewhere different most days, to confuse *Daesh* – often they would be firing at our position of yesterday, which never ceased to make us laugh.

I didn't say anything to my friends before we went out; I wanted to be sure the house was good, before alerting them. We were getting tired from the lack of food and the exhaustion from the battle by this stage, so it was better to save energy for talking about only the most important stuff. I ran towards this house, and when I went into one of the downstairs rooms I found an injured *Daesh* fighter.

I checked his hands immediately, to see whether he could fire at me, but he couldn't, so I relaxed. He was bleeding from his leg, and the smell of blood hung heavily in the room. Every woman knows what blood smells like, but just imagine the smell increasing in proportion to the amount spilled. He was fully alert, and could hear me and the others going from door to door, looking for a spot and trying to find some supplies. He grimaced as I entered and closed his eyes, expecting to be killed. If I expected to be killed, I would have my eyes open and a smile on my face, looking my enemy directly in the eye. But if I had done something I wasn't proud of, I too would have closed my eyes. I entered the room as I always do, quickly, away from the window or any open shots. But I didn't shoot him. Right then I didn't see him as an evil Islamist fighter, but as a man in need of help.

I put my rifle down, to show I wasn't a threat to him, and moved closer to hold him. He was shaking as he bled and his hand wouldn't stay still. He was bigger and taller than me, and I could have shot him, but in that specific moment I couldn't do it. It was my natural reaction to help. I thought I could bring him back to the others in my unit and we could tend his injury, but he wouldn't trust me, so after I helped him up, he limped away out of the house. Before leaving he looked down at me and said something in Arabic, but I told him I didn't understand. He then said in broken English: 'I will find you.' His words confused me, and I wondered what he meant. It didn't sound like a threat – it sounded more like a promise.

That was more than three years ago now, and he has yet to get in touch. He's probably dead. I fixate on this one act of kindness that I performed in Kobani, because it's really the only reminder I have from that time that I was a human being capable of empathy, and it makes me feel just a little bit less terrible and less like I am a zombie murderer.

When I told the others about him later, I was a bit nervous in case he had gleaned any information that could have been useful to his group. The others were angry and annoyed with me; by saving his life, I might be taking that of a YPG member. It didn't help with the trust that I was still building with the group. I was very much seen as an outsider, and because I come and go so much to Rojava, there are still some suspicions about me. The reason I didn't shoot him – as I explained to my comrades later that night – was because according to our ideology, if someone is shooting at you, you have the right to shoot back before he does, but in that moment he was injured and was not capable of hurting me; he was not a threat and his capacity to kill had been eliminated. So it would have been a war crime, but my explanation fell on deaf ears. The others weren't happy. 'This man could go on to kill one of our people,' one of the senior YPG fighters told me.

But the man I saw was just a man in a different uniform from me, who was badly injured. He was older than me, but there were many *Daesh* fighters younger than me in Kobani, including the first few that I killed. I didn't realize how young they were until I saw their bodies after they were dead. It was disgusting. I didn't come to Syria to kill small boys. I saw their faces after we cleared the area, going forward, a few hours later. Initially I wasn't sure if I had killed them, and I had hoped it was my commander, but Gökhan, who had been watching from higher up, came over and said it was me – which I think I already knew. The first boy had delicate little lips and an oversized Adam's apple he clearly hadn't grown into. He would have killed me had I not killed him, and his killing was entirely justified in our ideology and in the rules of war, but when I saw that kid's face, I felt like a murderer. In his uniform he looked like a real threat and a soldier; without his uniform, he looked like just another young kid from the block, who should have had a football in his hand, not a gun.

A lot of fucked-up things happened in Kobani, and I had to do some things I will regret for the rest of my life. I was ordered to do things I didn't like, and did things I didn't like off my own bat, in order to survive. Taking a life is nothing to be proud of, and I still feel very guilty about Kobani. We dress it up and make it sound lofty and worthy: defeating the enemy, conquering *Daesh*, vanquishing evil; but some part of me said it was just one kid from the Middle East, like me, killing another kid from the Middle East. The weapons us kids held in our hands came from afar: sometimes from Russia, sometimes America. We never had the .50-calibre sniper rifle in the Middle East, before Russia delivered it at the start of the Syrian war; and we never had the weapons *Daesh* used against us, before they looted them from the Iraqi army who had been supplied by the USA.

That's not to say I regret what I did: I fought for the YPG and I am proud of that, but when you break down what *Daesh* actually is: behind the fancy videos and viciousness, they are made up of ordinary people and they made mistakes in combat that led to their deaths. Mistakes a soldier knows not to commit, that they should have been trained not to do, such as shooting a sniper rifle from an open spot in a window. That's what I mean when I say their fighters are easy to kill – it is their black ideology that continues. Unlike the later deaths I was responsible for, I haven't been able to leave behind those I killed on the streets of Kobani. They stay with me still, as do my friends who died beside me. I wasn't sure what I was expecting: I had endured tough times – in training camps, in Aleppo, with my family – but nothing could have prepared me for Kobani. It was just hell. Animals couldn't survive there, all the dogs starved to death. The only animals that survived were those burrowing beetles that eat dead flesh. They would become the only meat.

We ate whatever we could get our hands on; stray animals were found and cooked, and any kind of vegetable we could get. We relied on the protein sources that Captain Cliff Dive had taught us about. With food stocks running low, we started eating boiled grass and I got really unwell. I went with one of the other girls to the bathroom, and *heval* Amara noticed my stomach was really bloated. I think for a moment it flashed across her mind that I could have been pregnant, but she didn't mention it.

The house we slept in at night would change, depending on what we were doing that day; the most that we would spend in any house would be a few nights. And the rules would eventually become more relaxed regarding sleeping; we needed to stay together to survive. We were right on the frontline, and when *Daesh* heard our voices, as women, they would become really agitated. So we would make a high-pitched *yala-yala* yell, to let them know we were hunting.

Mainly the houses were grey and cheap, and we moved further into the south. I didn't have any kind of input on decisions, I simply followed the other girls. After Medya was shot, we had a lot of discussions about a change of approach. We needed to find an actual safe house, slightly away from the others; so if we were to head south, as we were instructed to do, we should do it from a different angle, instead of charging straight into a firing squad.

Abu Bakr al-Baghdadi, the leader of the newly formed ISIS, vowed to wipe us out, and said that every Kurd in Kobani would be killed. These words, like so many other things he said, turned out to be false. They lost more than 1,000 soldiers, but the city became our graveyard, too. There was a Kurdish guy from Sweden whom I became close to, who was shooting with a PKM machine gun and an SVD – he was a proper sniper. Around dusk one night he, two YPJ fighters and I went out together as we had spotted a high house, with four storeys and a half-built roof at the top, which we believed would be a good spot to fire from and to cover from as we moved forward, street by street.

Every street took a lot longer to negotiate than we expected. Our job was to get to our house and set up our spots. All of us had sniper rifles: mine was an SVD, like those of the two other YPJ commanders who were more senior, and they also carried a huge Russian-made Dragunov.

In our army we have a tradition of salvaging parts so that we can learn about them and build better weapons than our enemies, and we even created our own 'Zagros' sniper rifle, named after our mountains. The 12.7mm home-made Zagros rifle uses a trigger from an RPG. Our creativity with weapons is not a choice – making new weapons can be dangerous and requires a lot of time and effort, but we are forced to improvise. So weighed down with our rifles that night – I only had my sniper rifle, not my AK, as I was exhausted and hungry, and the weight was unbelievable – we crossed the street and crept quietly into the house. The girls went to the second floor, while the Swedish *heval* and I went up another set of stairs to the fourth floor. It was still hot, as the sun had just gone down. The building was narrow, painted a sun-faded red and really high – but quite small. I think it might originally have been one small apartment that the family just kept building on top of.

We figured we could shoot from four different places in the one building, and we started setting up our firing positions. I wasn't feeling very confident, but I felt better having the rifle near me. Or course no one in Kobani needed a sniper rifle – we were so close that we could have used swords half the time – but the scopes were needed to peer into the distance and watch for *Daesh* snipers, who were, I have to give them credit, really good. Our job in this house was specifically to find *Daesh* snipers; the others were taking care of the regular fighters, who were not our concern, unless they were a threat to us and our friends, which of course they were. If we were to take them out, it took the pressure off those going further forward, but that wasn't our mission.

I think by this stage I was in my second week in Kobani, and although I was hardly adjusting, my response to the stress and trauma was to be super-alert and creep around like a ninja, whereas my Swedish friend had been in Kobani longer than me and was quite nonchalant about everything. He had been in Syria since the start of the *Daesh* takeover. I had my SVD rifle and was nervous, but I was ready. I know how to shoot. There were others who only did sniping in Kobani; including those who went behind enemy lines, such as Heda Musa, who was one of our greatest snipers and died in Kobani in October, just after I left. He killed many of the Chechen sniper mercenaries who impeded so much of our movement in the city. He killed more than one hundred *Daesh* himself, just in Kobani, and saved so many of us. We were so few, and they were so many. No matter where you were or what you did, you would get shot at. It was like no film you have ever seen; it just rained and rained bullets and explosions, all day, all night. The only times I don't remember the sounds of gunfire were when I think the sight and smell of the dead had engulfed my other senses.

We settled in our room; I had the SVD – it was a Romanian copy of a Russian SVD – and the Swedish *heval* had the PKM, so we were sharing ammunition between the two guns. He had his bag with him, with all the cleaning equipment; the worst part about being a sniper is the cleaning fluid that we had to cart around with us when we set up our positions. Particularly when you are using the slightly wrong bullets: the ones for the PKMs are just 0.2 grams heavier than those for the SVD, so while it's okay to use them in the necessary circumstances, it's not ideal, because it could damage the gun; but as I said, we improvise. Inside our bags we had hammers to make holes in the walls to put the sniper rifles through. I had been trained to do what is called 'loophole shooting', which is basically shooting through two holes; it makes you invisible to your target, but is a little more complicated. My Swedish friend started hammering the wall to make his first hole, but I had to tell him to stop making so much noise. I was feeling a bit confused; I had the sniper rifle in my hand, but I knew I wasn't a proper sniper. My hole was at the nine o'clock position and his was at the twelve o'clock position, meaning that we could shoot across and behind each other.

The plan was to stay in the house for that one night only, and wait for our group to come closer – so that when they launched forward we could protect them, hopefully by having already found a few of the *Daesh* snipers. Nothing went to plan in Kobani, but as the cool curtain of twilight began to fall, I started to relax a little at least and talked to the Swedish *heval*. In Kobani the rules about being alone with the opposite gender for too long didn't really apply by this point. So we spent our time oiling the cartridges together and chatting.

At the end of summer in Kobani it suddenly becomes very cold when the sun sets, and because we were hungry, we felt the cold in our bones. We had some tea before we left, but one thing that many of us do on the frontline is smoke. It makes you feel less cold, less freaked out, but most of all, it makes you feel less hungry. Of course it's just a feeling, but it was a good one, and good feelings are important for surviving. So I had found my spot, I was lying in position and looking up at the stars, debating how I could ask my Swedish *heval* what I was ashamed to ask the others: were we staying here for ever with no logistics, nothing to eat, no water and no supplies?

I was lost in my thoughts when I saw a plume of smoke go past my scope and immediately turned to my *heval*. At dusk, when the air is as cold and moist as it was on this particular night, we are not supposed to smoke on the frontline. Especially not snipers, once in position. It's like sending a smoke signal, and it provides a torch for the sniper who is looking for you.

'Relax, Joanna,' he told me when I warned him. He took out his packet of Arden cigarettes – they were from the USA, and I think he had bought them cheap in duty free – and offered me one.

I was really tempted, but I was uneasy: nothing had gone to plan so far in Kobani, and even though he had a better gun than me, he was a little inexperienced to be flouting a pretty sensible rule so fearlessly. 'You will get used to life in war,' he coaxed, offering me a cigarette again, as I had been complaining about being hungry, and he promised it would soothe my stomach cramps.

'Don't be like that,' I said and we began to tease each other a little. 'I was born in Ramadi, it's a little different from Stockholm.'

He still had his cigarette in his hand when he bent back to his spot to look through his hole: it wasn't very big at all, but as he crouched in his spot, a bullet blasted through the hole and into the front of his face. I froze and stayed completely calm after it happened, remaining exactly where I was. Whoever shot him probably didn't know there were four of us in the house; they had only seen the ember of his cigarette, which his blood would eventually put out as it pooled around him on the floor. I stayed quiet and crawled completely flat on the ground beside the wall and kept my head down, away from what had become of his face. Their bullets were better quality than ours, I could see that much. It wasn't the nice clean kind of kill you see in a film, with one bullet hole and blood coming out of the back of his head. It had hit his nose and seemed to have exploded the flesh off his face. I could see his skull, and his eyes had come out of their sockets.

The girls were a floor below us, at the better vantage point, and we should have gone with them to see how they had made their holes in the concrete. Ours were too big – or maybe the *Daesh* snipers were too good. I was still learning in Kobani. We drew too much attention to us because of the noise, the girls told me later, and I could hear them moving downstairs as I remained face down on the floor, away from the Swede's spot. When his blood began to reach my leg, I cursed him for smoking, and myself for not insisting he put it out. I couldn't believe that less than a minute ago we had been joking together.

I could hear shots from below me and somewhere behind me, so I crawled over to his body to take his ID card. I couldn't carry his body, I was too exhausted to carry my own weapons and there was no point. He was dead. I had to take his card and bring it back with me.

I took his PKM and his sniper rifle and left his body. I went slowly downstairs to the girls – I had thought they were coming up, but they weren't. I banged on the wall to alert them to where I was; obviously I didn't want to blow their location, and if I was being tracked by a sniper now, then so were they.

I hit my rifle against the wall again and didn't hear anything, so I thought they might have left. I crept downstairs to leave the way we came in, when suddenly one of the girls appeared from nowhere and hissed at me, 'What are you doing down here?' I explained what had happened. They thought we had fired out – not that we had been shot at. 'How did they get him through his hole,' they asked, incredulous, and I had to explain that he had been smoking. 'Why did you let him smoke?' they accused me, as if it had been my decision.

The building was bombed a few days later, so I'm not sure if anyone actually retrieved his body. His family are still in Sweden, and I don't know what – if any – of his remains were returned to them. But his mistake will always be a lesson for me.

We made our way back to the safe house, and I went to the yard to drink some tea and smoke a cigarette. 'How can you smoke after that episode?' one of the girls who had been in the building with us asked me. I felt very guilty, but feelings of guilt are not new to me, for my family taught me that feeling decades ago. In the house the Turkish guys smoked, but those who had done the proper training in the mountain camps didn't smoke and were against it. We didn't smoke when we were stressed; we smoked instead of eating food, instead of crying. Smoking was often the best part of our meal times. We were waiting for the blockade by Turkey to be lifted, and for the international community to help us. The night my Swedish friend died is among the scariest of my life because it made me realize, finally, how unlikely it was that any of us would make it out alive. If my intention was not to die, I had made a fatal miscalculation in coming to Kobani.

We didn't do a debrief and I didn't have to give my *takmil* to the whole group, which is what normally happens after a big day of fighting, but by then these kind of formalities had fallen away somewhat. Everyone stood up when they heard and looked down at their feet – they all knew what had happened. The Swede was a strong and clever *heval*, who spoke Kurdish and was really popular in our *tabur*, as he was incredibly knowledgeable about our ideology. One of the guys he was closest to took his PKM and spent the evening cleaning it alone. Another asked me what had happened, so I gave him my *takmil*, stressing that we had made a stupid mistake by hammering our sniping holes too big, and by smoking in our firing position that night. My hole was not too big and I didn't smoke, and I did tell him not to smoke himself because it was stupid; but in the end, it was me who survived and me who felt stupid, as it was my job to look after my *heval* in those circumstances.

I bowed my head in shame when telling the others what had happened, because hearing myself say it made it sound even starker and more stupid than it was. I didn't say it was my Swedish friend's idea, because in our movement we take criticism as a group and we accept the blame of our mistakes together, so that we can discuss them and learn from them; but I wish I had taken the cigarettes from him. He was more experienced than me, so as his junior it was down to me to take the blame.

Thankfully, one of the older YPJ commanders asked me for more details: 'Did you smoke?'

'No.'

'Do you normally smoke?'

I stammered, 'No.' She put her arm on my shoulder and made me look into her eyes. 'How do you feel now, sister?'

'Shocked and sad, because he smoked and I know we are not allowed to do this, especially at night.'

We sat down together around our tea, and Medya, who was still recuperating from her leg wound, spoke first, after a long silence. 'Everyone is under pressure here at the moment, and we are taking a lot,' she began tentatively, 'but remember, *hevals*, if we don't fight for what we love and we lose it, then we can't complain about it.' Our philosophy – the ideology behind why we fight – is that if you are determined, nothing can stop you. This is why we rely on the ideology training, as much as the weapons training. The rifle training might help your body stay alive, but the ideology training is what enables you to stay in the battlefield and keep on going forward, instead of blowing out your own brains to escape.

Medya spoke really poetically, in a way I enjoy, and what she was saying was that we were learning how we cope in stressful situations, and we were enduring okay so far, so we could endure more together, if we stayed together and remained focused. She sang for us, her beautiful voice ringing through the night, and we stayed up talking – and eventually laughing – together for a few more hours. Our way to face death was by being alive; and after a few more songs and jokes, Medya and Amara finally helped me find my smile. If it was my turn to die tomorrow, being miserable was not how I would spend my last night.

CHAPTER NINE

Stuck in the Mountains

I left Kobani in September 2014, following the death of Cengiz in the battle between the two buildings, and in need of medical attention for my stomach. After a brief period recuperating in Erbil, I was back in Denmark for a total of three weeks; I came home determined to tell the world about what was happening in Kobani, starting with my government. On 28th September I went on hunger strike along with eleven Kurdish and two Danish activists, to try and raise awareness of what was happening and get my government involved in the war.

When the hunger strike was over, I went to the hospital for an operation as the pain of my swollen stomach was getting worse. My doctor wouldn't believe that I had only been refusing food for a few days, as he said my stomach had shrunk away to nothing, and I tried to explain to him that the shrinking was not due to the hunger strike, but to the conditions inside Kobani. I am not sure he believed me, or that he had ever heard of Kobani, and I didn't elaborate.

I spoke to journalists and told them what was happening, and I tried to tell everyone I could that they had to help us. A huge picture of my face was on the front page of the Danish newspaper *Politiken*. I also did a live television interview on TV2 News, one of the Danish national broadcasters, which was slightly trickier. I tried to answer the host's questions as honestly as possible, but I couldn't tell him I had already been on the frontline, for safety reasons. The host asked if I wasn't afraid that the YPG and the PKK would be seen as the same, and said that the PKK was a designated terror group. I told him I thought it was really sad in a country like Denmark, where there is freedom, democracy and human rights, that we view a group who are fighting for freedom, democracy and human rights for Kurds as terrorists.

He seemed incredulous at the thought that I might hold a weapon and be a warrior, and I managed not to laugh at him as I said that I could become trained to be one. I had, by this point, already done many years of training. He wouldn't believe that I wasn't afraid of fighting, and accused me of trying to be a superhero. I told him I didn't think I could make a big difference, but I could no longer watch what was happening on television and do nothing. He finished by asking me the question I have been asked my entire life: Did I feel more Danish or more Kurdish?

The feedback from my interview was mixed, and I was shocked. Lots of people said it was impossible for someone like me to be in combat, because I looked like someone who would be busy 'having fun with men'. My family were furious, because they don't like the YPG and didn't want me to join them, but I lied to the journalists and said they were being supportive. My family had actually been really abusive when I told them I wanted to go to Kobani. I told them I was going to fight for our people, and if something should happen to me, I wanted their blessing. 'Make the milk you have given me halal,' I asked my mother in the Sorani Kurdish we speak at home, which means: I want your permission.

Instead of being pleased that I wanted to fight for Kurdistan, my father called me a Mafia hooker, and my brother threw a teapot containing hot water at me. I was shocked; I was trying to talk seriously to my family, but they could only call me names. My father pushed me down on the ground, and my brother slapped me in the face. I went into the toilet to get away from their yelling and the names they were calling me – words that no family member should say to a daughter. I thought to myself: How can the beatings from my father and brother hurt me in this way, when I can face *Daesh* on the frontline? Knowing that I had already survived Kobani changed the way I saw myself now, and made the opinions of my family matter less to me.

The Kurdish community in Denmark didn't like the interview, either; they didn't want me to speak publicly and said I was seeking attention for myself. After my troubles with my family, I started rejecting any phone call that wasn't YPJ or YPG-related.

I thought I could contribute to our cause from Europe by raising awareness and building support, but it didn't make me feel any better about being away from the conflict, so soon after I had my stomach operation I started making plans to get back to the friends I had left behind in Kobani. I didn't feel good that I had left under the circumstances that I had, and now that the international community was finally getting involved – or at least the USA was – I knew we would have a better chance of flushing out *Daesh*.

I started talking to a freelance journalist based in Erbil: he was Dutch, but was working on the frontline covering the conflict all over Iraq and Syria, and I offered to help him with translations, and he offered to let me stay in the flat he was renting. I flew from Stockholm to Erbil on 7th November 2014 and arrived at his flat that evening, where he lived with a photographer from Germany. The journalist was following the Iraqi army, and I went with him to the front in Gwer. I was wearing a flak jacket and a helmet, and he even lent me his PRESS sign, but I took it off to pose for a picture with the guys in the army. This picture was then picked up by the Danish press – and translated incorrectly, as it made out I was already fighting, when I was not. I just held the gun in order to pose with it, but as the only girl among men, I was criticized for posing.

It was very damaging for me that my picture with the Iraqi soldiers was interpreted in the way it was. The Iraqi army are the soldiers who ran away from their positions when Islamic State attacked. By doing so they gave more weapons to the group than any Gulf benefactor. Around Kirkuk, Kurdish fighters were pushing *Daesh* back from the frontline, and it was difficult, dangerous and slow work for them. I met some old friends that I knew from the mountains while helping the journalist with translations – including a woman called *heval* Kani, whose background is like mine, from eastern Kurdistan, in Iran.

Heval Kani and I were close in age, we both spoke Sorani Kurdish and had been briefly in the same Zagros mountains, and we spent a few hours talking together. The journalist (who has asked not to be named) started asking me questions about how I knew the fighters, which I didn't really want to answer. I was worried that he was becoming suspicious, and he seemed annoyed that I knew more about my homeland than he did. I got the phone number of one of the YPJ commanders who said she could help me get back to Syria, and so after returning to Erbil, I left the house of this journalist without saying goodbye and travelled with the YPJ commander.

By the time the pictures of me posing on the frontline had appeared on social media and on the news, I was neither in Kobani, as I had said I would be, nor in Kirkuk any longer. I had got as far as Derek, in the *canton* of Kobani. But instead of being sent back to the city, I was sent to a training camp. I was injured; I still had stitches in my stomach and, although I wasn't given any choice, I wasn't worried. I assumed this was normal and that I was going to wait for others to travel to Kobani with. But in Derek I met a commander who prevented me from fulfilling my plans. Her name was *heval* Jiyan, and she is still alive. I was already known in Derek, but there were a lot of people joining around that time and, due to the rapid expansion of the YPG since 2011, these new commanders were being given positions and responsibilities beyond their experience. *Heval* Jiyan did not like me, and to this day I still get furious even thinking about her.

The problem was that some of my notes showing my training and experience had disappeared. The note is a really small card that you fold up into a tiny square. When you open the note, you show it to your commander and then you burn it. It doesn't exactly feature information that you would put on a normal CV; it shows the locations of the training grounds you have attended, and everything in it is for your commander's eyes only. It's a secret and it's not something you share. I presented my commander with my note when I arrived in Derek – and gave it to another woman who was not my commander – and told her I had been back in Europe briefly, as I had to leave Kobani for medical reasons, but that I was better now and wanted to get back there as soon as possible to help my comrades.

The next day *heval* Jiyan asked me if I wanted to go to her camp to train, and I repeated the story that I had told the other female commander – who I had thought was to be my commander – the day before.

'I've done a lot of training already, and I already have the note.'

'Which note?' she asked, as if she had not received it. I couldn't accuse my commander of losing my note, so I had to say that I had lost it, which is where my troubles on this mountain began.

Heval Jiyan hadn't been inside Kobani, so as someone who had, I anticipated a bit more respect, but this commander wasn't having any of it and our relationship quickly deteriorated. I asked why there were no logistics deliveries going into the city of Kobani: if we were still able to send fighters, then why not food? She seemed taken aback by my question, as if she had not heard how horrendous the conditions inside the city were, and regarded me suspiciously. Looking back now, I think perhaps already at this stage, unbeknown to me, rumours about me being some kind of KDP *Peshmerga* spy had started swirling around.

Heval Jiyan was from Bakur in Turkey and didn't speak any Sorani or Persian, or English, just Kermanji and Turkish, which I do not speak – nor do I have any desire to learn how to do so. She sat me down and explained that I would have to do a new round of training just outside Derek before going back to Kobani. Knowing how desperate the situation in the city was, I tried explaining to

her that this was unnecessary. 'I am not a stranger here,' I said
very directly, looking into her eyes and hoping she could infer my
meaning. I was trying to say that the fact that she didn't know me
said more about how new she was to the YPJ, and less about me.
We spoke in Kermanji – which I still wasn't very confident in – but
I knew she understood what I meant and what I wanted: for her
to back down and send me where I wished to go.

'Since you don't have a note, or anything with you, you have
to go to a training academy outside Derek, at least until your
injury has healed.' She spoke Kermanji very slowly to me, as if
I didn't understand Kurdish at all. I was certain I had handed
over my note the day before, though even that didn't show my
complete training. Generally speaking, our training is inferred
rather than detailed.

Once you have special-forces training you are allowed to make
a lot of decisions about where you can go. In the YPJ the ideology
and its policy represent only one part, while the command-and-
control structure represents another. As in every army, you show
your commander respect. For me to accuse *heval* Jiyan of losing
my note would amount to treason, so I had to choose my words
carefully, which was hard in Kermanji. I now think that perhaps
I said something, without realizing it, that completely offended
her. As *Apo* advises, I should think more than forty times before
saying or doing anything.

'I already have this training,' I said again, more softly now,
trying to coax her. I told *heval* Jiyan the name of my academy
in the White Mountains and the names of some of my trainers,
whom she should have recognized as senior founding members
of the organization.

Heval Jiyan insisted, 'That academy has shut down, *heval* Joanna. It's no longer there. Your training was some time ago, so it would be good for you to take it again.'

In our movement it's very uncommon to argue with your commander, and when she was forced to repeat herself, I knew I didn't have a choice.

So for the next six weeks I did another round of training near Derek, in order to get back to Kobani again. I was pretty seething for most of my time there, and I found it harder the second time around: the long ideology lectures, reading the same books over and over again; the physical training, because of my stomach injury; chanting together; the whole erasure of our individuality, while I just wanted to return to my unit in Kobani. I don't think you can really get enough training, no matter what for, but I really wanted to get back to Kobani at that very moment.

You have to go through a lot to get to the frontline. The whole process was tough, but part of my frustration was hearing the daily updates about the martyrs of Kobani: the girls who blew themselves up to take out *Daesh*, those killed by snipers and their superior weaponry. The YPJ established its name internationally because of Kobani, but that name was written by the blood of our comrades. We had too many martyrs, not enough food, not enough logistics, not enough support and too much glorifying and celebrating of the dead.

I had my phone and my passport confiscated, and did the new round of training as if I was some village girl from the mountains who had never held a gun before. Quickly the trainers realized I was in the wrong place, even if *heval* Jiyan refused to acknowledge the fact. Not even all of the trainers had the special-forces training I had completed in 2012, so soon I was asked to assist in running the classes and courses, which I did immediately, and this experience of training the girls was the only good thing about my time stuck in the mountains, against my will. I was still injured, so I couldn't crawl on the ground with the weapons for a long time, and I had to spend a lot of time cleaning my wounds. After about a month I removed the stitches from my stomach, with the help of the girls I was sleeping with at night. Normally the stitches should fall out by themselves after one or two weeks, but mine didn't for some reason, so I enlisted the help of my *hevals* and pulled them out.

After spending six weeks with the other girls, I had another ceremony and another pledging session, and older commanders came down from the mountains. When the session was over, one commander called me to her and informed me that I was being sent with the other girls up to Tel Tamir, because there was a big battle about to start there. I almost laughed at her, but she was deadly serious. 'You are a *cadra* now, *heval* Joanna – you have graduated from your training, so congratulations.'

I sat down slowly and explained quietly to her that I was not a *cadra*, and that I had no intention of becoming one: I was what is called a 'traveller' in the movement – a step down from the *cadra* – which meant that I still had the right to come and go as I pleased, as the international volunteers did.

She insisted that I was going to Tel Tamir, while I insisted that I wanted to go to Kobani. We agreed to discuss it the night before the cars were due to come and ferry us to another base in Derek, and then towards whichever battle we were assigned to. I hadn't heard whether anyone else was going to Kobani – it wasn't my decision to make – but I was as sure as hell that I was going there. That night I went ballistic at *heval* Jiyan, and we had another huge fight, after she said I could either go to battle at Tel Tamir or stay training the girls in Derek. I didn't intend to argue, of course, and went to the meeting near our *nokhta* (our word for base, which we use for our group base, but also for a sniper's base on the frontline) determined to keep a lid on my fury. Having spent the last six weeks speaking Kermanji, I was feeling more confident in the language now, so we sat quietly together as I made my case.

'*Heval* Jiyan, I am a fighter, not a trainer. I have finished my A-team training, which means I have pledged to fight, should I be needed. I am needed in Kobani, and I am begging you to send me back there.' I was so emotional I was almost crying – which is not something we, as female fighters, are supposed to do very often – but I didn't care about my pride at this point. I just wanted to get out of the camp and back to Kobani, and I wanted her to realize why it was so important. 'Why are you keeping me here when Kobani is going on? We have injured women who can do this kind of training. You don't need me. Someone else could take my place,' I pleaded with her.

She listened until I started suggesting that someone else could take my place, and then she held up her hand to stop me speaking, and said that I wasn't being respectful of the structure of my movement, and called me arrogant. 'You can't just come here and do what you want, Joanna. That isn't how it goes. You know that.'

'I also know that I have been a member of the movement for a long time, and part of my involvement involves travelling home to Europe.'

I saw her face flinch when I described Europe as my home, and she practically spat the next words at me: 'You, Joanna, have become a spoiled daughter of capitalism.'

Finally her true feelings had shown themselves. Although she didn't scream or yell or curse me, she insulted me in a profound and shocking way. To call someone in the YPJ the daughter of capitalism – in a real way, not as a joke – was a horrible thing to say. Particularly to someone like me, who had given up the pleasures of capitalism to come and join this movement. I recoiled briefly in shock, and protested that I was as much of a Kurd as she was – more, seeing as I still spoke my mother tongue, and not the words of the fascist Turkish state that sought to destroy us. I had by this point abandoned all ambitions to stay calm. 'You know it's against our policy to force anyone to be a *cadra* against their will,' I said.

'If you are a Kurd, you belong here. Are you not here to fight for freedom?'

'I will fight for freedom for all Kurds, but I will never give up my own to do so.'

'Fine. Run away and be a traitor.'

For *heval* Jiyan to accuse me of running away, when all I wanted was to go back to the front, was her way of trying to humiliate and shame me in front of the others. By this point our argument had attracted a small audience, and I could feel eyes boring into my back, though I didn't turn round. The other trainers had come into the room to listen. A few of them knew what was going on, but they had all stayed out of it so far. They gathered towards Jiyan protectively, and I became aware that I was in a minority and they weren't understanding me very well.

I was so furious with them, but I was also powerless; *heval* Jiyan was my commander and she didn't know me – and what she did know of me, she didn't like.

'I will never run: not in battle, not from you,' I screamed at her. 'Women like you make female solidarity impossible.' This is a very harsh thing to say to a female commander; our entire *jineology* training is about solidarity and uniting for freedom for Kurdish women, and for women all over the world. *Heval* Jiyan was very hurt by my words, but when they came out of me, I was still spewing with anger, so I didn't care. She went out of the room and I was left with the other girls, who eyed me coolly and seemed annoyed on her behalf.

'Joanna, you are Kurd. This is where you belong,' *heval* Aria, one of the girls I had been friendly with, said to me softly. She came towards me – the others were still staring, and a few had left with *heval* Jiyan – and I cried into her shoulder.

I pushed her hand away from me and said to the whole assembled group, 'No, this isn't where I belong. I would never take away the freedom of someone who came to fight for your freedom. I would never kidnap anyone.' *Heval* Aria didn't say anything, but just looked at me sadly and we walked into the yard together.

So I stayed doing more training. I had no choice. This was one of the most disappointing times in my life. I was isolated and they backed me into a corner. They had my passport and my phone, so I was stuck. This was the movement I had quit school for, given up my comfortable life in Europe for, and they repaid me by holding me a virtual hostage in a training camp for new members. This was not what I had signed up for.

What we mean when we say that we fight for public justice over personal happiness is that our small individual happiness (or unhappiness) is immaterial to the wider ideology, until we achieve our military objectives. That's how it is in most armies, but it's a hard lesson to learn. That is not to say I was really miserable in the camp, I wasn't; and really, apart from Kobani, I had nowhere else I wanted to be.

I acted as a drill sergeant, a training commander, and fulfilled the role better than either I or *heval* Jiyan expected. I did enjoy training the girls. They were young girls from Turkey or Shingal mainly, who were incredibly sweet and liked me because I seemed to have more in common with them than those who had been living in the mountains or in desolate parts of Syria before joining. I tried to train the girls just as well as I had been trained, and I worked hard in the camp to win the respect of the other trainers.

Christmas passed and the new year of 2015 came and went without me really noticing. I hadn't spoken to my family and I hadn't called anyone since arriving at the camp, as I had no way to do so. In the YPJ the girls aren't really allowed to have phones, although it's normal for the boys in the local YPG to have them. Nor do they have social-media accounts, and back then I only had my personal account from Copenhagen and I kept very quiet about that. *Cadras* aren't allowed to have such accounts, or any contact with the outside world.

The international volunteers are treated differently when it comes to these rules, but the problem I faced back then – and continue to face now, to some degree – was that I was not viewed like the international volunteers. There were very few girls who volunteered

back then, and when I first joined I had my own reasons for being in the movement. I was always part of the main movement, but was permitted to work on my own projects outside it. *Heval* Jiyan thought I was looking for special treatment, compared to the way the other Kurdish girls were treated, and I suppose in some ways I was. I wanted to choose where I went, and I wanted to keep my phone on me and have the elements of my freedom that I enjoyed in Copenhagen with me in Kurdistan. This was how it had always been for me, so I couldn't accept that this new commander from Turkey could suddenly change all that. I didn't respect her authority over me, but I had to accept it.

I realized, after our bust-up, that there wasn't much I could do to form a friendship or a personal relationship with this *heval*, so I dedicated myself to proving to her that I was a professional and was ready to take a lot of responsibility for the training. My idea was to convince her that I was wasted in the training camps and that I needed to be at the front, but I also knew that these girls would be at the front soon, and it was my job to increase the chances of them not being killed. We have a saying in our army: the more you sweat in training, the less blood you spill in battle; and I worked these girls hard.

Our academy was called Badik and it's now closed, which is common, as we operate under the radar – our camps near the Turkish border spring up and close down frequently, which keeps us safer but can cause confusion, such as the misunderstanding between *heval* Jiyan and me, in terms of how commanders assess different levels of training.

The girls I trained were mainly Yazidi girls from Shingal or girls from Turkey who had been brought up Muslim, which led to some small cultural misunderstandings. The whole Yazidi community was traumatized by the genocide in Shingal, while the girls from Turkey were fighting more for their rights as Kurds than out of vengeance. All of my girls were very highly motivated and I loved getting to know them. They always wanted to hear stories about Europe, and I would scandalize them with stories about boys and boyfriends. I even told a few of them about my cheerleading days, and laughed at them as their eyes widened in disbelief.

I would get up every morning at 4.15 a.m. to make sure everything was ready, and I tended to start my morning by going to speak to whoever had been in charge overnight – the role we call *supeye*. That person would be aware of what the schedule for the day was: who was making breakfast, what time classes were; and it was their job to be on guard, should we be attacked overnight. They would make sure the weapons were in the right place so that we could mobilize quickly, and they would have to stay awake and alert to keep the rest of us safe.

At half-past four I woke the girls and at 4.45 we would have the *takmil*. I was responsible for the physical training, while the more senior commanders were responsible for the ideology training. I took part in all the ideology classes, because it was mandatory, and it was like watching an old film or reading your favourite book over and over again: you get something new every time. My trainings took place in the morning from five till six, six-thirty or seven, before breakfast. Ideology classes started at seven-thirty, meaning that everyone would rush around for the half-hour before that, washing their faces and brushing their teeth.

Our biggest meal of the day was around noon, and after lunch we were allowed to smoke. Classes would start again at around one and would go on until 4 p.m., then we would have our dinner and in the evening there would be more classes and lectures until about eight, when it was homework or self-study before an early bed. My classes were physical training and fitness; it's impossible to overestimate how important it is to be able to run quickly, as a YPG soldier. We fight with minimal armoury, so we have to be fast and outsmart our enemies using our minds, as well as our weapons. Our bodies are our weapons, and our brains are our explosives. Both need to be cared for and fed well.

I would make the girls run slowly for five minutes in a jog, then for five minutes they would run quickly, then five minutes slowly again, before running fast for fifteen solid minutes, while I shot at their legs with my rifle. Using my AK, I would aim for their ankles to make them run, just as my commander had done to me, as a youngster. It makes the girls run faster. Of course there have been instances where girls have been injured during training, but that's normally when they are being stupid and messing around with their weapons, before they know how to control them. I loved the girls, but I had to show my love for them by being strict and making them train hard, so they would have the best chances of staying alive. They would get mad at me and were very vocal in their complaints, and sometimes I felt bad. But trust me, when you are running from being bombed, you will wish your trainer had shot you through the legs.

In the YPJ we tend to go ahead of the boys, so if we were doing mixed-gender training, the girls would practise going in front. In single-sex training I just needed them to be as quick as possible. Of course for the first few days I would be less strict, and I wouldn't use a timer until they had built up their level of overall physical fitness. In Kurdistan, as in most Muslim countries, women don't play sports much, and although none of my girls were ever very fat, their fitness levels weren't great, so this was the first challenge.

The girls hated the wall-jumping most; it's a hard part of the training, as you need a lot of upper-body strength, and women don't naturally have much arm or upper-body strength, but to be a fighter you need it. So we would do hours and hours of wall-jumping until they could finally get over. When you fight from house to house, and from street to street, these urban survival skills are what will make the difference between being a heroic fighter and a heroic martyr. My job was to make them the best fighters they could be, and I took enormous pride in my work and I was good at it.

The weapons training I gave was very basic, for those who had no weapons experience. Weapons training isn't like some kind of *Rambo* shooting and target practice; before you get there you need to know how to hold the gun, how to sit in the right position and how to clean it. I didn't know the Kermanji for the different gun parts, so I wasn't responsible for weapons-handling training, although I had to attend. In weapons classes the languages are Kurdish, Turkish and Russian; most of our weapons are Russian, or rip-offs of Russian weapons. Many of the books in the training camps are Russian, because Russia has trained many Kurdish fighters in the Middle East over the past couple of centuries, so their methods are still used. Some of the books we have in the mountains are older than me. These books are our ancestry as female fighters; we are democrats and we are ready for peace, but we are first and foremost freedom fighters, trained to fight and win wars.

The new recruits really liked the fact that I was an 'outsider' and yet Kurdish. One day right after training we held a *takmil*. *Heval* Jiyan arrived while I was speaking loudly to the new recruits, as my trainers had done. I was telling the girls: one mistake you make on the battlefield will surely lead to your death. If you are successful in life, and with training, then you are more likely to be successful in battle. The new *shervans*, as we call them (from the Latin for 'servant'), would call out to me, saying they wanted me to show them the exercises and fitness trainings that we did in Europe. They liked these games especially: they loved what we were doing and wanted more. *Heval* Jiyan stood watching the girls and saw the standard of training that I was providing, and she could see that I was ready to go to war. I gained her respect in the end – against her will perhaps, but I know I did.

When the girls first come to the camps, they are kids, and when they leave they have to be fighters. They have made the decision to join the YPJ, and the younger ones can surprise you on the frontline; the adrenaline can make them braver than a thirty-year-old man, and they have such pride in their achievements. Why would they leave this to get married? They have more courage than I had when I was their age, worrying about cheerleading and planning how to escape my family. The options for girls in Kurdistan are not many, particularly if your family does not have money. And wealth is not evenly distributed – Kurdistan is still almost feudalist in most areas: there are a few wealthy families, and everyone else gets by on scraps.

I would like to set up shelters for some of the younger kids who join the YPJ to live in, so that they can finish their education before learning how to kill. I believe everyone should fight for their own goals and live by their own dreams, rather than fighting for someone else's ideology, or because they have nowhere else to go.

While stuck at this camp, I thought a lot about the parts of the movement that I didn't like, which I couldn't justify in my head or to my family, or talk about to friends in Copenhagen. There are two main things that are challenging for me about our movement: the restrictions placed on YPJ fighters, in comparison to YPG fighters; and the young age of some of our fighters. Our movement is based in the Middle East and is born of the injustices that we, as women, suffer there, so obviously it will reflect that culture. We are like the diamonds created by the pressure of the Earth – and we wear this struggle with pride. It's complicated to understand, and it's something that coverage of the YPJ has yet to seriously reflect, perhaps because the journalists who meet us tend to be men, who fall in love with the movement and are therefore blind to its imperfections.

You are not allowed to have sex as a YPJ fighter; relations with men on the frontline must remain professional and distant at all times. If you become pregnant while being a member of the YPJ, you are forced to marry that man or you may be imprisoned in one of our camps in the mountains. Likewise, if you are a *cadra* and you try to leave, it simply is not permitted. When you are part of the YPJ you are fighting for freedom, but you must give up your own freedom to do so.

There is a women's group that is responsible for women's health and issues to do with gynaecology, and so on. These are the same women who come whenever someone dies – they will mourn whoever the martyr is; they don't need to know their name. These women's councils are a vital part of our movement, as they are slowly changing the culture. We are all in a continuum; as the YPJ, we fight on the battlefield, proving that women are equal to men in this regard, while the different women's councils fight in civil society to ensure that women's issues are taken into consideration at all levels of the different decision-making processes. We have separate but equal parallel organizations, but changing the culture is the longer, more difficult goal. A free Kurdistan, where women are treated as they are currently treated, is not the goal for the YPJ. We see women's liberation and a free Kurdistan as interlinked ideas, and we fight for each of them together. But it's difficult, because we have to be so patient. And stuck in this training camp near Derek, I thought long and hard about how far we had yet to go.

The recruits graduated after three months of training, and I became emotional on the day they left to go to the front, as we had a really close bond by this time. The cars came to pick them up, but also to bring visitors to their ceremony. We had the flag up, the picture of Ocalan, our AKs and the pledge to the women's movement. Everyone was standing in a line, and a senior commander came from the mountains to make a speech. Afterwards we were dancing and singing, eating special food and then the cars came to take them away.

I stood watching them leave and cried as they waved to me. 'Be good. Honour yourself and each other,' I said to each of them as they left.

One of the commanders – a trainer who had softened towards me while I had been in the camp – came over and held my hand as I cried. 'I know you love them, but don't cry so much.' I was happy just to have her holding my hand. I felt responsible for the girls, but I was also crying because I wanted to go with them, but instead I was stuck in that fucking camp.

These girls were so much braver than me, and younger than me, and I took my responsibilities to them seriously; in our movement we say that a student can't be wrong – it's only a trainer who can be wrong. One of my favourite girls got out of her car and ran back towards me, when she saw me crying through the window. 'We knew you were going to cry. Don't play tough any more. You love us.'

I still couldn't say it loudly, but I took the girls in my arms and cried, while kissing them goodbye. One of these girls later died, and I regret not telling each and every one of them that I loved them more than they would ever know. But even the words 'I love you' are hard to say for me. In my culture these words are often used to trick women to feel ashamed, even when there is nothing to feel ashamed about.

A group of girls was due to head into battle a few days later – I thought they were going to Kobani, so I didn't say anything; I just kept my head down and waited for the call. The night before they left, *heval* Jiyan woke me up when I was sleeping and told me to be ready before the girls woke up the next morning. Finally I was leaving. So I packed all my gear, my clean uniforms and my toiletries, and was put in a car and taken by a male YPG fighter to the main transport base in Derek.

Heval Jiyan was at the base in Derek, and she smiled at me. I asked her what was happening; Kobani was on the other side of Derek, and the car that I was told to get into was going in the opposite direction. 'No, you are not going to Kobani, Joanna.' And I was instructed to get into the car when it was ready to leave.

There was another girl at the base, who asked if I had done something to annoy *heval* Jiyan. 'I didn't mean to,' I said quietly, as Jiyan approached me. 'What is happening? What are you doing to me?' I asked her.

'*Heval* Joanna, save it. You know what is happening.'

'No, *heval* Jiyan, I don't know what is happening.'

'If you are not going to be a *cadra*, you cannot stay here. You are leaving us.'

'What do you mean, I am leaving? People are coming from all over the world to join us and they don't have to stay here for ever – they can be volunteers. You can't force me to stay here, just because I'm a Kurd.'

'You are leaving. You are going back to Iraq, and into the KDP.'

'You can't do this to me. You know who I am now, to this movement.'

'Joanna, I know you have been here a long time, and it's time you were no longer here.'

As it started to dawn on me what was happening, I became really fearful. 'You can't do this. I am a female fighter, and this is against our policy,' I said.

'You are not one of us, you are *rarib*' – which means 'outsider' – and with that, *heval* Jiyan turned away from me and didn't look back.

At Rabia, I was told to get into a car with four *Peshmerga* KDP soldiers. One of them was a captain, an older guy. Rabia is close to the border of Iraq inside Syria, and they were travelling across the border into Iraq. I didn't have my passport, but at that moment this was the least of my worries. I was dressed in my military fatigues, with all my uniforms inside my bag, and my toiletries and supplies packed as if I was going to war. I was in shock.

You have to understand that in our movement there was no difference between handing me over to the KDP and handing me over to Turkey. In our training we are taught to kill ourselves instead of being captured or handing over anything to our enemies, and though the KDP are Kurdish fighters like the YPG, we are enemies. It hurts me to this day that people think I left my friends and our movement to join the *Peshmerga*. I never did. But I couldn't explain it at the time, and I was reluctant to criticize anyone within the YPJ. To settle disputes in our movement, we have what we call 'platforms': if someone has had a problem with someone else, or something has gone wrong and there have to be consequences, we have a big open meeting. Those involved stand up on a platform to speak their criticism of whoever has done them wrong, or to take criticism for whatever they have done wrong. Accepting criticism together is a key component of our movement; pointing the finger at someone, or speaking about it outside the group, is unusual.

In the car, the soldiers asked me whether I had a boyfriend and were obviously trying to find out whether or not I was a virgin. Because I am from Europe, I knew they would consider me a slut, and initially I feared for my sexual safety as much as I feared for my life. Thankfully, the older captain was a Zebari Barzani, related to the Barzani family (that of the president of the KRG) and a tribe connected to my mother's tribe.

I tried to tell the men that I was just a journalist and a translator, but they laughed at me. They were kind actually, and brought me to their base, gave me some food and allowed me to call my family. I hadn't spoken to my mother or sister for six months. It took me some time to remember the phone number, and I misdialled it the first time.

'Hello, it's me.' I spoke in Sorani Kurdish, as I always do with my mother. 'How are you?' I continued, really happy to hear her voice and her breath. It took about three seconds for her to begin yelling at me, but I could tell she was happy to hear from me.

'What happened? Why haven't we heard from you? We have been going mad with worry. We heard you were killed.'

I began to weep gently as they rambled on about their efforts to locate me, and hearing how hurt they were made me feel guilty. My sister came on the phone and was crying and screaming, but behind all the yelling I could hear their love for me and it felt great.

'I even called my *Baba*,' my mother wept, 'and told him you had joined the PKK.' My mother is a particular kind of Kurd who believes that everyone who is not *Peshmerga* is in the PKK. She doesn't understand the new movements in Syria, or that the YPG is a separate organization. My grandfather – her *Baba* – was a captain in the same army as Barzani, the president of Kurdistan's father. His advice was to go the mountains in Qandil, where the PKK headquarters are, to find me.

'You were going to go to the mountains in Iraq to find me?'

'I just wanted to get my daughter.'

'Oh, Mama,' I sighed, imagining her going all the way to Qandil for no reason. She's a very strong woman, my mother, and she doesn't get enough credit.

The captain and my mother spoke for a long time on the phone, sharing some stories about our tribes and relatives, some of whom he knew. This is what it's like being part of a tribal culture; everyone knows everyone else, and many people are related to one another in some weird, distant way. After being alone in the mountains, and having all that trouble with *heval* Jiyan, it felt good. The captain reassured my mother that he would take care of me, and asked me to go with him to his house in Sulaimaniya.

In the car, I still felt confused and angry. I couldn't understand why *heval* Jiyan had done what she did to me. I am the first YPJ fighter ever to be handed over to the KDP by another YPJ commander. This is nothing to be proud of. I was trying to think what I had done to make her hate me – had I been disrespectful? Had my body language been offensive? I was still reeling as the captain tried to talk to me.

After the call with my family he was much nicer to me, and explained that many YPG fighters had joined the *Peshmerga*, and it was something I should consider doing. He knew I was with the YPG, as they had gone through my bag before letting me call home. 'You are the daughter of *Peshmerga*, why did you go to the PKK?' (In Iraq, the KDP *Peshmerga* call the YPG and the YPJ the 'PKK', as if we are the same organization, in the same way that Turkey does. The KDP hates the YPG, and we hate them back; politically and ideologically, we are very different, but personally I found these men to be kind, polite, open and generous towards me.)

I told the captain about the photos of me that were already in the Danish press, from my time working as a translator, and the press attention I had attracted. He talked about the need for international support to defeat *Daesh*, and for the world to unite behind the Kurds. He was a smart man, and discussed how the Kurds could use this terrible war to show the world how inept the Iraqi government was, despite its funding from the USA. I could see the wheels of his mind turning, thinking about how he could use me for propaganda purposes for the *Peshmerga*. I didn't have that many options at the time, so I listened to him, but my mind was still on *heval* Jiyan.

By this stage, international volunteers had started travelling through the training camps in Derek. These men were regarded as heroes for coming to join our fight, and they didn't have to give up their whole lives to do so; they were free to come and go as they pleased, and this made me furious. They were admired by our community, while I was called a traitor for the stupid pictures taken with the *Peshmerga* army, and was accused of seeking attention. I was treated like this because I am a Kurdish woman, and the movement considers my rights less important than the feelings of Western men who volunteer. This is not how it should be and is another example of how imperfectly our ideology is applied, and how far astray it can go when it's forced to interact with real life.

I have waited before speaking out against what *heval* Jiyan did to me, because it would be seen as a further act of betrayal; but I have now decided to release myself from the lies that have engulfed me these past few years. And who would I really be betraying? Only those whose silence has betrayed me. I thought then it was better for people to believe the lie – that I had left because I was fame-hungry and wanted attention – rather than risk damaging our movement. But I am through with lies and, looking back now, I don't blame our movement for what *heval* Jiyan did to me, and it didn't prevent me from returning to the movement.

My experience with *heval* Jiyan taught me that women will not always fight for women; they can be just like men in a war, or more vicious still. There are horror stories of what Arabic women can do to other women in times of war, or even in peace, but I don't hold them 100 per cent accountable for their actions. When you grow up in a culture that hates you, hates your rights and any sign of you asserting those rights, it's easy to turn that hatred towards yourself, or towards other women like you. This betrayal felt at the time like the biggest betrayal of my life. Never in the history of our movement has a YPJ member crossed over to the KDP, although several YPG fighters have, as you can get a salary and support and can have a family if you fight for the *Peshmerga*, whereas you have to give all this up with us. But I did not choose this path willingly.

I am not *Peshmerga* in my heart, and throughout my time with them I never spoke badly of our movement, nor did I tolerate any criticism of the YPG or the YPJ.

As I travelled in the captain's car along the long road to Sulaimaniya, I had no idea what lay ahead of me. Even though I was back in my homeland, I felt alienated and confused. But as I watched the mountains disappear behind me in the mirror of his jeep, I was grateful that at least I was no longer stuck in that camp.

CHAPTER TEN

Peshmerga Poster Girl

I arrived at the captain's house that evening, having passed the time in his car pleasantly enough. Being born in Iraq had its advantages, and we spoke Sorani Kurdish together, which was nice and reminded me of my mother and her Iraqi family, whom I am still very close to. That night I stayed with the captain's family, who seemed kind. The captain had a huge house that my mother would have loved, but she would not have approved of his wife. She was very pretty and wore revealing clothing, in the new way that Kurdish women are dressing themselves. She would have been in her thirties – a decade or so older than me, but not quite a decade younger than my mother. Even though she is only in her forties, my mother dresses like an old conservative Muslim woman, and always has; she sees it as a way of staying true to her Kurdish culture, whereas this woman dressed quite sexually.

This is the generation of progress in Iraqi Kurdistan that passed my mother by: a new Kurdish culture that has nothing to do with Islam. The clothes of the captain's wife were modelled on our traditional Kurdish clothing, where the bra is worn on the outside, to emphasize the breasts; and around her skirt was a gold chain that fell close to her groin. She was incredibly kind, gave me lots of meat in my meals and asked me many questions about Europe. When he got home the captain changed into normal civilian clothing; he was kind to his wife and doted on his kids. He was clearly a family man, and they were a happy couple. You could see how committed he was to working so that his family could better themselves; they were fighting *Daesh* and fighting for their freedom as Kurds, but without giving up their personal life in the process. It might sound silly, but to me this was a revelation: he could have a private life that was his own, and still be a soldier.

The next morning I had breakfast with the driver and the captain. Still slightly fearful and aware of my precarious legal situation, as I had no passport or papers with me, I listened carefully and fixed on my face an expression of what I hoped was earnest humility, trying my best not to let the anger flash across it.

'My dear sister, you are the third generation of *Peshmerga*. We know the *Peshmerga* from eastern Kurdistan are able and strong fighters. Why did you join the PKK? Don't you know what they do?'

I explained that the YPJ and the PKK are not the same movement, we simply share the same ideology; and that the PKK don't operate in Syria, where I was. But the driver interrupted me before I finished. 'They bomb civilians, they kill babies, they kidnap people, they use human smuggling, they traffic drugs. Why would such a pretty girl want to be part of this?'

I had heard these accusations many times before, but it was hard to hear it from a Kurd instead of a Turk. I squirmed in my seat and glared at the driver, but said nothing, until the captain spoke again. He knew about the child training camps I had been to with *Lawan* and seemed keen to recruit me.

'You are a Sorani Kurd, not a Kermanji. You should join the other girls who are fighting our revolution. Kurdistan is changing, and you have skills that we could use, and you could have a good life here. You are obviously very determined. Why don't you use your passion to fight for your own people, and for Kurdistan? Fight wearing Kurdish clothes, under the Kurdish flag and speaking your own Kurdish language.'

'Do you speak Turkish?' the driver interrupted again.

'No, of course not,' I snapped.

'Then you must have had a lonely time in the mountains,' the captain finished. And they were right in some ways, it had been. These men were clever and they made valid points; most of the Kurds in the camp had spoken either Arabic or Turkish, languages I was not fluent in. And the YPG don't fight under the Kurdish flag – we have many different flags that we fight under.

Fighting under my Kurdish flag would not be a betrayal, but I still felt I was being pushed down a road I didn't really want to travel. I didn't want to stay in the house, because much as I liked the captain and his wife, I knew I wouldn't have very much say in what I would be doing. Kurdish women don't have many rights in northern Iraq, just as women all over Iraq don't. This fact of life is an unwritten law, on the occasions when it's not actually inscribed in the law. And the people are very conservative – often more conservative than the laws themselves.

I knew the *Peshmerga* wanted to use me as propaganda and dress me up like an army doll, to try and show the world that women in Kurdistan have equal rights to participate in war. Although there are many women in Iraqi Kurdistan and in the *Peshmerga* who have fought, it's not the same as the army I had just been evicted from, and my heart was still then – as it remains – with the YPJ.

'In Zahro we have a military college you can attend. They are like the YPJ, but they get paid,' the captain stressed, taking another tack. I really didn't want to commit to that, as my head was still all over the place from what had happened with Jiyan.

'I might like that, but not right now,' I said as firmly as I could. I don't have anything against the *Peshmerga* women fighters, as women or as Kurds, but I was suspicious. These men were being very nice to me, in the way that people often are nice when they want to manipulate you into doing something. I didn't want to join the female fighters of the *Peshmerga*, because they are just an army paid for by a conservative government, they are not a revolutionary fighting force, but I didn't have too many options. I promised them I would contact a female commander in Zahro to enquire about doing some training. In the meantime, the captain agreed to drive me back to the apartment of my friend, the journalist in Erbil.

After staying in his apartment for a few days, I was contacted on Facebook by a guy from the *Peshmerga* called Murad. I had met him on the way to Kobani the first time, and again when I was in Rojava, and briefly while I was in Derek. He was one of the guys from the *Peshmerga* who came to fight with the YPG in Rojava, with a group called *Yekitiye Soresgeri Kurdistan* or YSK. I had heard of his group, but hadn't made any enquiries into what it was. The YSK originated in eastern Kurdistan, Iran – like my family – but fights all over Kurdistan. In Syria they fight with the YPG; in Iraq they fight with the *Peshmerga*. They also call themselves *Peshmerga*, because this word can apply to any fighter who is willing to sacrifice his or her life for Kurdistan, or to stand in front of death, so that Kurdistan will live.

Murad said he had been contacted by a commander in the KDP and told that perhaps I was interested in joining them. This commander knew who I was, and where my family was from, and he wanted to meet. 'We fight for Kurdistan, as everyone from our region does; we don't fight for ideology, we fight for nationalism,' Murad said. It sounded interesting to me. We talked for a while and Murad explained a bit more about the YSK to me; the YSK had originally been founded by a man called Leheng, together with his brother, but they fell out, and Leheng's brother went on to set up a group called the Kurdistan Freedom Party (PAK), who are an Iranian Kurdish fighting group with thousands of fighters inside Iraqi Kurdistan, seeking to defend Iraq's Kurds from both ISIS and the Islamic Republic of Iran. PAK are very religious; they are Sunni Muslims, which places them at the more conservative end of the wider spectrum of Kurdish movements, but they are known for being good fighters and had been part of some great victories in this war. Obviously they are outlawed in Iran, because they fight the regime directly.

There are lots and lots of different fighting groups inside both Iraq and Syria, working together to defeat ISIS under a broad coalition, and I had heard of PAK, as they are connected to the KDP, so I started taking this guy more seriously. Murad arranged for me to meet the leaders of the YSK in a house in Erbil: Leheng, along with his bodyguard, Shahpour, and another guy called Aram. The commander who had first suggested the introduction, Pashaa, is a Kelhouri Kurd – one of the old Kurdish tribes from Iran, where my mother's family came from.

The meeting started by them asking me why I, as a Sorani, was fighting with the Kermanjis. 'I was fighting, just like you were, in Rojava. Your people died there for them.' The older man, Leheng, had been wounded in battle, but it wasn't clear how old this battle wound was. I told them about being with the YPJ, and glossed over the misunderstanding that had resulted in my current situation, but I think they got the picture.

'There are many cases like yours,' Leheng told me, and he assured me that he would help get my passport and phone back. Instead of me returning to my friend's apartment in Erbil, he invited me to attend a meeting they were having. 'You can see who we are, and what we fight for. You might be pleasantly surprised,' he said.

Leheng led the meeting. He was an impressive leader, an internationalist who had spent a lot of time in Colombia with different armed groups; he spoke English as well as several other languages, and he was very modern, by Kurdish standards at least. He viewed Islam as the enemy, which is quite a radical position for a Kurd inside Iraq to take. 'Islamic culture limits our Kurdish identity,' he told his group. 'Kurds will always have enemies just because we are Kurds; our identity – our very existence – is a threat to the states that have colonized our lands and our minds,' he continued, as everyone nodded in agreement.

I found myself agreeing as well. He spoke very poetically, and he had a way of talking that gave me confidence. The others in the meeting I didn't know. I heard they were from another group that had recently broken down. This is how our movement is: one group starts, it gets shut down, it opens with another name. There's a certain fluidity to it, which works to protect the people involved, but can make it confusing to follow, even as a Kurd.

I was impressed by what I heard at the meeting; those attending it were very modern, they were militants, but they respected others' privacy. As I was about to leave and go back to my friend's house, Leheng came out to the car. 'Joanna, you can always join us. We are open to a woman like you. You have the skills and experience we are looking for, and we want younger people to join us. We owe it to the younger generation.' A few others had gathered around him as he continued this impromptu speech. 'The future has been built by our ancestors. Our grandparents aren't living here any more, and I won't be here for ever, but for the younger people who will inherit this place, you are part of it, and you should be a part of creating it. We need a fresh start and a new Kurdistan, and a new Middle East.'

I felt like clapping when he finished. I liked Leheng a lot; he was a reformist more than a revolutionary, but he accepted and acknowledged the need for both. His ideas about the change in culture that we need in Kurdistan reflected my own, including his views on the role of women. I decided that joining his group was the least-bad option for me, and that I would commit to it. Having decided to join the YSK, I went back to stay with my friend in Erbil.

Leheng wanted me to join him and Aram in gathering new recruits, and they wanted to get more women involved. I said I would help. The transition was not too difficult, because both Leheng and Aram had already fought in Rojava and had worked with the YPG, so I was satisfied that I wasn't betraying my leaders. They were nice guys; they weren't trying to take advantage of me, or perv on me. They respected my experience and wanted me to be part of building something bigger. I knew they wanted to be larger than PAK, but with better politics, and any group that is aligned with the YPG operating in Syria is a group I knew my YPJ commanders would be okay with me working for – or so I hoped.

When I got back online, I had lots of messages from people telling me that a journalist from Denmark was trying to find me. He had visited Rojava when I was there, but had not been able to get hold of me, as I had been in Derek. Someone gave me his contact details and told me to get in touch with him through Facebook, which I did a few days after he arrived back in Copenhagen. It was nice to speak Danish again, as I explained that I was back from Syria and was in Iraq, and that I wouldn't be going to Syria for the foreseeable future.

The journalist told me that he wanted to make a documentary about me, and flew out to Iraq to visit me the following week. By this stage my relationship with my friend in Erbil had deteriorated, and I was now living in the main YSK base in Shaqlawa, which was very basic and conditions were difficult there; the windows were broken, the toilet was a hole in the ground and it looked like a slum. If you are an armed group based in the Kurdish region of Iraq (the KRG), you have to register with the government and get a licence to be in a particular place; the licence the YSK had was to be in Shaqlawa, even though the buildings they had there were terrible. The area itself is very beautiful, though, and I would stare at the snow on top of the Safeen mountains every morning when I woke up.

Pashaa invited me to stay in his house with his wife and family, due to the terrible conditions at the base. The house was really busy, with different fighters and trainers coming and going. I slept in the same room as his wife and kids; the family didn't sleep together, as there were so many people passing through that the women and children slept in one room, and the men in another. There was also a basement where people could sleep.

Pashaa was in his forties, I think, but his wife, Basan, was really young and glamorous, just a few years older than me. They had two kids. Some journalists who were visiting the frontlines also stayed from time to time, plus the documentary crew from Denmark. Basan would cook for everyone, but there was a rota so she wasn't just a skivvy, and the others would pitch in and help her. When I was there, we were eleven people: me, Pashaa, Basan, their children, Aram, Leheng, another woman who came and went like me, and the crew.

We were waiting for a group to come back from Rojava in Syria to join us before going to the front with the documentary crew, but around that time some problems started between the YPG and the KDP *Peshmerga*. The group from Rojava were delayed, because the road into Syria was closed by soldiers of the KDP. So we waited a few days and were debating where to go: our options were Gwer, which was the last point where the soldiers were on the way to Mosul, or Kirkuk. In Gwer the *Peshmerga* soldiers are affiliated with the KDP, the ruling party, while in Kirkuk they are affiliated with the PUK *Peshmerga*. They are both *Peshmerga*, but are divided along party lines.

In the end we went to Gwer, because the PUK-affiliated *Peshmerga* in Kirkuk historically don't have a good relationship with the Rojelati *Peshmerga* – which is what the YSK are. The different groups in Kurdistan can be so difficult for outsiders to understand, but I hate this 'the Middle East is just a mess and nothing will ever change' attitude that I often hear about my region, even from some of the international volunteers in the YPG. The groups have slightly different aims, and sometimes confusingly similar names, but they are just like different political parties in Europe – the main difference being that each one has an armed wing to its civil structure.

So we travelled to Gwer, and I felt awkward because I was the only woman; I didn't particularly care about this, but I know the region, and I know the people there do care about such things. We were being shown around by the local frontline soldiers, who knew Pashaa and Leheng. They were really friendly, but it was like a circus: there were dozens of people who shouldn't really have been there; different journalists from different organizations – many of whom were freelancers, like my friend – but there were so many of them, it was alarming. There were different news crews with what seemed to me basically loads of war tourists coming to take pictures. There was a guy who showed everyone round and told the cameras where to point. It was like a horror tour: here's the blood of this soldier, he died a few weeks ago; over there is the fresher blood of this soldier, he died a few days ago. Over the radio we could hear *Daesh* from their positions, which they had no intention of leaving, and which they were not cleared out of for another two years.

We watched them, and they watched us, and literally dozens of people filmed the whole thing. Everyone wanted to take my picture, and I had to try and ignore this and stay focused on what we were actually supposed to be doing. I had seen some other KDP *Peshmerga* soldiers there, who wanted selfies, but I didn't want to have my photo taken with lots of men I didn't know, in this new uniform that I wasn't entirely comfortable with. The attention was overwhelming, and the whole situation was chaotic.

I was told to follow with my rifle a white car that was full of *Daesh* fighters and to shoot at the car, by Pashaa, who was clearly delighted to be filmed and happy that I had brought the European journalists to promote his group. I looked at the car, surveyed the madness all around me and found myself a spot on the ground, lying prone and being careful not to spread my legs too wide, in case it attracted even more attention from the *Peshmerga* soldiers who were there.

My first time shooting for this new group, the YSK, was going to be filmed on camera. I found the whole situation slightly preposterous. I knew none of these *Peshmerga* soldiers expected me to be able to shoot; they saw me as a doll, which made me determined to prove them wrong. I also wanted to prove to Pashaa that I didn't let my nerves get in the way when it was time to fight, no matter how mad the frontline was. I had held a sniper rifle before and I'm a good shot. My rifle was .50-calibre, a Chinese copy of an M99, and a really nice piece of kit.

I could immediately see the difference in the quality of arms, compared to the YPG; the chamber that holds the gun is much more stable, and much easier to operate. So I focused on this white car, which was driving out at a ninety-degree angle, perpendicular to me. I had the camera on me, and several other journalists who were there – plus about a dozen *Peshmerga* guys – waiting for me to miss. I wasn't going to give them that satisfaction. I was using .50-calibre cartridges, which meant that if I shot one of the *Daesh* fighters in the head, it would explode, so I was aiming for the midpoint of the car.

One of the senior commanders, a guy called R whom I had met back in November, before I was stuck in the mountains, was there. I remembered him because he is incredibly handsome. He hadn't spoken to me, but I noticed him immediately and his eyes were on me, which I was very excited about in some ways, although it made me more nervous was well. I tuned out everyone – and everything – and concentrated on my breathing. When shooting, you have to focus solely on the target, but be able to take into account a myriad of different factors: the wind, the atmosphere, your exact position on the earth and how that will affect the bullet. It's totally absorbing.

Huddled with my cheek close to the butt of the gun and both eyes open, I aimed low. My best chance to hit the driver was to go for his midpoint – if I missed, or the wind took the bullet a little high, he would still be dead. I was on his left and he was moving fairly quickly, but he was far enough away that I could track him, and his movements. I held the weapon tight with my left hand and cocked my right on the trigger. I'd already started slowing my breathing down as soon as I spotted him, and the extra oxygen had done the trick and calmed me down, allowing the tension to leave my body and silencing the background noise behind me.

I could see his beard, and he had some kind of black hat on. Which would make the mess of his brain easier to clean up afterwards, I thought. He wasn't very young, and he was driving at a speed that suggested he was on the way to an attack; he was certainly in a hurry. Holding my breath, I pulled the trigger and let the bullet go. I held the gun tight into my right shoulder, so that it would absorb the force of the blowback, and listened to the explosion as the bullet left the gun and – bingo! – hit the car. Shot!

The car stopped, one of the YSK guys on their scope announced, and I could see that everyone was impressed, but mainly surprised. 'Oh, she's good,' I heard one of the guys who was filming me say to his friend. Yeah, damn right, I thought, although I tried to stay cool and magnanimous.

Getting a hit on a *Daesh* vehicle travelling out of their state is as big a hit as you can get for someone of my level on the frontline, so everyone became very excited and I could feel their attitude towards me warming. The car had stopped, so it looked like I had killed the driver. It was my first kill in a long time, and certainly the only one that had ever been captured on camera. I have to admit: it was an easy kill and it felt pretty good. I was back where I belonged. *Daesh* started firing back towards us immediately, which confused me; I was lying flat on the ground on the roof of a building and out of view, so they shouldn't have been able to locate me. The incoming fire came in sudden bursts, and started a firefight between the soldiers who had been watching me and the *Daesh* fighters who had been covering the man in the vehicle. The Danish journalist and the photographer almost got hit and had to hide. If they had been killed, it would not have been good publicity.

'Have you been fighting from this position before?' I asked the guy from the KDP *Peshmerga* who had been filming me.

'Yes, every day, sister.'

'What? Why are you fighting from this spot, then? Why are you bringing people here? They know our spots?'

'Oh, she's good,' he said to R, instead of answering my question. I didn't respond, because I caught R's eye and had to look away. But I thought to myself: I might be good, but these guys clearly are not. As cute as that commander was, I needed to get out of there.

My first firefight for the *Peshmerga* was captured by the Danish documentary crew, which was bizarre, but I tried not to think about it and settled into the fight. At one point I started filming it on my phone. I thought: If everyone else is going to have a record, then I should, too. They filmed me filming the shooting, and they kept coming up onto the roof to get better pictures, which was stressful for me. 'It's not going to be good for me if you get killed. Really. Get back and get out of the way.'

The firefight ended after a while; I'm not sure if *Daesh* took any more injuries that day, but luckily we did not. I stayed with these KDP soldiers until about five in the morning, and I spoke to some of them. I was impressed by how they were holding the line; they were sleeping on the frontline under blankets, and they offered me the chance to stay with them, but I knew this wouldn't be safe, even with the protection afforded by the documentary crew. They were good guys, but they were Iraqi men, so I had to be on my guard. They were not used to having women at the front, and men can get weird sometimes when they see women at the front – sexually, I mean.

The next day we went to the ghost areas of the city – where the airstrikes against *Daesh* were being fired from. Everywhere I went, the *Peshmerga* soldiers wanted to take pictures of me, and I could see there were some international volunteers with them. I posed for some photographs with locals, and particularly with young girls and families, as I wanted them to see that it is possible for girls to be soldiers. I tried to avoid being in too many pictures, though, and politely declined as many as I could. You can't be taking photographs with lots of men in Iraq, because it's seen as sexually inviting.

I didn't realize that refusing to take photographs would mean that these men would take pictures anyway, then write horrible things about me on the internet. The international volunteers, for their part, were no better. I knew by then that I was interested in R, and I thought he was interested in me, so I wasn't looking for any kind of romantic relationship with these men, but this meant I inspired some kind of fury in those whose sexual advances I declined. It was a fury that would be punished by their nasty words online about me. This was when all the internet attacks on me began, and was probably when the early trolling started. It's hard for me to pinpoint the exact date, because I was in combat at the time and so I didn't really notice it take hold. I only gradually became more aware of it after the Danish documentary article about me, and then after another article, in *Vice*, went viral and the spew of hatred began.

We went back to Gwer the following night, and I ran into R again. I felt I was slowly starting to get to know him. One of the soldiers was telling me his story about killing a *Daesh* soldier there that day, when a group of very pretty girls turned up at our spot on the frontline. This spot, like a lot of the *Peshmerga* positions I visited, was an open frontline – the international media, particularly the American media, were all over the place. One of the girls came over and interrupted our conversation. 'We heard there was a woman *Peshmerga* and we wanted to meet you,' she said. She was caked in make-up and was wearing some kind of Spice Girl version of the *Peshmerga* uniform, with her top buttons open to reveal her cleavage.

'We are also *Peshmerga*,' she told me, and she and her friends smiled and kissed me. All of these girls were very young, and they didn't look like soldiers to me. Looking at them, the YPJ Joanna came out; they were clearly visitors – they were with a news crew and had no weapons with them, and seemed to think they could become *Peshmerga* simply by dressing up in a uniform. There were about 1,400 *Peshmerga* stationed in Gwer at the time – men who had not seen a woman in a long time, and who were desperate for female company and attention.

You don't go to the frontline in high heels. It makes my job as a woman soldier on the frontline harder, because it makes all women look ridiculous. These girls, with their make-up and their breasts pushed up and puffed out, came as a shock to me, after the harsh and deliberately gender-neutral rules of the YPG, and I felt a tug for my old comrades and our regulations. As a woman on the front, you are viewed very differently from men already, so you don't emphasize your femininity at all; it's dangerous to do so.

Perhaps these girls were trying to show solidarity, but sometimes I feel that those who show solidarity take credit for something they have no role in. For me, these girls fell into that category.

Our kind of nationalism in Kurdistan supports this sort of thing; as if whether we are KDP or PYD, we are all one, when actually the fat man who goes to a protest every once in a while and holds a flag does not deserve as much credit as the young mother who blows herself up to stop *Daesh* capturing our position. One of those people has made no sacrifice or very little, and the other has made the greatest sacrifice it is possible to make. They are not one and the same; they are completely different. It annoyed me that these girls had clearly never been properly at the front; if they had, they wouldn't have dressed as if they were in a show.

I stayed on the frontline for another few days and slowly began a relationship with R. His boss was still being an asshole, but once I was 'claimed' by R, I belonged to him, according to the beliefs of this primitive culture – and it made it easier to operate without the constant threat of sexual advances. I missed the mountains, and I missed Rojava. I even, in some ways, missed that stupid camp. I was more comfortable; I had a clean uniform, enough to eat, somewhere soft to lay my head, shampoo and even a toilet some of the time, but it was a different feeling from being in the YPJ. I was glad to be fighting again, though, and my rifle was definitely better. The superiority of the weapons was probably my favourite thing about being with the *Peshmerga*.

CHAPTER ELEVEN

Pregnant Little Girls

I spent another few nights on the frontline at Gwer with the documentary crew, before travelling back to Shaqlawa with Pashaa and saying goodbye to the Danes. As the YSK, we worked with the KDP *Peshmerga* that R was a part of, and there was talk of joining a special-forces operation inside ISIS territory. Such operations were done on the quiet; officially the *Peshmerga* were not going behind enemy lines, but were simply holding the line, calling in airstrikes and preparing their tactics for the eventual push to take back the Kurdish villages outside Mosul.

This joint operation was going to be led by the YSK, officially, so that if anything went wrong we would take the blame, Leheng said, which was fine with him. At the time the YSK were still very small, although he had ambitions for it to be bigger than PAK, the group founded by his brother. The other reason was that the KDP didn't want to risk their soldiers going in, or the press attention this would receive when they got killed.

Leheng briefed us on the plan – or rather, in the typical way a commander does, as much as we needed to know – and I was invited to attend another meeting where more details were to be disclosed. This meeting was between the KDP *Peshmerga* commander and a few of us from the YSK. It took place in the evening and was definitely unofficial. We were due to go in from villages outside the north of Mosul that were under KRG control at the time. I thought then that the operation was a rescue of another KDP soldier from a mission like this one that had gone wrong. I wasn't sure and I didn't ask, I was just listening carefully, excited at the possibility of getting back out.

The plan was to approach in the vehicles, get out at a safe enough distance that we couldn't be heard and then split into two groups: one group would go forward to attack, and the other would stay behind to protect civilians if there was a firefight. There were only a couple of us YSK members – myself and a sergeant – accompanying the KDP guys. During the briefing the KDP *Peshmerga* captain drilled into us that there could be no civilian casualties; absolutely none. This is something, I assumed, that the USA was insisting they include in their training, and I was happy to hear it was important to them, because in a war it's often civilians – women and their children – who are the first to die.

We were warned that, if anything happened, we were there unofficially, but that we had the necessary permissions from the right people. A bit of a murmur went round the room, as people asked why exactly the plan was being kept so quiet, but the commanders didn't give away any more than that, and I didn't ask. The *Peshmerga* warned that if anything went wrong, we were not to link the operation to the party – their KDP. In Iraq everyone is linked to either the PUK or the KDP, and I thought it would be a bit obvious, but I kept quiet.

When we could see *Daesh* spots with our eyes, we got out of the car and went on foot. It wasn't a defensive attack, so before we got out of the cars, our commander radioed everyone to say again, 'Civilians: keep them out of it, and don't fuck up.' I went with my sergeant and one of his friends. 'Maybe we are getting a snitch,' he whispered as we crept through the streets, and I thought he was probably right. Many men – including those in the army – simply took off their Iraqi army uniform and put on a black headband to join *Daesh*. Then, as the horror of *Daesh*'s rule began to affect them, they wanted out and started contacting their former comrades. All war is messy, and snitches can provide vital intelligence, but they are universally despised by rank-and-file like us, so I thought perhaps that was why the commanders wouldn't actually say why we were going inside.

I went forward on patrol with the two men: we were just behind the initial part of the attack crew; there was the first group, a group behind them providing cover, and then us behind, covering them. Behind us was another group covering us: each of the groups contained three or four people. I was the only woman and, as I walked around, it became clear that we were in a ghost town; it must have been an old Christian or Jewish area, because most of the houses and gardens were empty.

The shops were closed; there was no thriving Islamic State; everywhere was just dead. The houses were small and clustered together, and we were trying to listen for the sound of civilians so that we could be mindful of their position in relation to where the groups in front of us were going.

We went forward slowly, particularly at the start; house by house initially, but everywhere was really quiet. I could hear a mosque in the distance, but our area was still. After a few minutes of this, we all relaxed a little; we knew we were advancing towards *Daesh*, as opposed to being in their actual lair. After about half an hour of quietly moving forward, the streets became slightly more lived-in, but we were staying low and I was feeling more comfortable, and the thrill of being inside their territory with my rifle overtook any fears I had.

We came to a clearing that was full of rubbish, and my first sergeant was walking ahead when I started to look through the rubbish. It had been burned fairly recently, as there were large black soot-marks on the walls that looked fresh. I crept over, slowly, as one of the fires was quite close to a window, so I had to be careful: there could be a sniper hiding near any of the windows, waiting for me. I had a look in the rubbish and saw lots of used sanitary napkins; most of them were only half-burned and so, using my feet, I kicked a few of them out of the fire to look at the stains on them. The blood was still quite red and hadn't dried up, so they must have been soiled by someone recently. My sergeant turned round at this point, as he was ready to go round the corner of the yard into our next street, and I called him back.

He looked at the rubbish, then looked at me quizzically and gestured for me to come forward – the group we were covering was advancing. I made him look again at the rubbish, and pointed to a freshly soiled sanitary towel: 'There are girls here,' I whispered. He looked at me and he knew, and gestured to let the others know we were stopping, so they needed to slow down.

This sergeant was about twenty-four, just two years older than me, but a lot more experienced. He was a good soldier, and we agreed that we needed to check this out. We also agreed that I would go in first. When entering an enemy house, it's normally the second soldier who needs to be the more experienced one, as the first may catch the enemy off-guard. Statistically, the second soldier is more likely to be killed. He stayed close behind me, with a young KDP *Peshmerga* behind him, and we tried to open the door. It was locked, so he started to kick it, while I began looking through the windows to see if I could spot anyone inside. I could – there was evidence of families in the property: kids' things were scattered around, but the house seemed deserted. Eventually he shot the door down with the KDP guy, and we crept slowly inside.

Several of the rooms were blacked out and there was complete silence. We didn't speak as we made our way into the hallway and towards the stairs in the centre of the house. Acting on instinct, I moved slowly and carefully through the property, certain I was going to find people somewhere, but unsure of everything else. Upstairs was empty, and so was the roof, so we followed the staircase down into the basement of the house, and as we descended the steps I heard their breathing: shallow, dusty breaths that they were trying to keep hushed. I pulled my weapon and walked slowly downstairs.

At my ten o'clock position five girls were huddled together at the other side of the room. You could tell immediately what they were: a few of them were wearing *abayas* – the loose dress. They had cuts on their knees, elbows and faces. They were very calm and stared at us listlessly through their pretty green and blue and brown eyes.

I was ashamed to look at them at first, as I could see they were hungry, with huge sunken eyes in their emaciated little faces.

There was so much fear; as if they were expecting us to hurt or kill them, but they also seemed resigned. By now they knew better than to attempt to have any say in their own fate, or the way the events of their life unfolded. They made no effort to cover the parts of their bodies that were exposed. I was frozen to the spot in silence for a few minutes, as were the two guys with me. The place stank – of blood, faeces and fear. I will never forget the stench of their little bodies in that filthy basement.

I could see some kind of painful-looking rash down the legs of the girls whose flesh was exposed. My first thought, bizarrely, was that these girls were being sold to Afghanistan from Iran; we have a lot of girls from Iran who are trafficked in this way. But that was the stress of the situation making me confused. I took off my helmet and untied my hair so that they could see I was a girl: and I said in Kermanji who we were, and what we were doing.

'We are not here to hurt you. We are not here to hurt you, sister.' I just said it over and over again, like I had gone mad. I was quiet, because I didn't want to scare them, but I struggled to find anything else to say. The guys didn't speak at all; the KDP kid retreated out of the room entirely and went to call the others, while my YSK friend just stood with his mouth frozen in horror. 'So it's true,' he said eventually, to no one.

I put my weapon down – deliberately away from them, in case they decided to use it on themselves or against us – and approached the girl who looked the oldest, and as if she was in charge. 'We need a doctor; we need medics,' I called to the retreating soldiers, and I suddenly found myself alone in the room with them. The ones who had been looking away slowly began to raise their eyes when the men left; they may have suspected we were here to take them. This kind of trafficking of girls was not invented by *Daesh* in our region; others have done it before. Part of me suspected the girls had been drugged; there was a heaviness about them, a listlessness about this older-looking girl, as if she was talking to me through some kind of invisible glue. She didn't move, but pointed to the other side of the room, where there was another girl lying on a urine- and blood-soaked mattress in the corner.

I found out later that this older girl was much younger than me. Yazidi girls sometimes age differently from the boys in their community, because many of them work in the fields after they begin menstruating, while the boys continue their education. Her body was young, her breasts just small buds and her hips not yet developed. I could tell by the parts of their bodies on display that these girls were still children.

I walked slowly over to the corner of the room, and saw a huge swollen belly before I saw the child's face. She was pregnant – I found out later with twins, or some kind of foetal abnormality caused by her age – and the monstrous life growing inside her was killing her slowly and painfully. Colonized by the forced pregnancy resulting from the rape, the babies had turned her small body into something abysmal; something even the other girls being held there couldn't bear to look at. They had tried to make her as comfortable as possible, but she was barely conscious. Her feet and knees especially had swollen to double the size of her tiny legs, which were two spindly sticks that looked as if someone had attached bright-red boxing gloves to the middle. There were blue veins all over her hands, neck and stomach, and I initially thought she was covered with blisters and bruises – and she was, to some extent – but when I went closer I saw that much of the discoloration was beneath her skin; the capillaries of her blood vessels had burst, so that her skin was blue, purple, red or greyish-white.

Seeing this girl, something kicked in – maybe it was shock, maybe terror – and I became very calm; my focus was on securing the area, and on communicating clearly with the others to get the cars to us, so that we could take the girls to the hospital. It was much easier to distance myself in this way than to engage emotionally or connect with what was going on around me; and it was better for the girls as well. The senior KDP *Peshmerga* officer arrived soon afterwards, while I was still holding the hand of the pregnant child, and immediately everything started happening at once.

Blankets appeared from the cars, and we covered the girls in the relatively clean ones and escorted them to our Toyotas. I was put in the van with the pregnant girl and the younger, more scared-looking ones, and I knew then why I had been invited on this mission and I was glad. 'There's too many like this,' the driver said as we pulled out, and I wondered whether the other, more senior soldiers had been fully briefed as to what we were doing and why I was there.

I don't mean to sound clueless about the mission, but I was shocked and scared, though I didn't let it show as I stroked the girls' faces and we distributed some water and found some sweets for them to eat. We drove out quickly but in absolute silence, with me still holding the pregnant little girl's hand. Some of the girls started to cry. The pregnant girl cried and screamed in the car. 'Make it stop, stop the pain,' she groaned on and on; we didn't have any medicine to give her, so I just held her down as she shook. Around her nipples blue veins were popping out. She was twitching and moving, and I was worried she was going to fall out of the car, so I held onto her tightly.

The other two girls were very polite and quiet, still too scared to speak, or maybe drugged, or drowsy from lack of food. They ate greedily. The pregnant girl was a very beautiful child; her eyes were big and surrounded by a thick forest of eyelashes, and there were deep dimples in her cheeks. The other girls were older, and beautiful in the way that Yazidi girls especially are.

The other soldiers were clearly shocked by our mission; you can have many years of combat experience in the trenches and never have to face this kind of horror. Nothing can prepare you for it. You just have to stay calm, and hope your training kicks in. We all knew we had to get the girls out, so a clear chain of command was established, and everyone did their part.

We were all taken to the military hospital in Erbil – the one used by the KDP soldiers, where the best surgeons and medics are stationed. It's the main hospital in Erbil, so some of the doctors are civilian, but there is a military wing that only *Peshmerga* or KDP officials can use.

The doctor's reaction to the girl released the emotions that all of us soldiers had so far managed to hold in. We half-carried her, half-walked her inside, before getting her into a wheelchair. There were two of us pushing her together, and as we entered each corridor everyone's head turned to look at us. Initially I thought the doctor was blaming us because he thought we were responsible for the rape and pregnancy that were killing the child, but now I think it wasn't the first child like this that he had seen. The *Peshmerga*, though they didn't do enough of these kinds of rescue missions, were familiar with holding houses like this one, and I doubt these were the first hostages to pass through the hospital doors.

The doctor took the girl's pulse and put her on the bed, and felt her freezing feet and hands and started shaking with anger. 'Everyone who carries a weapon is responsible for this. It is all your fault,' he hissed at the soldier I was with. He didn't really look at me initially, but I stood between him and my soldier and forced him to look at me, as I thought he was going to hit my sergeant. He had his fists up and at one point I thought he was going to hit me when I got in between them.

I stayed polite, and so did my sergeant; we needed the doctor on our side, helping us out. Everyone was totally out of their mind, but I was shocked by the doctor's initial response, as I hadn't fully grasped the situation, whereas of course the doctor had. He was a doctor taught to save life, but what he had realized, and I hadn't yet, was that there was no way he could save this child. It was up to him now to take away her pain and let her pass into the next life.

The girl was moaning and begging for medicine. 'Make it stop – take the pain, make it stop.' This calmed everyone down and we all turned back to the doctor, who focused on the grim task at hand. He injected her with something and she fell asleep soon afterwards. We found out from one of the other girls later on that she had been sold by *Daesh* to a family, who weren't aware that she was pregnant. Then she was sold back to the holding house, when it became clear she couldn't be a domestic servant. This aspect of the Yazidi and Assyrian Christian girls who were captured wasn't really well known; yes, they were sex slaves, but they were also domestic servant girls.

It was not just the *Daesh* fighters, but also the Sunni families living under them who condoned this behaviour, though clearly they might not have had too much of a choice. But even so, their cruelty was hard for me to swallow, as I am from a Sunni Muslim family myself and I was born in Iraq, so something about this wider societal role in the trafficking of girls felt especially sickening.

Someone came in with some cola and sweets for the other girls, but the pregnant girl – who was Assyrian, according to the other Yazidi girls – was out by this stage. Everyone in the hospital was very sweet with the girls; the nurses came round and kissed their hands. Several people came in to see the Assyrian girl. It was surreal; like they were visiting a body before burial, but the body was still alive. The little girl died that night – she was all swollen up and there was nothing the doctors could do. It was too late to remove the dead foetuses and it was too late to save her life.

The other girls were off being treated for malnutrition, skin infections and dehydration. Some might need abortions, treatment for STDs or for worms; and for things there aren't really proper treatments for. The methods of sexual torture the *Daesh* captives endured are too numerous to describe and too painful to consider. It doesn't help the dignity of survivors to go into the grisly details of what happened to each of them, but these details are known by some and, once you know, it's not an exaggeration to say that your feelings towards humanity change for ever. This is why the doctor snapped, I think. And although I was shocked at the time, I can't say I blame him. What happened in Shingal was genocide, but surely those shot in the first few days around 3rd August 2014, or those who died on the mountain, were lucky compared to this girl. This girl had been rescued; she didn't know she was dying, but she was begging to die.

The sergeant left the room and I followed him as he paced about and muttered to himself, 'This is what we are dealing with.' The nurses had taken off the girl's clothes and had changed her into a white gown, but she was still wearing her Hello Kitty bracelet around her wrist, and in the hours before she died it looked like she was sleeping. Looking at her, I thought of all the ways little girls get hurt by men, and of what I went through at the same age. Though I grew up far away, in a country where there is peace and stability, I recognized what we had in common: an awful experience of being a girl. It's not something I talk about, but the pain of sexual abuse as a little girl is something I recognize. What happened to this child happens across nations and oceans far away from the Middle East and Islamic State. It comes in many shapes and forms, but it happens all over the world, every day and every hour.

Sexually abusing children is not unique to *Daesh*, but this pregnancy – this outward sign of something that is normally so well concealed – was a shock. The doctor said he thought the girl would die within twenty-four hours, and she was gone in ten. It was too late; we were too late. The babies had been rotting inside her for too long. Until she actually passed, I hadn't really realized this was the plan; I had thought the doctors could do something to save her, or at least some small childish part of me thought this, and I clung to it. During her last hours she slipped in and out of consciousness, but at last her whimpering stopped. She died surrounded by strangers who were shocked by the sight of her, sickened at what had happened to her, but were stroking her carefully and whispering sweet thoughts in her ear.

A group of anti-terror soldiers called *Hezem Drezh* came to talk to the surviving girls. These guys wear all-black uniforms, keep their faces hidden at all times and operate as a militia who report directly to the official KRG government. They don't allow anyone who is not KDP or part of the two main Barzani-linked tribes to be involved; anyone with even a vague link to the PKK in their family is forbidden to join. These men don't fuck around. They came, looking scary, with their faces covered and fully armed, and told the doctors to get the girls ready to leave.

The girls were being separated into three groups, to go to three shelters, and would be taken out of the region. I am not sure if the soldiers meant that would be outside Kurdistan, and I didn't speak directly to them, as they were busy arguing with the doctors and nurses, who didn't want to release the girls to these intimidating-looking men. 'You will scare them. They have been through enough trauma and they need to rest, and be treated,' the doctor was pleading. But there wasn't much discussion to be had. I left the room as I heard the soldier come over to the doctor and speak directly into his face. 'Doctor, your job is saving lives, ours is to take these girls.'

The doctor started to call people and went outside, where the anti-terror soldiers were waiting. 'You have done a good job getting the girls,' one of them said to my sergeant, 'but now it's time for us to do our job. They have been in Islamic State territory for more than a year; they could be radicalized, they could blow themselves up. We are taking them away – they have valuable information for us, which we need while it is fresh, in order to take more of those who do this to children.' I was outside in the hall at this point, listening as the argument continued. The girls were taken away by the masked men later that evening.

The thing is, you don't really argue with *Hezem Drezh* – the law lies with them. Our mission wasn't officially sanctioned, either, though it was known about. The soldiers told us they were taking over the mission now and we could stand down, so we did. The sex slaves had had a unique experience, and they did have vital information – I just wish they had more of a say in what happened to them next. They were very vulnerable, and at the time I doubted many of them would ever acknowledge what had happened to them; as long as they weren't pregnant, they would tell their parents they were still virgins, so that they wouldn't be rejected by their community. All of these men talked together about what was going to happen next to these girls – and the girls didn't have any say at all.

I was proud of myself that day for the first time in a long while, and some new ambition had settled inside me. I could use my position to go on such rescues, and the *Peshmerga* could benefit from the propaganda associated with me. I knew I could be useful in the *Peshmerga* – actually useful to my fight for women's rights, instead of simply useful as a pretty face to get some headlines for the KRG. I could spot a woman's touch in the way that a man could not, which made me think of my sabotage training; you can spot a bomb made by a woman easily, as things are placed together with such delicate attention and care.

Back in the house, I just wanted to be alone, so I went outside with my crappy cheap cigarettes and spent some time on my own. Everyone was talking about how to use the sex slaves for propaganda – to promote their own ideology, by claiming that they, as rescuers, are the true opponents of *Daesh*. I didn't want to do this, but I really wished I could somehow have shown how these girls were being used symbolically – this is what happens when Islamist women-hating is allowed to flourish in a military army. The girls were the most extreme symbols of what all women who lived under *Daesh* could become. I was also keenly aware that the only reason I was allowed on that rescue was because of my last name; the KRG wanted to use me to show that the *Peshmerga* are where the first daughters of Kurdistan fight, the real rebels. I went to sleep feeling furious and distracted, and tossed and turned the night away until the sun came back out.

The next day my sergeant was going back to his base near Mosul, and I was returning to the YSK base where Pashaa was. But instead of going back to my base, I went to Erbil, to a bar called the T-House, bought myself a packet of expensive cigarettes and a few beers. It was stupid, but I was all cut up from the day before. I was thinking of what possible effective punishment there could be for the *Daesh* fighter who I believed had killed the Assyrian girl. I wanted revenge. I wanted to bomb them with hot water and watch them disappear in front of my eyes. I thought of an old method of punishing rape in Iran – you place resin around the cocks of the men and let the rats eat their cocks and balls alive. This was a medieval punishment that I believed *Daesh* would appreciate.

I was lost in my own thoughts and just starting my second glass of beer, having successfully avoided various offers of beers from the men attempting to leer at me, when two Asayîş officers came in and, seeing my uniform, came straight over. Asayîş are part of the security and the intelligence agencies in Iraq and are very close to the executive leadership of the KRG. They are not people you want to catch the attention of.

'What are you doing?' they said, and sat down on either side of me. 'What is a female *Peshmerga* doing drinking in a bar?'

'I'm Christian,' I replied stonily and started another cigarette, hoping the smoke would push them back out of my personal space. I wasn't drunk, because I don't tend to get drunk. Also, in Erbil they put salt around the top of the glasses of beer – even Tuborg – saying it's Mexican-style, which makes it gross, obviously, so my beer was going down very slowly. I was just mad at everyone that day, and they were about the sixth group of men who had approached my table and, without asking, sat down. I didn't have the tolerance to take any shit from anyone.

'Where are you from? Who do you belong to?'

'I have no idea,' I said, rather philosophically. I showed them my card, and they called my commander. Leheng was furious with me. The Asayîş officers handed me the phone, smirking. 'What are you doing? Why are you drinking?' Leheng screamed at me.

'I'm allowed to drink. I wasn't working.'

'You have a responsibility. You should not be drinking. You are not allowed to do certain things, particularly as a female *Peshmerga*. Particularly in a group where there are not many female *Peshmerga*,' he thundered. It was back to the rules. I wasn't breaking the law, but I was breaking some unwritten rule.

So the Asayîş officers put me in their car and drove me back to Shaqlawa. The drive was long and difficult and I had some trouble talking to these guys. I called R and, probably because I was annoyed and thinking that, as a woman, I was only expected to be useful in the kitchen and in bed, I started being very dramatic.

'I'm going to jail now. I'm being taken away by two Asayîş guys because I have been drinking in a bar.'

R laughed. 'You are kidding. Drinking in your uniform?'

'Yes. I was not the only *Peshmerga* drinking in that bar.'

'Do you think you are in Europe now?'

I handed the phone to the officers, thinking that Bashur (northern Iraq) was more similar to Saudi Arabia or Iran than I had thought. The officers were super-nice and friendly to R. Suddenly it was all: 'Oh hi – yes, she's drunk. We are taking her back to Shaqlawa.'

It was dark when I arrived and everyone was annoyed with me. I told them about my relationship with R, and that I wanted to go and be with him in Gwer, and leave Shaqlawa.

'How does it look for us that you have done this?'

'You know what happened yesterday. I was having a day off.'

'You don't get a day off in war, Joanna.'

'Don't tell me about war.'

'No, Joanna, don't talk to us like this,' Pashaa interrupted and everyone was silent as he continued, 'You have done something really stupid and violent towards us. You got us in trouble with the Asayîş.'

Then I said something stupid: 'I don't belong to you. I belong to the KRG now. Ask the captain.'

'What do you mean? You are betraying us now? You are leaving us? You are having an affair?' They were furious and told me that my actions as a Western woman had made them all look stupid. They said I needed to decide between them and R – that wasn't fair and it wasn't a choice. If I had been a man, there would not have been any problems, and I resented being forced into an impossible decision. So often women are made to choose between a series of bad options. No one would look me in the eye. I tried to explain to them that I just wanted to fight *Daesh* and be on the frontline; not at the constant meetings that I had to attend as a YSK member. I was exhausted by constantly trying to prove myself.

R came and picked me up later that night. He is a high-up commander, so there were no angry words when he came; everyone was very polite. Pashaa's wife, Basan, wished me luck in my love-thing before I left, and we went back to stay at his base together.

R and I started renting a house together in Erbil. I didn't have my passport on me, so in some ways I was stuck there. I had a meeting with the head of the PYD in Iraq, which is the political wing of the YPG, to try and get my passport, but it was unsuccessful. I'm not the only girl who came from Europe and had her passport confiscated; there were others like me, who were stuck in the mountains, but they all managed to leave in some way, without being kicked out.

My card said that I was YSK and that I was hosted in Shaqlawa, but R had made me another card, which said I was part of the KRG *Peshmerga* fighting officially under the KDP as part of his group – anti-terror. It was pretty stupid of me to accept this card, but when I first moved in with R, I was hopeful that I could do some good fighting with this group. The KDP *Peshmerga* I had worked with on the rescue were professionals and I had liked them; they also had the resources to do the kinds of work I was most interested in.

I started to try and open a women's office in the KDP *Peshmerga*, as a place for women to come and talk specifically about their complaints. I was trying to make a structure similar to what we have in the YPG, where women's issues could be discussed and given greater prevalence; this suited the KDP's aims as well, as they were actively recruiting women.

I was interested in training with the female fighters, as I knew my position in Gwer was going to be dependent on R, and it would be difficult to establish myself separately from him unless I was with other fighters. I was already having doubts about the viability of our relationship; he was quick to anger, and prone to violent outbursts. I had a meeting with R's commanders, and they put me in contact with an older woman in charge of military training for women in Zakho camp, the only place at the time where women were being trained. The military training there takes eighteen months, but it's still not as good as the special-forces training within the YPJ.

At the initial meeting with a commander called Chimen, one of the trainers for the female *Peshmerga* in Iraq, they wanted to see what training I could offer them, in addition to what they were setting up themselves at the time. We met in a hotel lobby and I told Chimen about my background and training. I explained my experience in battle, and how I wanted to do more. I was honest with her: 'I'm not one hundred per cent with the KDP ideology; but I'm willing to train girls, and I'm willing to risk my life.'

Chimen was polite enough, but there was a coolness about her. 'Are you a girl or are you a woman?' she enquired – was I a virgin? – and so I answered her honestly. Telling her that I had grown up in Europe and we do not classify women in this way,

I said I was a woman. 'So you are a woman and you are not married?' she asked.

'Yes, sister,' I said quietly, shamefully. I know it's not really shameful to be a woman, and that this classification of women is primitive, but part of me felt shamed by her line of questioning.

'I will have to ask my superiors whether you can join us; we normally only take girls.'

'Why is this necessary?'

'Because you have had sex and you are not married, you could lose your concentration in battle and focus on other stuff.' I said nothing and let her continue. 'You know, from being in battle yourself, that you can get horny in those intense situations. This is not something that could be acceptable to us.'

I tried to explain that the feelings I have on the frontline are nothing like those I had when I was intimate with a man. 'These are entirely separate things, sister. On the frontline I think about my survival, protecting my friends and protecting civilians, and remaining calm. I don't get horny in battle. No female fighter does.'

'Well, that is not what your body is telling you.'

'How do you know?'

Chimen was silent and we ended our meeting. I gave her my phone number and told her to get in contact with me again when she heard back from Zakho. Like my mother and so many other women, this commander was subjecting me to these questions because she was enforcing the patriarchy that she was forced to live under, and forcing me to live under. No man would be asked these questions; again, it was my sex that prompted them.

I knew after my meeting with the commander in Erbil that my virginity status was going to have an impact on my chances of getting work training at the academy in Zakho, which made me miss the YPJ and begin to regret my decision to allow R to get me a KDP card. I didn't say anything like this at the time to R, of course, and we spent some good times together in our house in Ainkawa.

He would take me to the frontline quite a lot and I would do guard duty, which I loved, but it was difficult to see any actual action, as R became very 'protective' of me, which was how he tried to justify his controlling and paranoid behaviour. I would do a lot of translations for the commanders, but R didn't like this. He was working very hard at the time himself, so thankfully he couldn't watch my every move, as he was coordinating a lot of the frontline work around Gwer.

I wasn't accepted for training at the KDP academy at Zakho, which was fine as I didn't need their training, but I also wasn't allowed to teach, which was disappointing, and I knew it was because of the status of my hymen. But a few days after I met Chimen, Pashaa from the YSK called me again, saying they had a new group of girls coming and would I train them? I asked R, who didn't really want me to accept the role, but I decided to do it anyway, as I was getting bored and it would be an opportunity for me to do more training myself. I still really liked the YSK, who were good to me and I preferred their politics to the KDP's, but I thought at the time that I was in love with R and I am very romantic in my outlook, though this might surprise you. I wanted our relationship to work, and for this reason I stayed with him long after I should have left.

I gladly took up the invitation to go back to Shaqlawa and see my friend Basan again, Pashaa's wife. I stayed at their home the day before the training. She woke me in the morning and I got to the training base at around 6.30 a.m.; I wanted to start early, as we do in the YPJ, but no one turned up on time. They finally started to trickle in about an hour later. The first day there were only four girls and six guys; it all started quite casually, so I think everyone was surprised when I started the physical training.

We started with sprinting up the hill, then jogging, then walking. The girls were fit, but they weren't pushing themselves to their full ability – I think possibly because they were embarrassed to be running and training with the boys. Careful not to scare anyone on the first day, I focused more on games; we did this game where I held a coloured scarf halfway up the hill and everyone had to hide in different positions, then compete to grab the scarf from me. This task is about being quick; you are not allowed to touch the person, you have to only touch the scarf.

The next stage of training was with tyres: everyone takes a tyre, ties a rope to it and ties the other end around their waist and runs up the hill – I started them halfway up the hill initially, to make it easier. This exercise is about building core strength as well as speed. Another training exercise with the tyre is when you tie a really long rope to it, go to the top of a mountain and then pull it up, starting slowly and then racing each other. I taught everyone how to put bark sap and leaves on their hands so that the rope doesn't burn, and which leaves were the strongest for this task.

Part of the challenge when you are training anyone is team-building, and this is a vital part of a being an effective fighting force on the frontline. Getting girls and boys to work with each other in a society where they don't normally speak is really difficult, so a lot of my training exercises are designed to teach this vital skill. The first one was to get everyone to use their strength together to carry a guy up the hill. One of the guys was placed in the middle of the tyre – he was having a great time – and the rest of us had to pull together to heave him up. This exercise is about upper-body strength, again something that girls need to work harder on than boys. I tend to focus my training on upper-body strength exercises; some trainers start with the legs, but I prefer to do lots of running, which is good for the legs, and lots of upper-body strength. I trained them until they couldn't walk any more, until they couldn't hold each other up any more, because you need to get used to the exhaustion and learn to push past the pain that comes from holding a weapon all the time. This, in my experience, is the hardest thing – being strong enough to carry a weapon – so this was the aspect I stressed most.

Slowly I got to know the girls I was training. I tried to be like my trainers in Rojava were with me – tough during the training sessions, but friendly and kind elsewhere. They were all girls from eastern Kurdistan, like me; Rojelati girls, and all very fit. It was really important to Leheng that the girls were trained quickly, as his brother's group – PAK – already had girls fighting at the front. So for a few weeks I would travel from where R and I were living to Shaqlawa every few days, whenever Pashaa called me in to provide training.

I would be in the training camps during the day, and would either stay in Shaqlawa or be with R at night, which he preferred. There wasn't any structure and every day was quite different. My trainees developed quickly as the summer progressed and the days got hotter; more girls came to train and they became more confident around the boys. There was a lot of competition – over how many Kurdish nationalist songs they knew; about fighters in their family; about everything really. It was quite flirtatious at times, which was not the vibe I was trying to cultivate.

Alongside this training, I still wanted to open a women's office with the *Peshmerga* and work with local women, but because I was an outsider, and a woman, this was made much harder for me. My aim had been to establish a link with NGOs and women's-rights organizations, as we have many instances of FGM within the Kurdish communities in Iraq, though no one likes to talk about it. In Halabja and the surrounding areas the majority of women are still circumcised, as it is expected by the men. I wanted to open a women's office so that we could start gathering information, with the aim of running campaigns about the harm FGM causes. When I was with the YSK, I always asked to speak to the woman of the houses we visited, and had already started compiling notes about their complaints. I asked people to write to me, to tell me in greater detail their complaints with regard to their rights. About ten women wrote to me in total, and I added this information to my body of work.

R's commander, who was responsible for the entire frontline towards Mosul from Gwer, agreed to a meeting so that we could discuss the women's office; he was keen to attract female recruits and funnel them to the Zakho academy, but I was the first female fighter he had actually had in his ranks. He liked me, but as usual, a little too much. He lived in Erbil and invited me to his home to discuss my plans.

I had a map of different areas where I thought we could set up the women's information centres, to attract recruits and engage with local women. He listened and seemed interested in the project, as it made sense and they needed as many recruits as possible in the lead-up to the eventual take-back of Mosul, which was already being planned at the time, although it wouldn't happen for another eighteen months. He told me he thought it was a good idea, but that he had no money from the KRG and didn't have the facilities, but that I could work from his home. 'We could use an old house and slowly renovate it,' I suggested.

'There is space for you to work in my home, Joanna.' He moved closer to me and looked directly into my eyes, in case I didn't get what he was inferring.

I could no longer ignore the feeling of dread rising inside me. This man was old – in his sixties at least, and fat and ugly, yet he believed he would be attractive to me, because he had power and could help me achieve my aims for women's rights. I asked him to get his driver to take me home, and called R on the way back, furious. He didn't answer initially. 'Your boss is a pervert,' I texted, and he called me immediately.

Instead of seeing my point, R accused me of flirting with his commander and some of his colleagues. 'What the fuck is wrong with these men?' I asked him. 'I wasn't flirting.' R was of the opinion that there was something wrong with me instead.

Things weren't great with R by this point. He wanted to own me, completely and totally. What I had thought was passion was actually extreme possessiveness, and what I initially dismissed as small cultural differences were, by this stage, transforming into actual cruelty. He thought that because we had been intimate I was his property now – I was unclean for anyone else. I realized, as he was pleading with me after he had hit me, that there was something profoundly wrong with me; I had chosen a man as violent as my father.

It was June at this point, and I finally had some success in locating my passport. I'd been away from Denmark since the previous November and I thought perhaps it was time to leave. I wanted the KDP to commit seriously to the plans I had for various projects, in return for the propaganda work I was doing for them, while they wanted me to continue doing the propaganda work and make no demands on them. There were rumours swirling as to how I had got my passport back: that I was a spy for the PKK and was just there to gather information that could be used against them. None of the rumours were true, but the feelings of mistrust were established, so it was difficult for me to move forward.

I wasn't gaining anything by being with the KDP, other than a bad reputation, so I decided it was time for me to think of a new plan.

CHAPTER TWELVE

Over Borders, Under Scrutiny

At the end of the summer I resolved to go back to Denmark for a while. My relationship with R was deteriorating, and I was also missing school. It's one thing missing out on education opportunities to be on the frontline, but quite another to be missing out in order to be someone's trophy female fighter. I decided to fly back to Copenhagen.

It was a really bright autumn day when I arrived home; the sun blinded my eyes when I stared down from the plane as I approached Copenhagen. I was happy to come home, and this time it felt like the right decision; I wasn't sure if it was really over with R, but I was definitely open to that possibility. When I got back I saw there were lots of different articles in the news about me, with pictures of me on the frontline at Kirkuk, which were published when I was in Derek and had no time to examine some of the coverage that the article generated. The vast majority of the feedback was positive.

I lived with a friend in Christiania called N, and his girlfriend, Lana. They are a happy couple, and it was the first time I had seen a really happy couple up close. It was great to be around them; they were supportive but gave me space, and I called them my adoptive family. I lived in a small room in their house with no wardrobe, but I was very content there: I could eat and sleep whenever I wanted, and I started putting on weight slowly, from eating normally again.

An official government email dropped into my inbox on 29th September 2015 telling me that I could no longer leave Denmark and that my passport had been confiscated. I didn't understand why, or what was going on. I had been in the news, talking about what I had done and why I believed it was everyone's responsibility to join the fight against *Daesh*, and I had already made enemies.

The legislation under which my passport was confiscated was designed by the Social Democrats and passed with a broad majority by the Danish parliament to stem the flow of *Daesh* fighters who were travelling to join Islamic State, but the actual statute doesn't name *Daesh* specifically: anyone leaving Denmark to join an armed group was targeted. I knew the intelligence agencies had been watching me for a while but I had some kind of relationship with them, having passed on intelligence related to the mosques that were recruiting fighters back in Copenhagen, so I was shocked and felt very betrayed by what they had done.

Their premise was that anyone who has fought in a foreign army has skills that could make them a potential threat to Denmark. I found this accusation very painful indeed. I love Denmark; I always have and always will. I wouldn't dream of doing anything to threaten the country. I believe Kurdistan should emulate Denmark, in terms of women's rights, freedom and democratic participation. The country is not perfect, obviously, and the idea that many people have that Denmark is some kind of libertarian la-la land is false. Denmark, like any European country, is both racist and sexist in its own muted way, but it's also beautiful, free and a place of opportunity and relative wealth.

I believe a lot of *Daesh* fighters and sympathizers goaded the police about the 'special treatment' I had been getting, before having my passport confiscated: I'd been in the region since 2012, on and off, and I had not been shy about what I was doing – I believe transparency is a vital component of a democracy – it was known that I was in Syria with the YPG and in Iraq with the *Peshmerga*. Not many politicians spoke up on my behalf, although I remember that a few did. A man called Naser Khader spoke up, saying that I was not a threat to Denmark. I felt betrayed by the Social Democrats, as they were instrumental in bringing in this law. I still can't understand why those fighting on the side of the coalition are covered by the same legislation as those fighting for *Daesh*. How could I be a threat to a value system if I was ready to die to defend it?

I was, however, glad that the authorities had realized the extent of Europe's involvement in the wars of the Middle East; before social media, this had not really been appreciated. These people are a danger to the public: there are literally tens of thousands of men across Europe who support *al-Qaeda*, *Daesh*, *al-Shabaab* and various Islamist groups all over the globe. They raise huge funds, through fake charitable giving, to provide supplies to militant groups who wish to establish a Salafi-style Islamic republic. They are getting trained online and offline to carry out terror attacks against civilians all over the Western world. They should be prevented and their propaganda taken down from websites all over the internet, and I believe they should be imprisoned and counselled out of their extremist views. They hate Denmark; they hate democracy; they hate every good thing about our life and our culture in the West. They hate women, and they hate me. I have been subjected to threats from individuals like this for the past several years, with no official protection from the state. When I learned about the law itself, I was happy; but I just couldn't accept – nor can I still – why I was the first person this new measure was imposed on. I understand it, but I just can't accept it.

My lawyer at the time reflected my predicament: he is a great prosecutor, but he was also defending *Daesh* fighters, with more success than he had with me. This lawyer was recommended to me by friends in Christiania. Apparently he had saved a Palestinian militant who murdered a police officer from going to jail for the rest of their life. This group, which I cannot name for legal reasons, is active against the Israeli state. It plants bombs and murders police officers. My lawyer came with the recommendation that he could literally get you away with murder. But this lawyer was an asshole. He wouldn't accept that the YPG were the main partners in the coalition to defeat ISIS; he would only let me talk about my work with the *Peshmerga*. He believed that because the *Peshmerga* were an official army of a region – the KRG – I couldn't be found to come under this new law, as it specifies non-state actors; the *Peshmerga* are, broadly, a state actor. But I hadn't left the *Peshmerga* in the most elegant of ways; and I wasn't sure whether the card they gave me was officially sanctioned, though R had the authority to do so.

My trial was due to start early the following year, in January 2016. As the end of 2015 approached, Lana and I talked about my future, and she asked me whether I was pregnant. I had no idea at the time – she knew before me, and she was right. I thought I was just putting on weight as part of recovering from finally not being in Syria, but no, I was having a baby. I had been having sex without protection, as I believed I was infertile due to injuries from the violence I had suffered as a young woman, so I was surprised that I was able to get pregnant without medical assistance.

I miscarried the baby in late November. While I was in the hospital, the Christmas decorations were already up. I was in hospital for one day, but I stayed in bed for the following fortnight.

My trial started in January 2016 and was held in a closed court. There was a lot of media attention, and I had a great deal of online support before going to court, but no one to actually go with me on the day. My lawyer and I continued to disagree on how to approach my defence, right up until the trial began. In the end I followed his advice because I thought he knew better than me, and I regret that – if I had followed my own instincts perhaps I would have had more success.

I had just re-enrolled at school, and term started the week that the trial began and I had to miss a few days, but the toll of the trial wasn't too great, as I now had my adoptive family, a place to stay, hot food every day, and I realized I was lucky.

During the court case I was still trying to go to school and to the library as much as possible. One morning during the week of my trial I had gone to school, but when I got there my class was cancelled. I was annoyed because normally we would get a text telling us not to come in, but we hadn't received one that morning. I was on my way back to Christiania, and was on the high road where my adoptive family was living, when I heard the sound of footsteps very close behind me. I turned round and saw three big guys behind me; one of them had his switch-blade out and was looking directly at me, while the two others had their hands in their pockets, as if they had weapons inside – but I didn't spend much time looking. I ran as fast as I could, as I recognized two of the guys from the news; they were Danes who had been to fight in Syria, against Assad, but also against the Kurds. They had joined *Jabhat al-Nusra*, like the majority of Danes fighting in Syria in the early years, before *Daesh* became more popular. They were taller than me, with dark hair and jihadi-style beards. The one with the knife was wearing red Adidas, while the others were in black. I knew they had Danish wives who had converted to be with them and were wearing the headscarf. Two of the guys were quite light-skinned, like me.

I hadn't spoken to these guys before, but I knew their faces and as soon as I realized who they were, I ran. One of the ones without the knife was a fast runner; he caught up with me, overtook me and managed to grab my left wrist, yanking me backwards. Using all of my weight, I tried to swing it over his head so that it would catch and break, but by that stage the man with the knife had caught up with me. I put both of my hands together, near where he was holding my left wrist, so that I could break out of his grip – by pulling my hands towards the centre of my body and him towards my stomach, then raising my fists high and then back over my knee, to break the lock he had.

The guy with the knife was yelling and was close enough to stab me, but his friend was in the way, as I was wriggling around frantically. They were yelling at me in Arabic and Turkish: 'Kurdish slut', 'fake Muslim'; I was like a dirty cloth you use to clean spilled water, I was a doormat, I was dirty. Horrible stuff. As a woman, I don't have the same strength as a man, so I had to be quick and use my weight in a focused manner. We don't learn a lot of self-defence methods in the YPJ, but probably more than in a regular army; we engage in hand-to-hand combat, so I had some training to rely on. I kept my heart and my face covered, wriggled out and ran. It wasn't the type of running you do on the frontline, though, where you are among friends and someone is covering for you. I was totally by myself; I was in a quiet corner and, had I been stabbed, no one would have noticed for several hours. Running was the most logical thing to do, so I ran without looking back, for about a mile and half. I don't think they followed me, but I was completely focused on getting away. Looking back now, it might have been smart to run into a more crowded area where there were a lot of cameras, so they could have captured the men's images, but this might also have put others at risk.

I ran as fast as I could for as long as I could, and when I stopped I grabbed my phone and called the police. I explained what was happening as calmly as possible; they asked me for my identification number. I scrabbled around my pockets for my card, and explained to them where I was and that I needed the police immediately. I couldn't have predicted their reaction. 'We don't have the resources to send anyone at the moment. We will check up on you again tomorrow.'

'Is this a joke?'

'I'm sorry.'

'Okay.' I hung up the phone. I ran through Christiania to get home to my adoptive family's house. The whole thing had lasted an hour. When I told Lana she was really worried about me, and urged me not to go about so openly. 'Maybe you should dye your hair,' she said. 'By being on television and doing interviews you make yourself a target.'

I didn't think it was fair for me to have to hide what I was doing; I felt as if Lana was asking me to do what my lawyer wanted me to do: hide who I was, unnecessarily. I told her I would think about it, and stayed in helping her cook for the day. Someone had captured wild boar while hunting and we were making a special dish for the family to enjoy together.

I called my lawyer and he brought it up during the next trial day, asking why the police wanted my personal identification number before deciding whether or not to send help. The judge said it was human error, and that the police didn't feel comfortable because they don't tend to go inside Christiania. This isn't strictly true; and while I was close to Christiania at the time, I wasn't actually inside it. I was shocked that the police would just leave me, when I needed protection from fighters who posed an actual danger on the streets, while trying to prosecute me for the same reason. The prosecutor then used this as evidence against me in my later court trials – claiming that I am a threat to public safety, although it was me who was being attacked, not me who was attacking anyone else.

Growing up in our community, as a refugee and as a Kurd, we have a primal distrust of the police, as simple as it is complete. You don't call the cops if there is something going wrong in the home; the elders of the family will decide what to do. These elders are our men, and while they may not have been as successful as they hoped to be in Denmark, they still maintained their privileged position within the families and within the clans that we trace our history through. The police not helping me when I needed them most – against armed Islamists, the reason I was in all this trouble – shocked me, and taught me that the authorities were no longer on my side. As well as losing faith in the justice system, because of their inclusion of me alongside those who threaten Denmark, I began to lose my faith in the police – in the whole state apparatus. The police never seemed to have any problem finding me when they needed me for something, but when I needed them, I was on my own. I got the message.

I lost my trial. On 4th February 2016 the prosecution successfully argued that it would be better for me to remain in Denmark, as leaving would make me a threat. I was banned from leaving the country, and my passport was confiscated, but was not physically removed. It was a big blow to bear, and I felt very let down.

I went to my lawyer's office and just ahead of me was a guy I recognized as an Islamist fighter, for a group operating near Turkey who are linked to *Daesh*. I had to wait outside while this guy was inside, getting advice. It was horrible being in the same building as him, and when I asked my lawyer why he was representing him, he said everyone has the right to a fair trial. I baulked. 'He can say he's a jihadi fighter, but I have to pretend I am something other than a YPJ member?' My lawyer wanted to go back to court and appeal against the decision, but I didn't want to. I didn't like how he was in court, and I didn't like his lack of understanding of who the YPG were, and I hated that he also represented my enemies.

After the trial and the attack I focused on getting healthy. I went to school, went to the gym and tried to get strong again. I started to make new friends in school, and slowly began going out more. I didn't talk very openly about what was going on with the court case or about my trips abroad, only to some close friends in Christiania and to my adoptive family of Lana and N. I made some friends in my society and biology classes, and slowly I was building up friendship groups offline, but particularly online. Lots of people wanted to get to know me, and I felt proud of myself and content.

In May 2016 I agreed to do an article with *Vice* about my experience on the frontline, and almost immediately was swamped with attention. The reaction to the article – 'The Girl Who Ran Away to Fight ISIS' – was overwhelming. I was cyber-bullied by people who didn't believe my story, and was contacted by literally hundreds of men from all over the world asking me to marry them, then turning vicious when I wouldn't agree to get involved with them.

I was trolled, I would say without exaggeration, in half a dozen languages. It was incredibly personal, and often sexual. The original article was picked up and plagiarized by lots of different newspapers in the UK, the USA and Australia, and even as far away as Korea, China and the Philippines. Small details of the original article were changed in every plagiarized version – it was like a huge game of Chinese whispers, so the final stories that were being told about me bore little relation to the truth. They went through my personal photos on Facebook and selected the ones that were most revealing. My body, face, words, every part of me was picked apart by men and some women, all over the internet. It was insane.

Every morning for a month after the story was published I would get hundreds and hundreds of messages and friend requests on Facebook, Instagram, Snapchat. Most of it was sexual or vicious in nature; often both. If I didn't respond to some sexual request, very quickly it would turn violent. When I look back now, I was very naive. The journalists were trying to use me for their own purposes. I hadn't realized how ugly people could be, behind the screens on social media. Because I didn't have close friends, it was hard for me to know how to cope with what was going on; people who I thought were my friends – people I was friends with on Facebook – suddenly started being horrible to me. Everyone was accusing me of lying, saying that I was a prostitute and that I had only been in Iraq on the frontline because I was sleeping with a commander.

Two fighters with the *Peshmerga*, a guy called Peshmerganor and another called Peshmergawe, were particularly vicious. They accused me of making everything up, and they spoke to a so-called journalist called Jack Murphy from a website called SOFRED, who continued to spread these lies and encouraged the hatred against me. This so-called journalist was one of the hundreds of people who contacted me after the article went out, but I didn't respond, as I was being questioned by the police that day. Instead of researching his story, he published the words of these trolls, and I became a victim of this vicious fake-news cycle that swirled on social media. My life was apparently too unbelievable for them. It caused me many problems with various people in my life; other international volunteers seemed jealous of the attention I was receiving (though I didn't enjoy it), and basically no one could accept that I could look as I do and do what I did.

derstand why they wouldn't support me publicly. I
yself, 'Where are they? When will they speak out?'
ears I have been involved in the movement, their
nce was the only answer I received.
ome YPG commanders about what was going on,
rumours being spread about me, but they were
busy – gearing up for the battle of Manbij as we
Daesh back to Raqqa. It came out on the Kurdish
016 that the SDF was undergoing its first major
anbij. At the time they were saying that the SDF
men; they weren't talking about the YPJ being part
ost impossible to contact an active YPJ fighter on
female fighters are not entitled to have phones.
to find a YPG fighter, and I spoke to a few of my
commanders. They told me it wasn't true that
nposed solely of men; this was just being said to
men to join. A friend of mine told me about two
died fighting with the SDF and were not given
's burial or funeral honours. I was incensed that
women was not being recognized.
I needed to get out of Europe and get offline.
, whom I was still living with, that I would be
give them the full details. They thought I was
the Danish units that were slowly beginning
st the international coalition, but this was not
orrecting this misunderstanding, as they were
st me out of their life for this reason. Lana
ieve I would go back to the YPG, considering

Male fighters who post online multiple sexually explicit pictures
of their girlfriends, wearing nothing but a G-string while posing
on a bed, were praised by people who said they 'deserved' such
sexy partners; but because I had a picture taken with a beer in
my hand while in a uniform, they called me a war slut, a war
tourist, an infidel and a liar.

I was caught between my legal situation and the potential trouble
I could find myself in, if I spoke too loudly about my time in the
YPG, and the need to defend myself online. Everything that had
been going on-track seemed to be unravelling. I supposed I was
naive to think the men in the *Peshmerga* in particular – most of
whom had seen very little frontline action in Iraq, and absolutely
none in Syria – wouldn't take offence to what I said. Here I was,
a small blonde student who looks a little like a doll, saying that
ISIS fighters are easy to kill, when experience was showing that
they were not. What I meant was that on the actual frontline,
those few of us who were killing *Daesh* soldiers were finding they
were human after all – not the monsters they wanted us to believe
they were – and, like any human, they could be killed. What is
not easy to kill is their myth-making ability, and the ideology of
hatred that they had been so effective in spreading.

I lost a lot of weight, very quickly, as I can't eat when I am
stressed. A few weeks later I was skin and bones – just not too
much skin, and a lot of bones. The feedback affected my personal
life; I lost a lot of confidence, as the Kurdish pages on social
media picked up on the negative stories about me and ran their
own. People were contacting my family, who of course were
not exactly singing my praises. I stopped wearing make-up, I
stopped training, I stopped going out; I became consumed by

this web-storm of vitriol against me. I am still deeply affected by this trolling, and it's hard to explain how much it impacted on every aspect of my health and well-being. The trolling is still going on, and is still taking the same toll.

It would come in waves. After that first tsunami of attention hit me and everyone around me, I could track what was happening. It started in the USA and UK, after the original article, then slowly travelled across Europe. On a Thursday it would be French requests on my Facebook page, then the following Monday lots of people from Germany. Mainly it was men, but there were women as well. Not all of it was negative, but it was the negative comments that I remember. That's what trolling does; you forget all about the positive things and take in everything harsh they say about you, because truly it's difficult for anyone to have a lower opinion of me than I have myself, at times.

To my Kurdish community, who were shocked by the pictures pillaged from my personal social-media profiles and distributed around the world, alongside boasts about how easy *Daesh* soldiers are to kill, I say it was my camouflage within the system. I was living in a particular society and I was expected to fit into that society. People of my age – as well as old women and young girls of every age, and also boys – post multiple pictures of themselves every day: in different outfits, different locations, different contexts. I did not intend my words about being a soldier to be accompanied by the pictures from my Facebook page. I approved the photographs from the *Vice* shoot, where I was covered up. I know what this says about sexism in capitalism, but what I want to ask is what it says about sexism in our movement as well. Why were my pictures allowed to explode my words and

deeds on behalf of our ar
offensive? Who does that
you must understand tha
liberating its people, and
trolling would not have

Our movement's lea
a broadly supportive ba
must be embraced in pr
right to show her bod
about my body? Why
taught me that my bo
me to feel proud of m
hard-earned. You ha
there, and I was inte
Kurd and a Kurdish
am both simultaneo

I started sharin
pictures that I had
were wrong, the ne
at war, but only t
international volu
to go through this
we are taught to
so everyone was
stand up to defe

I thought of J
if that was why
of that inciden
good soldier ar

I couldn't un
kept asking m
After all the
deafening sile
I spoke to
and about the
understandabl
began to push
news in June
operation in M
comprised only
of them. It's al
Facebook, as ou
It's much easier
old friends and
the SDF was co
attract more Ara
women who had
the official marty
their sacrifice as
I decided that
I told N and Lan
leaving, but didn'
going with one of
to mobilize to ass
true. I regret not
hurt enough to ca
and N couldn't be
how I had left.

But I knew I wanted to go back to the YPG and into Manbij. I couldn't just sit at home and watch the news from my couch all day. It's hard to look back and say why I made the choices I have made so far in my life. The decisions I make depend mostly on my heart, which I continue to trust.

CHAPTER THIRTEEN

Evolution of Tactics

Before I returned to Iraq at the start of June 2016 I kept a low profile, staying with friends around Christiania, aware that I was on the radar of the band of *Daesh* brothers in Europe. After the article, one of the more terrifying strains of trolling that I received involved pictures of my face being Photoshopped onto an array of dead YPJ corpses. As YPJ fighters, we keep our last bullets or a hand-grenade to end our own lives in battle with, because of the distinct propaganda value our tortured corpses would provide for *Daesh*. *Daesh* have beheaded a few foreigners and several dozen YPJ and YPG fighters, and most kills are captured on film footage, which is edited for maximum gruesomeness and posted online for their fans all over the world. Our orders were to never join these ranks. I had threats that they would behead me in Europe, or find me and rape me, because I was a slut who obviously loved sex.

The trolling from Kurdistan reached me before my return to Erbil in June. My name preceded me there, along with certain parts of my body. I knew I would get some nastiness from Iraq and Kurdistan for my photographs, but what I was surprised at was the impact this had on the way people treated me when I arrived.

Before Manbij, I was not the kind of girl who took photos on the frontline. A lot of the international volunteers spend a great deal of time taking pictures, particularly in the early days, when they are held back from being on the frontline. In the beginning there was a lot of debate about how best to use the international volunteers, and a general consensus that we should keep them for propaganda purposes, but this has evolved on an individual basis, depending on how long the volunteer has stayed with us. As a Kurdish member of the YPJ, I am treated very differently from an international member of the YPG, and I first became aware of quite how stark these differences were when I travelled back to Manbij.

Although I had my passport officially confiscated, and there was a whole court ruling against me and forbidding me from leaving Denmark, no one actually came and took my passport off me. I'm not sure if the police or the PET were looking hard for me, but either way, after the attack on me near Christiania I went underground for a while, as they had made it clear they were taking no responsibility for my safety and would not protect me from *Daesh*. Now I was planning to flout the travel ban, but I wasn't sure what would happen at the airport: would an alarm go off? I doubted it, but I was nervous all the same.

I needn't have worried. I flew out with another YPG fighter, JM, after only a minor argument with the check-in assistant over whether or not I needed a visa. When I arrived in Sulaimaniya, a friend called Mohammed picked me and JM up and brought us back to the house where several international YPG volunteers were staying. There was a Canadian YPJ volunteer staying there, but apparently she was given special exemption to do so, because she was in her forties. I was told that she was trusted 'not to do anything' with the men, because of her age, while my body – the body that, along with my life, I was ready to give up for this fight – was apparently in prime sexy season, and therefore I would be staying elsewhere. It's the whole shame thing again, and it's hard to swallow within a feminist army.

So I was driven to the home of a family who were working with our movement. I wasn't sure if they had seen the pictures of me with the KDP, but I hoped not. The man, Shorash, was one of our drivers, and he and his wife, Nasrine, lived in Sulaimaniya with their two boys. They would keep people like me and be paid for it by the movement – a smaller version of a safe house, one that is more embedded in the community.

By this stage, international guests were very common. Hearing my accent and my story, the family considered me one of their own, and didn't modify their behaviour as if they had a guest with them. The mother would beat the two boys senseless; and they were small boys who had no chance of fighting back. It was incredibly shocking for me, but I think it was her weird way of saying I was part of their family. Because I had told her I wasn't married, she must have assumed I had been living with my Iraqi Kurdish family, when in fact I had been living with another family – without violence – for a few years now. It triggered sad memories of what I went through in my own family, and I hated being near Nasrine when she was vicious to her kids. She was full of fury, as any woman would be who was married to her husband.

Male fighters who post online multiple sexually explicit pictures of their girlfriends, wearing nothing but a G-string while posing on a bed, were praised by people who said they 'deserved' such sexy partners; but because I had a picture taken with a beer in my hand while in a uniform, they called me a war slut, a war tourist, an infidel and a liar.

I was caught between my legal situation and the potential trouble I could find myself in, if I spoke too loudly about my time in the YPG, and the need to defend myself online. Everything that had been going on-track seemed to be unravelling. I supposed I was naive to think the men in the *Peshmerga* in particular – most of whom had seen very little frontline action in Iraq, and absolutely none in Syria – wouldn't take offence to what I said. Here I was, a small blonde student who looks a little like a doll, saying that ISIS fighters are easy to kill, when experience was showing that they were not. What I meant was that on the actual frontline, those few of us who were killing *Daesh* soldiers were finding they were human after all – not the monsters they wanted us to believe they were – and, like any human, they could be killed. What is not easy to kill is their myth-making ability, and the ideology of hatred that they had been so effective in spreading.

I lost a lot of weight, very quickly, as I can't eat when I am stressed. A few weeks later I was skin and bones – just not too much skin, and a lot of bones. The feedback affected my personal life; I lost a lot of confidence, as the Kurdish pages on social media picked up on the negative stories about me and ran their own. People were contacting my family, who of course were not exactly singing my praises. I stopped wearing make-up, I stopped training, I stopped going out; I became consumed by this web-storm of vitriol against me. I am still deeply affected by this trolling, and it's hard to explain how much it impacted on every aspect of my health and well-being. The trolling is still going on, and is still taking the same toll.

It would come in waves. After that first tsunami of attention hit me and everyone around me, I could track what was happening. It started in the USA and UK, after the original article, then slowly travelled across Europe. On a Thursday it would be French requests on my Facebook page, then the following Monday lots of people from Germany. Mainly it was men, but there were women as well. Not all of it was negative, but it was the negative comments that I remember. That's what trolling does; you forget all about the positive things and take in everything harsh they say about you, because truly it's difficult for anyone to have a lower opinion of me than I have myself, at times.

To my Kurdish community, who were shocked by the pictures pillaged from my personal social-media profiles and distributed around the world, alongside boasts about how easy *Daesh* soldiers are to kill, I say it was my camouflage within the system. I was living in a particular society and I was expected to fit into that society. People of my age – as well as old women and young girls of every age, and also boys – post multiple pictures of themselves every day: in different outfits, different locations, different contexts. I did not intend my words about being a soldier to be accompanied by the pictures from my Facebook page. I approved the photographs from the *Vice* shoot, where I was covered up. I know what this says about sexism in capitalism, but what I want to ask is what it says about sexism in our movement as well. Why were my pictures allowed to explode my words and deeds on behalf of our army into nothing? Is my skin really that offensive? Who does that remind you of? My dear fellow Kurds, you must understand that we simply can't have a land without liberating its people, and half of those people are women. The trolling would not have happened to me if I was a man.

Our movement's leaders need to learn that in order to build a broadly supportive base across Europe and America, feminism must be embraced in practice as well as in ideology. It is a woman's right to show her body without shame; what was so shameful about my body? Why should I feel ashamed? It was the YPJ who taught me that my body was strong and vital, and who inspired me to feel proud of my strength, which was hard-trained-for and hard-earned. You have to integrate into a society in order to live there, and I was integrated into Danish society. I am a Danish Kurd and a Kurdish Dane. I can't decide which one is which, I am both simultaneously and I should never have to choose.

I started sharing some pictures of me in combat – older pictures that I had previously hidden. Instead of admitting they were wrong, the next wave of trolling suggested that I had been at war, but only to take pictures. This made me furious. The international volunteers that I helped to get to Syria never had to go through this, because they were men, and they looked like we are taught to believe a soldier looks. I do not look like this, so everyone was sceptical about me, and my own people didn't stand up to defend me.

I thought of Jiyan and how I had left the group, and wondered if that was why they were annoyed, but I was sure the full truth of that incident had not made it to senior command. I am a good soldier and I have a good reputation in our movement, so

I couldn't understand why they wouldn't support me publicly. I kept asking myself, 'Where are they? When will they speak out?' After all the years I have been involved in the movement, their deafening silence was the only answer I received.

I spoke to some YPG commanders about what was going on, and about the rumours being spread about me, but they were understandably busy – gearing up for the battle of Manbij as we began to push *Daesh* back to Raqqa. It came out on the Kurdish news in June 2016 that the SDF was undergoing its first major operation in Manbij. At the time they were saying that the SDF comprised only men; they weren't talking about the YPJ being part of them. It's almost impossible to contact an active YPJ fighter on Facebook, as our female fighters are not entitled to have phones. It's much easier to find a YPG fighter, and I spoke to a few of my old friends and commanders. They told me it wasn't true that the SDF was composed solely of men; this was just being said to attract more Arab men to join. A friend of mine told me about two women who had died fighting with the SDF and were not given the official martyr's burial or funeral honours. I was incensed that their sacrifice as women was not being recognized.

I decided that I needed to get out of Europe and get offline. I told N and Lana, whom I was still living with, that I would be leaving, but didn't give them the full details. They thought I was going with one of the Danish units that were slowly beginning to mobilize to assist the international coalition, but this was not true. I regret not correcting this misunderstanding, as they were hurt enough to cast me out of their life for this reason. Lana and N couldn't believe I would go back to the YPG, considering how I had left.

But I knew I wanted to go back to the YPG and into Manbij. I couldn't just sit at home and watch the news from my couch all day. It's hard to look back and say why I made the choices I have made so far in my life. The decisions I make depend mostly on my heart, which I continue to trust.

CHAPTER THIRTEEN

Evolution of Tactics

B efore I returned to Iraq at the start of June 2016 I kept a low profile, staying with friends around Christiania, aware that I was on the radar of the band of *Daesh* brothers in Europe. After the article, one of the more terrifying strains of trolling that I received involved pictures of my face being Photoshopped onto an array of dead YPJ corpses. As YPJ fighters, we keep our last bullets or a hand-grenade to end our own lives in battle with, because of the distinct propaganda value our tortured corpses would provide for *Daesh*. *Daesh* have beheaded a few foreigners and several dozen YPJ and YPG fighters, and most kills are captured on film footage, which is edited for maximum gruesomeness and posted online for their fans all over the world. Our orders were to never join these ranks. I had threats that they would behead me in Europe, or find me and rape me, because I was a slut who obviously loved sex.

The trolling from Kurdistan reached me before my return to Erbil in June. My name preceded me there, along with certain parts of my body. I knew I would get some nastiness from Iraq and Kurdistan for my photographs, but what I was surprised at

Shorash was appalling, and it felt to me like he tried to sexually abuse me almost from the first day I arrived – during the Holy Month, and him apparently a good Sunni Muslim. He was lecherous and weak, he talked too much, all of his stories were about himself, and he had obviously carved out some credit within his community due to his work in our movement, and with the international volunteers in particular. He had called me slut on social media before he even met me, having seen some of the photos where my cleavage was on display. He is part of the group of Iraqi trolls who said I was a prostitute, or that I was sleeping with different KRG soldiers while touring around the frontline with a camera crew. I asked him why he had said this, and he told me he thought I was just trying to get famous. He didn't delete his comments about me, nor did he appear to revise his opinion.

'I'm here for you to drive me to Manbij,' I told him.

'I'm to drive you where you need to go,' he responded threateningly. He always wanted me to travel in his car alone with him, so that he could try and force himself on me. I became afraid of leaving the house, although I knew I had to leave because, after a few days, Shorash began attempting to molest me in his home. I think Nasrine was beating up her children because of the frustration she felt; I would always look from Shorash to her when he asked me to go in his car with him. Everyone knew what was happening.

One morning, after Nasrine had gone to the women's meeting, I woke to find Shorash's hands down my pants. The women's meetings are always early, because the women are not allowed out later on in the day – they have to stay at home and provide snacks for the husband and children, or for any of his friends or work colleagues who might drop in. Waking up with him on top of me was disgusting. I texted JM and a few others and told them I needed help, and decided I needed evidence; because of the trolling, everyone at the time thought I was someone who exaggerated things. I recorded Shorash later that evening on my phone and sent the file to my friend on WhatsApp. I debated my options: should I go back to Denmark? I knew that if you break the travel ban you can get up to six years in jail, but I needed to get out of this house – and soon.

Shorash forced me to wear an Islamic headscarf because it was the Holy Month. He told me it was to keep me safe, because my hair colour was so recognizable; YPJ girls at the time didn't tend to be blonde. People would know who I was and would target me, he said.

I went to find the PYD senior figure to complain; in the YPJ we are under no obligation to dress according to Islamic tradition, and no man can force us to do so. I urgently needed to find some comrades within the movement and tell them what was going on, but I was very isolated in the house and this took some time. I had started fighting with Shorash, who had become even more blatant during his wife's frequent trips out. I began to dread hearing her leave the house.

'Who are you to touch me like this? How dare you?' I would scream at him, which, considering the way sound travels through the walls, should have alerted the neighbours. But nobody ever came. Shorash's sons would leave the room if it started in front of them. They were ten and sixteen, but they looked about six and ten. The little girl was four years old and absolutely adorable. Shorash didn't like the girl and would hit her, while Nasrine would hit the sons and he would try and protect them from her. She would punch them in the head, step on their heads and kick them. It was horrendous.

I finally got to meet the PYD member – the political representative of the YPG – the same man called Metin who had helped me get my passport back when it was confiscated from me in the mountains. I told him I was waiting for the appropriate permissions to get into Syria; I didn't mind waiting and knew there were some border issues, but I could not stay in this house any more and I needed to leave *now*. 'Are you a *cadra* or a volunteer?' he asked, as Shorash listened.

'A volunteer,' I responded.

'Then you stay where we tell you, like the others.'

The others, I knew, were getting food, safe accommodation and were generally having a nice time. I asked Metin if we could talk privately, but he wouldn't permit it. Asking to talk privately to a man in his house can be seen as a sign that you are sexually propositioning him. Unable to speak freely, I begged the PYD guy to take me to the YPJ house in Sulaimaniya. It was just a normal safe house, but it wasn't for volunteers; everyone who stayed there had pledged to be a *cadra*. 'If you don't like it in Iraq, then why don't you go back to Denmark?' he asked, and he and Shorash laughed together.

'I can't now, because I have broken this passport ban to come here and join,' I responded.

'You could do a Leyla Zana.' I didn't respond, but just glared at him.

Leyla Zana is a very famous female politician with the People's Democratic Party (HDP) in Turkey, who was sentenced to ten years in jail for speaking Kurdish, after becoming one of the first Kurdish women elected to parliament in Turkey.

'I have permission to send you to Rojava as a *cadra*.'

'Sir, you are not a *cadra* yourself, so how can you ask me to do a Leyla Zana and give up my freedom for ten years, or ask me to give up my freedom as a European for ever, when *you* have not done the same?'

'I'm sorry then, I can't help you; perhaps your other contacts can.'

I returned to Shorash and Nasrine's house for another glum meal of rice and sauce. In the car on the way back, Shorash put his hand down my top, into my bra and started to grab and pull my nipples. 'They are slowly getting bigger again, my dear.' I pushed his hand away, but he persisted, so we drove like this until he finally had to concentrate on the road.

I went back to the PYD and told Metin I needed to see him again. He was eating, so I had to wait a long time, and the smell of the food made me jealously hungry. 'You need to take me to the YPJ house. It's my right to speak to a female commander,' I said.

He finally relented and drove me to the house. Inside were three YPJ *cadras* who were not expecting us, and who didn't seem pleased to see Metin. I tried to talk to the girls and explain that I needed to stay with them. One of the girls I recognized from my first time in Kobani; we had trained on the same mountain together, so had passed each other on our training camp. 'Do you recognize me?' I asked her.

'No,' she responded.

I had lost about a stone and a half in weight and dyed my hair blonde, so I wasn't completely shocked. 'I met you on the White

Mountain,' I said, specifying the camp. Looking directly in my eye, she smiled at me in pleased recognition. 'I need to stay here, as I am waiting for permission to get to Rojava and it's taking longer than I thought. But I was sent to stay in the home of Shorash.'

He was still in the room as I was talking, as he seemed to be stalking me. He appeared to be close to the PYD guy, and I wondered if they were deliberately trying to ignore what was going on. Did the PYD know all along?

I went into the kitchen of the girls' house and started to wash some of their dishes and clean up, while the men waited for tea to be made. None of the YPJ girls wanted to serve them, and eventually Shorash came in and told me we had to go.

'Sister, do you wear a headscarf on your head because of the Holy Month?' I asked.

'What Holy Month?' the younger one answered, and I had to laugh. She turned to Metin. 'You can't just show up here unannounced. We train here, and it's annoying for us to have to cut off our training to entertain.'

'I'm sorry – she told us she was lonely in the house and wanted to see you.'

'Do you wear the full headscarf?' I asked them. 'This man wants me to wear it while staying in his house, but I do not wish to wear it. I'm in Sulaimaniya, not Iran.'

'We don't care if it's the Holy Month or not. We are still not Muslim, and we are still not religious. You can make your own decision if you wish, but we do not wear the scarf.'

I took off my headscarf and we left: the girls didn't want us there and there was no way I could speak to them privately to tell them why I needed their help.

Back at the house, Nasrine was angry that I wasn't wearing the scarf, but served me meat and vegetables first, and we joked about fattening me up. Shorash's eyes never left my cleavage, and I wanted to be sick. He was older than my father, but on the way back from this sad visit to the YPJ house he had proposed to make me his second wife: an honour that his mistress had been trying to achieve for several years, he stressed.

He touched my legs, my knees and put his hands inside my top again, claiming that he wanted to check if his wife had been taking good care of me, and to see if I had been putting on weight. Exhausted and defeated, I looked out of the window and let him get it over with. The kids were writing and drawing, so I went straight to play with them and tried to avoid Shorash until I would be forced to sit near him for dinner.

I filmed a few videos, subtly, of what was going on in the house: Nasrine's behaviour towards her kids, and Shorash's towards me. I contacted a Kurdish guy called *heval* Givara, who was in charge of coordinating the volunteers, and told him to come and see me in the house.

Givara arrived and was treated very respectfully by Shorash, and together with his friend *heval* Diyar, we went out together. After seeing me for the first time in a week, Diyar looked aghast: 'How could you get more thin than you already were?' *Heval* Givara also seemed concerned about my weight, and I played him the recordings from the house. They listened through the headphones, but didn't say anything.

The next day Givara came to visit me in the house. I had fresh recordings from the early morning, when Nasrine went out and I was assaulted by Shorash again. Givara put the headphones on and, sitting right next to Shorash, listened to what had happened. I could see his eyes widening in alarm, and he looked from me to Shorash and back again, as if he was following in the present the conversation that he was hearing between us. Shorash, by this point, knew something was up and was getting increasingly agitated. 'What have you done, you whore?' he spat, but by now *heval* Givara had finally heard enough to believe me. Everyone stood up and they had a fight for a while, as *heval* Givara told me to get my stuff. Finally, I was leaving.

After we all left in the car, we drove slowly to the centre of the town. As we reached the corner of the street, Givara stopped the car. 'If Shorash follows you, then we will know for sure.' I couldn't believe it; I had sent him two recorded attacks, and he had seen the reaction from Shorash that morning, but he still wasn't certain? Sure enough, Shorash followed us in his car, so we took a long diversion, before going to a hotel called the Dolphin, where I stayed for the remainder of my time in Iraq, at my own expense.

While I was staying there I bought *heval* Diyar a gift, as I knew he had helped convince *heval* Givara to get me away from Shorash. It's common, when going back to the front, that you receive small gifts from friends. He gave me a YPJ flag that was printed wrongly: instead of having the YPJ symbol on the red bit, it was on the yellow part. 'I know it's got a mistake on it,' he apologized. I loved it anyway, and kept it.

'That's fine,' I said, 'I like mistakes,' thinking by this point that I had just made a fresh one by coming back to Iraq.

Since I had left Kobani and Rojava, the flag of the YPJ had become more important to the movement, as the sacrifices made

under our flag could no longer be ignored. In the hills of eastern
Kobani, the YPJ flag now flies where previously a *Daesh* flag did;
when I had left in 2014 the area was still flying the *Daesh* flag. I
was looking forward to going back through Kobani, as I knew
the strategic headquarters for the Manbij operations were based
there and it was likely I would see some of my old commanders.
I was hoping they could shed some light on why I had been
forced to leave the last time, and on why they had not defended
me from the trolling.

I stayed in the Dolphin for a few days and helped to pick up some
international volunteers. We don't pick up the recruits directly
from the airport, due to the security risks. My job was to translate
for the commanders when the volunteers arrived at the safe house,
take their phones and batteries and explain why they wouldn't be
seeing them for a while, and explain the next stage of their journey
towards the camps near Duhok, where they would get some basic
training, before heading into Rojava for more training and then
on to the front.

   I had made it clear to everyone I spoke to that I was not
doing any more training: I was coming back to fight, so I had
an appointment arranged with a female commander in the YPJ
in Duhok before I crossed the border. Because of my language
skills, I helped with translations; occasionally I had to do some
questioning and translate some reports, writing down the details
of the new recruits and passing the information up the ranks, for
the commanders of the new international recruits. Nazzareno
Tassone, from Canada, was one of these guys, along with Josh
Walker from the UK, a guy from South America and a guy from

Spain. Beyond this, I had no idea who any of these recruits were, and they had no idea who I was. In our movement we don't really care what you have done before you join; we just accept anybody who wants to fight *Daesh* and will work for the movement. Nazzareno was eventually killed, along with the British YPG fighter Ryan Locke, a chef from England whom I did not meet. I was sent a video that *Daesh* made of their bodies, for propaganda. They were demanding huge sums of money for the bodies of both fighters, and getting them out took longer than it should have done.

Heval Diyar came to the safe house and told me to get everyone ready to go to the camp. 'It's now.' Diyar took his name from his older brother, who had performed a suicide mission in the battle of Kobani when he was twenty-nine. As the younger brother, in another time Diyar would have had nothing to do with the war. 'Make sure you call me, when you get there,' he said as he put us into the vehicle. His job at this early stage was shuffling the volunteers, so I knew I wouldn't see him for some time, and I am sure he was thinking that I might be one of those never seen again. I had to fill out an address for the *hevals* to send my body to, should I be killed. I wanted to send it to Lana and N, but they wouldn't permit it, so I put the address of the Danish PET. They could have me for good, if they wanted me so much.

The drive into the training camp near Duhok was hilarious; there was me, a driver from the mountains who was playing 'Jingle Bells' – in Holy Month, no less – a guy who was half-German and half-Russian, Josh Walker and the gentle and solemn Nazzareno. I had my phone on me and we were still in an area where the internet and reception were good. I was still getting abusive messages, saying I had lied about being in Syria, but I turned my phone off to save the battery and we passed the long journey from Sulaimaniya to Duhok, through the mountain route, easily enough. Although I was careful not to be too open with the new recruits, it was great to be back in their company again and away from Shorash's house.

When we finally arrived at the camp, the guard who let us park and helped us come in was someone who had been there a long time and recognized me. 'You are back again? How many times?' I said I was like a cat with nine lives, and I would spend every one of them fighting. We were due to cross the river into Syria that night, as the moon wasn't out, which meant it was going to be darker, and there was space for us on the dinghy.

I couldn't find the female commander I was supposed to be looking for, so I asked the driver if I should cross or wait. 'If it's important – you should talk to her. You never know what happens, once you cross.' It was important: it was a case of clarifying that I continued to be a volunteer, despite what Jiyan had said. This commander, *heval* Parwin, is a senior fighter and I knew she could settle any issues I had. So I waited until the next day to cross, after I had spoken to her. I was tasked again with helping to usher the international volunteers, and there was a guy from America who was joking as we crossed. I thought of how I had entered Kobani the last time, compared to how I had left, and told him to stop messing around. 'You have to be quiet and focus – you can get yourself killed all you want, but the rest of us want to die on the battlefront.'

He was really annoyed that I called him out in front of everyone, and that I had the authority to do so within the YPJ. He became one of the international volunteers who started to bad-mouth me to others, both in person and online. It didn't cross my mind at the time that he would behave in this way: I was saving his life. Once we were inside Syria, on our way to the base in Karacho, he kept running in front of everyone like an excited child, instead of going carefully, because of mines.

I didn't like the foreigners who came and found it funny; they had no decorum at times. At the funerals we have for the dead, some of the international volunteers don't know how to behave: they will be laughing and taking photographs with babies, when we are there to mourn our friends. It could be something about the way we mourn: we shout as loud as possible, and walk in long formations, making lots of noise; but it's the noise of grief, not a baseball game.

There was another volunteer, when we were inside Syria but near a *Daesh* outpost, who put his head straight up above the rock he was hiding behind – basically offering his American face to *Daesh* and risking getting us all captured to co-star in whatever propaganda film they would make. I suppose I felt a little of what some of my Kurdish friends feel when they are with me: by being European, I am more of a target, which puts everyone in slightly more danger. And by being not from Kurdistan, you are more prone to make stupid mistakes. After this other American gave away our position, I had a word with him, but I did it less publicly than the first telling-off, because at least it was an honest mistake and he was actually trying to be helpful.

I didn't meet that many international fighters on the front, as it takes a long time to build up the experience to make it there. If one volunteer comes from the UK and goes on TV, then ten more will come and join our movement. But similarly, if one UK volunteer dies, it makes it less likely for others to come after him. This is bad for recruitment, so our leaders were careful about letting the internationals to the front. Our job, as Kurdish soldiers fighting with them, was mainly to keep them alive. The internationals I met on the frontline impressed me a great deal; they were experienced, tactical and contributed greatly to their battalions, despite the insane circumstances.

At the base in Karacho, our headquarters in Rojava, I saw there had been some changes to training, and new tactics briefings and general training points were given every day at *takmil*. The mistakes of Kobani were being learned, and there was a renewed focus on better after-reports from fights, and patient listening to experiences where our fighters had died, in order to get a fuller picture of the tactics *Daesh* were using.

We called this kind of training the 'evolution of the revolution': we had to learn from our experience by examining it carefully. In Kobani we had been caught out by *Daesh*'s heavy weaponry. In Manbij this wasn't going to be such an issue, as we were supported by airstrikes from the US-led coalition. There were several foreign special forces along our frontline positions: British Special Forces, French Foreign Legion fighters and even some American SEALS. Lots of impressive men, and one woman.

When I got to the mountain camp in Mount Gara, I showed them my passport and was hoping we weren't going to have another episode about whether I was a *cadra* or a volunteer. Nothing was taken from me this time, and everyone was very polite. In Gara I slept with the YPJ girls in an underground cave in the mountains, as Turkey flew their F-16 fighter jets overhead. One bomb from them and our entire camp would be destroyed. Our caves are designed to withstand their bombing, though: they have two large entrances, so that the pressure can come into the cave and leave again quickly. Because the pressure leaves, the caves stay intact, and inside we slept on my favourite fluffy duvets.

Being in Gara and hearing the F-16 planes overhead as we were trying to sleep, I felt so excited to be back, despite the constant fear of being bombed. I love camping in the mountains with my comrades. I have not found anything I enjoy as much in this life so far. It was freezing, yes, but we managed to have a small fire inside the cave. We had hot tea, and I met the Italian girl who had been staying with Shorash just before me. She was on her way back out of the mountains now, having done some ideology training and learning about *jineology*. 'That fucking house,' I said, knowing she spoke good English. I offered her a cigarette and waited to hear what had happened her. 'Can you believe that guy? How is he still working for our movement?'

She didn't seem to want to speak, so I asked her again in Kurdish, and she looked me directly in the eye and said simply, 'Don't talk about it.'

In Kurdistan, no matter what kind of movement you are in, or what kind of rank you have, if you are a woman and are accused of something by a man, they will check you to see if your virginity is intact, and that will determine how they proceed. Even so, I couldn't believe this girl's reaction: had she not just been doing *jineology* training? What are they teaching now? Who is taking the training? Sexual assault, when it is not against a virgin, is something our culture doesn't quite grasp, but in our movement it is our belief that all women are entitled to live free of sexual assault or unwanted sexual attention. I was sure this girl wasn't a virgin – she was Italian and she was into radical politics, so of course not – but I was equally sure she didn't want any kind of investigation into this man, if it involved her.

We believe in the right for Women's Protection Units, but we fail to protect our own European recruits from sexual predators within our own movement. I didn't speak to the Italian girl again, as she went back into Iraq and, presumably, home. I do still wonder how many girls Shorash has abused. I reported what happened to my comrades, but I am not sure what happened to him as a consequence.

CHAPTER FOURTEEN

Selfies on the Manbij Frontline

A lot of people were coming and going from the Karacho headquarters, and before I had gone round and said hello to all of the people I knew, I was told to get into a car and join the sabotage unit in Kobani. Back to where I had been almost two years ago. My codename this time was Sofia, or Vashti (the modern version of Sofia), one of the earliest feminist icons in the world. We travelled to the headquarters of our base in Belka, inside the Kobani *canton*, and I waited for the sabotage unit to come and get me. The house was beautiful: we had our flags in the garden and there were trees and plants growing; even the internet was working. I was so glad to be out of the house of that awful man.

We had watermelon for lunch and I fell into conversation with some girls I knew from Derek, who couldn't believe I was back in Kobani. I normally hate watermelon as it reminds me of my father, but I accepted it to be polite, and it was delicious. I had this sense that things could change: I could make changes in my own life. I wouldn't always hate watermelon, I could enjoy it now, without allowing memories of my father to poison the taste. The girls were *cadras*, and I thought how much simpler my life would be if I became one myself. I could pledge to stay in the mountains and never go back to Europe.

I knew I should have a better CV before applying to be a *cadra*, but when I was in the house preparing to go back to the front, I was struck by how happy I was. I didn't care about the trolling; I was back with my friends and they were happy to see me, and glad that I had returned. It occurred to me that I had spent too much of my life associating with people who didn't like me. As I was thinking this, I also realized it was ridiculous to have come this far for that kind of peace of mind, and decided to stop being inside my thoughts and go back to enjoying the company of my friends.

A senior commander, *heval* Fidan, greeted me as Joanna, and I told her I was Sofia this time. She knew me from my time in the mountains, so she knows my real name. She is now the YPJ leader of the whole *canton* of Kobani. She took the *takmil* for the Manbij operation, and I listened to what was happening on the frontline. Mines were a problem: *Daesh* had daisy-chained them everywhere, and there was some consternation over land we were due to take back. Manbij was not Kobani, but it was a brutal fight where *Daesh* mobilized many of their men.

Our efforts were focused on an area called the 'Manbij Pocket', which is in the northern Aleppo governorate. The reason Manbij is so important is that it opens the corridor to Raqqa, and it cuts their fighters out of Aleppo. Immediately after *takmil*, I found Fidan and told her I wanted to get back to the sabotage unit and could be part of the teams clearing mines. Fidan just laughed at me and put her hand on my shoulder: 'Always in a rush, still the same old Joanna. You are never patient enough.' I laughed and told her how pleased I was to be back with my friends. 'I was told you are a sniper now, so I thought you must have developed some patience,' she continued. I laughed, because she was right. This woman was always right, and she was one of the commanders who would lead us to success in Raqqa.

'In combat I am patient, I promise. When I am not on the frontlines, I am impatient.'

'Hmm.' She raised her eyebrows as if to say, 'Really?'

'I didn't come here to eat food and look at my phone. I have already paid a high price to get here, and I want to be on the front.' I didn't want to have to wait until another commander who knew me came to the house, before I could be despatched.

Heval Fidan looked at me and I could tell I had won her over. 'There's a commander in the next room you can talk to,' she said. 'Her name is *heval* Leyla and you will be under her. You will learn a lot.'

In sabotage units we make the chemical parts of explosives, and dismantle explosives for parts. It's delicate, complicated work, which I had some training for in Derek. Explosives are one of our core skills as fighters, and I had a lot of observational experience from my first time in Kobani, but also from my time in Aleppo back at the beginning of the conflict. Sabotage units are the brains on the frontline, while forward-roving units called *haraketli* are the muscle. In sabotage units you have to be 100 per cent honest with feedback after missions, as this is how you learn from common mistakes. We do this briefing right after returning, when our memory is fresh, and we do it so that we can plan, but also learn from each other's mistakes on the battlefield. Experience of this nature, with different substances and explosives, is how you begin to understand them. No mistrust can be shown in creating a bomb; faulty bombs are made because of this, and if an explosive that you make goes badly, it will come back to haunt you, along with the responsibility for your friend's death. If there was mistrust between two people in a sabotage unit and they made a faulty bomb together, as a result of their mistrust, then they could be imprisoned in a camp for a while. Mountain prisons are not fun, so everyone is keen to make sure they avoid this fate.

Heval Leyla was the one of the area commanders of the sabotage units of Manbij. She had long, totally black hair, loved Celine Dion and Metallica and was the best commander I ever had. She had learned English at university, where she studied history. Leyla and I were introduced and she said she knew who I was, because she had been friends with someone from my *tabur* who had died after I left Kobani. 'You were with *shehid* Medya and you were in Kobani,' she said. She had been there as well – but in a different area of the city. 'I am very glad you are with me, and we all owe a debt of gratitude to your group, which suffered greatly for our revolution, sister.'

So our unit had been remembered. I was really glad to hear her say this, as those of us who survived are not really in touch. The only one from this unit who I am still in touch with is a guy called Samir, who is now living as a refugee in Germany. It was so nice to be with someone who knew me from my actual life, instead of through lies and rumours online.

'I need sabotage, but I know you have held a sniper rifle as well. Are you looking for an opportunity?' She laughed, and so did I: that's not an opportunity. Due to the weight of the kit that you need to carry for both these roles, that is a death-sentence, an invitation to die for the great revolution. On the frontline in the YPJ it is common to joke sometimes about the demands our commanders make on us, and so we developed this weird relationship where we were comrades, but *heval* Leyla was, essentially, my commander. Dying gloriously for the revolution against *Daesh* is one thing, but dying from exhaustion from lugging kit around is another entirely. I was very thin back then, as well, because the anxiety caused by the trolling made my appetite disappear; but nothing gets an appetite back like being on the frontline.

Leyla and I went to the car together and I met our incredibly cute driver, who I discovered, quite quickly, was spoken for, and *heval* Mijdar, our little explosives squirrel. Mijdar had just graduated from her training and was incredibly keen to get out and show us what she could do, but at seventeen and fresh out of Derek, she was to learn on the job first, under Leyla and with me.

She was not happy about this at all. 'How would you know how to make bombs?' she would tease me. 'Europeans can't make bombs.' Mijdar liked to state her wild theories on the world as solid fact, and mistook me for some idiot international volunteer, but I liked her immediately. She was funny and smart and committed to learning, and so keen. She said exactly what she thought – there was no filter and no self-consciousness. She was so refreshingly optimistic and energetic. She would squirrel around looking for mines like an acrobat walking a tightrope. She was really good at what she did. As long as she could be near the bombs, she would do anything to help. She reminded me of myself.

'At least give me a chance to fuck up, before I get all this. You can't say this chocolate isn't good, when you haven't even tasted it,' I told her that first time we met, while offering my chocolate bar to her, and she took it. Our friendship started well, I thought.

Our driver, Qatai, was quite simply beautiful: light-brown hair, perfect small nose, hazel-green eyes and delicate lips, like he was wearing lipstick. A picture. He and Leyla had a special thing going on, which I never snitched about, but they were eventually discovered. Qatai was twenty-five and was our driver in the anti-terror unit, so they weren't in the same battalion, but even so, this was not allowed. Leyla was sent to prison in the mountains for three weeks, and Qatai eventually managed to get up there to see her. He wasn't punished, but he was responsible for her punishment, and the way they treated Leyla made him question the movement. Up in the mountain camp in Iraq he begged her to run away with him and leave the YPJ, but she refused. She loved the movement too much: YPJ fighters don't leave. She did her time, was forgiven and released back to the frontline, where she, like thousands of other girls like her – and younger – was killed.

Qatai works as a waiter in Erbil now, or so I heard. I didn't care if they were in love, I just thought: Good for them. I don't agree that it was a failure on my part to report them. I was just back from the *Peshmerga*, where fighters have an actual life and, rather than making people bad fighters, a relationship actually motivates them. I understand why Leyla came back to the movement, of course; it was her life. It was the place she discovered who she was and who she wanted to be, as a woman and as a person. She chose as she was trained to: public justice over private happiness.

I know that feeling; in the YPJ we say let a man go, again and again, and we fight for equality between the sexes.

The sniper group I was placed with was named after a famous sniper called Herdem Musa, who was from the Iranian part of Kurdistan, like me. He was a solo fighter, trained in the special forces, and he killed at least 149 *Daesh* in Kobani alone. In Rojava there are two kinds of fighters: IOD and non-IOD. IOD means you belong to a commander, and non-IOD means you belong to a group. Our sniper group was autonomous, so we didn't belong to a group directly (non-IOD), but we did belong to a commander (IOD). Our sabotage unit was under Leyla's command, and she reported to a YPG and another YPJ commander. I was in both units; first in a sabotage unit, and then later in a sniper unit.

We travelled to the main sabotage house where all of the units like us were operating from. It was an old mill and bakery, with lots of shelves for ovens and long assembly-line tables. This sabotage house was our sleeping quarters, and also where some girls from other roving units were based. When I arrived someone had made popcorn, and the older YPG guys were distributing it around. In one of the rooms of the factory, explosives and electronics were made by our engineers. We disassemble weapons and munitions to learn who made them and how they were made. Leyla and I, instead of getting an early night, spent the evening surveying the remnants of old explosives that were on display in one of the workspaces. We stayed up late that first night, trying to learn the different names of the substances we found and talking about the women's revolution. It's kind of weird, because when you train to be a saboteur, you learn a collection of words: Russian, English and sometimes German.

Before we bedded down, Leyla showed me her sniper rifle. 'Are you a sniper?' I asked.

'No, Joanna, I was given this for you.'

I had pranced over to the gun to have a look at it, and grabbed it from her. 'I'm not a trained sniper,' I said. 'I had some training in Derek, and I have done some practising in Denmark. I wasn't a sniper in Kobani, though I was using a sniper rifle at times.' I needed to be clear about my level of ability: the rifle was a good weapon and I needed to make sure I deserved it, and that it wouldn't be more useful in different hands. 'I haven't done the sniper training from the mountains,' I said.

'But you have been using a sniper rifle?'

'Yes.'

'Do you want to be a sniper here?'

'Do you not want me to be a saboteur?'

'I do. I want you to be both a sniper and a saboteur.' So her joke earlier was nothing of the sort.

'So I have a normal rifle when I am out with the unit, as well as this one?' Normally when you are a saboteur, you will carry a smaller gun, not a sniper rifle.

Leyla looked at me, and I felt annoyed I was so thin. 'It's going to be hard for you.'

'Hard? Impossible, you mean.'

She looked at me and laughed. 'Joanna, nothing is impossible.' This was what Leyla was like.

That night we slept in our clothes near each other under the quilt. I was new and I was trying to impress Leyla, so the next morning I was up early to see where we were going that day.

We were going to start building small munitions, and after

takmil we drove to where the electrical engineers were: the guys who make the circuit boards and the wiring of the bombs, but don't do the chemicals. It was me, Mijdar and a few others. These electrical engineers are our senior experts. They basically make the device that is the trigger for the explosions, while we do the easier end-part of adding the chemicals to make them actually explode. Leyla had to test my level of skill, so I had to make a device capable of destroying a small animal, then a bigger animal and then eventually a large car, using three different techniques. I am aware that this is not common knowledge or experience and therefore I will be brief with the details, so the authorities cannot accuse me of trying to be a threat to society. The experts are on hand to help with basic explosive-making, though they are normally involved in their own larger projects. If you want to learn a new kind of trigger, they can help you, as they build all the explosive components in our munitions. They also did classes about the best ways to hide IED bombs, and there was some learning from things that had gone wrong before.

We stayed at the house all day as a team, with Mijdar bitching and moaning the whole time that we should be on the frontline. It was dark when we left to get back to our base, and there were only certain roads that were clear to go on, as not all of them in our area were cleared of *Daesh* at this point. We were at Belkan in Kobani, pushing forward towards Sarrin, closer to Manbij. Our driver, Qatai, hadn't been paying enough attention to our route, so there was some concern as to whether we were on the right road. Mijdar and I immediately assumed that this was a basic part of his task and that he had failed in his duty to carry it out, so we teased him. 'You all have eyes yourself,' Qatai said defensively.

Leyla took his side, which alerted me to their relationship, as Qatai was definitely in the wrong. In the YPJ we instinctively take each other's side in disputes, so Leyla not doing so raised my initial suspicions. We didn't have reception on our phones, just the GPS in the car, which we were trying to link to the instructions on the radio. We came to this roundabout and none of us could remember if we took the third or fourth road; none of us knew the area, as it was an Arab area newly liberated, and clearly Qatai hadn't been paying careful enough attention. There was a petrol station that I had noticed on the way down, which I thought I could see around a corner in the distance, so eventually I suggested that we took this road, and thankfully we were correct.

Back at the main house we cooked, cleaned up and went to bed. Mijdar hated any of the food or kitchen duties, but I quite enjoyed them: cooking nice food for my friends, waiting for them to come back. I spent the next day helping around the house and getting to know some of the others there. The following day we were due to deliver some munitions to one of the *haraketli* forward-fighting units that rove the front. These guys push forward in tactical assault units, killing *Daesh* and clearing areas of mines. That night when I was cooking I thought of my very first few days in Kobani, and of my kitchen-duty day there. We had no new supplies, so I had helped prepare bread and the last of the potatoes. I wasn't at the front the first day and had spent the time cooking this huge feast, but two friends died that day, so in the end no one was really hungry. The food ended up lasting us a few more days – some people even kept the bread for the remainder of the week. In Manbij we had food at least, and logistical support. The airstrikes that the commanders ordered in were instantaneous, and brave special-forces soldiers from all over the world were there with us.

Next day we went to Serê Kaniyê (Ras al-Ayn), and I thought of Lewant, who had died there almost two years earlier. That beautiful man, who died for his beliefs. I have too many friends who have died, and this final time being back in Syria I saw them everywhere. I have a huge hole inside me where I store all my dead friends. I keep them in this dark and silent place.

I met a commander called Sozan, who had short hair like Rihanna in her 'Umbrella' stage and wore her uniform tighter than usual, which we are not strictly allowed to do, although many of us do. She was another commander who was seemingly obsessed with Hello Kitty, which continues to have a big following in Iraq.

We spent time there sourcing the chemical compounds we needed for the munitions that we had picked up the day before. Sozan had lost her arm and the vision in one of her eyes during combat, so she focused on this kind of operational support. Her job was to make sure we had the right chemicals, and the array of munitions to drop with the frontline *haraketli* units that they needed, and to funnel through some explosives to one of the main factories. We were organizing some of the chemicals, to begin taping them up into munitions, and Sozan started to sing with the other girls. She had a beautiful voice so I recorded them on my phone. YPJ girls don't tend to have phones, but somehow I had kept mine on my way through. It seemed to be the only privilege I shared with the international volunteers, but then this was my third time travelling to join the conflict. The song was about Abdullah Ocalan – about a girl who wanders over the mountains of Kurdistan looking for our leader, but finding him nowhere:

> *I am looking with my eyes*
> *From mountain to mountain I am looking,*
> *My eyes don't see you,*
> *My dear leader, my eyes don't see you.*
> *You are in prison, my leader, so I don't see you.*
> *I send you greetings to Imrali prison.*

Once we had our munitions built, we had to carry them with us safely. I also had to carry around a bag of cleaning utensils for the sniper rifle, and my own small kit bag. We were going to deliver the explosives that we had made to another group on the front, who needed help. To get there we had to drive to a junction where a big fight was going on, get out of the car and run, one by one, across the street into our frontline house.

Our driver got out of the car when we got near, and all the car doors were opened to provide protection as we got closer, in case *Daesh* had seen us coming – which they surely would have – so that we could all jump out and go on foot. Another *heval* jumped into our car and we were helped out. There was a collection of houses: we had two guys to our right, who were snipers and whose position we did not want to give away; and then about thirty fighters occupying a row of five houses facing an old school and a shop where *Daesh* were. They also occupied a high position several houses further back, and more territory behind them. This is it, I thought, I'm back. I couldn't carry the bag with explosives, along with my sniper rifle, the chemicals for cleaning it, and the bullets – we were using the PKM bullets again, and we had to oil them so that they didn't explode halfway up the barrel and blow our arms off.

Qatai took the bag from me; he was in the anti-terror unit, so he had been trained in sabotage logistics – if not in how to actually make them. He needed to shoot from the roof, and so we rolled towards where the roadblocks began and got out, greeted our *hevals* and ran over the road. Mijdar ran first, as ever. She was gone before the car's engine had barely stopped. After Mijdar, Qatai ran next; and the plan was for me and finally Leyla to arrive last. Some other *hevals* then decided to cross with us as well. I think they were shooting from a car, but decided to come inside – maybe they needed a break or more ammo. One of these guys, Shervan, I had known when he was in Rojava, but before he was a full YPG member.

A guy from his unit ran over before me and got shot in his leg, but he kept running, so he was okay – or at least he would be. It was my turn next, and I sprinted over before more firing began. We entered the house and I saw a girl called Rozan, whom I knew from Derek. She was part of the group of girls who was annoyed that I kept leaving and coming back and was mad that I wasn't living with them and pledging to stay for ever. She is from Turkey, with very beautiful green eyes and brown hair. She was now stationed with one of the *haraketli* units, meaning she is a complete badass.

In her unit was an international guy who took the name of Militan. I knew by looking at him that he wasn't Kurdish, so I spoke to him in English, but he didn't speak English very well.

Militan had been with the French Foreign Legion and was the only international in his unit, which he said he preferred. He admired my sniper rifle, but then Rozan called me and Leyla to the room where Mijdar was already firing from the window. Hazan, who was the commander of the sniper units in that area, came to look at my rifle and asked me about my role. 'I'm a sniper, but I am based in the sabotage unit,' I said. I looked at him and couldn't help noticing that he had an injury. 'Were you in the battle of Kobani? Did you lose your hand there?'

'Yes. How do you know?'

'I heard on the radio; we heard you call for help over one of the radio channels in our unit. You were calling for help, and you were told to shoot, but you couldn't because you had lost your arm. You were very calm in battle, *heval*.' That was me and Hazan friends now.

We shuffled back from the frontline into the different yards and buildings that made up this spot. The house was filthy, and in chaos. The commander had just been killed and three fighters from this *haraketli* had been mistakenly killed in an airstrike while out on an unofficial mission, probably to get food. They weren't supposed to be out, so our commanders called in the strikes, because they were located somewhere very different from us and had no idea who was missing or why they had been forced to leave their spot.

Logistics hadn't been to the house in over two weeks, though some food was being sent in with people like us delivering munitions. But they managed to get us in; we made bombs, taped them up, wired them and brought them in. That's complicated work. Surely someone could have organized for a little bit of bread and some meat and vegetables to be delivered, too? In Manbij there was food – but only in the base houses, and never enough on the actual front. The YPG never managed to get this aspect of fighting sorted.

Conditions in general as a sabotage unit were good; our car was always full of food and water. As a *haraketli*, though, officially you don't get fed – you go through the special-forces training, and then go and live your life like this. It takes many years of training to be a *haraketli*, but because of the ferocity of the war with *Daesh*, some fighters without full training were also there, and the necessary logistics to sustain these less well-trained fighters never materialized.

Everyone wants to join *haraketli* – and the more friends you lose, the more you want to. You get to kill a lot of *Daesh* this way, but also of course you get into a lot of major fights. We went to have some tea, and met a few more *hevals* having a break. It was the first time I had met the SDF, and the Arab guys would call me Iranian, which annoyed me. The guys who came in with us were supposed to be rotating out the unit that was currently on the spot, but they were refusing to go until *Daesh* was cleared from the nearest building across the street – the school. About twelve *Daesh* were holding it, we suspected. Not a huge number for the size of the building, but more than usual. We were hoping it was a munitions factory or weapon store, which we needed, as there were a lot of political moves between Turkey and the USA that were depriving us of vital supplies. We knew that *Daesh* still had good weapons, having relieved them of several arms hauls by this stage.

The buildings behind the school were more densely populated, and then behind them, some were occupied by families. There were still civilians in Manbij; you may not have heard much about them on the news, but they were everywhere and many of them died.

Rozan gave us the briefing on the commander who had died, from an RPG. So *Daesh* were using them again. Using an RPG in the close-proximity areas we fought across is like dropping a bomb when you want to catch a fish. This time, however, we had airstrikes, though no one in this unit was feeling too positive about them that particular evening.

I went back to the front to find Mijdar, and discovered that around fourteen of our fighters were firing from the same position that the RPG had landed near, across two different rooms. 'Why are we still shooting here, when this position had been compromised?' I asked Rozan.

I said 'we' instead of 'you' deliberately. In our movement, we accept our faults and our flaws together, so we use the collective noun to describe this shared experience. It was my way of tactfully telling them they were being idiots. You never shoot or eat from a position where there has been previous incoming fire – you are setting yourself up for an ambush. You learn this on the first day of training. The way I learned, you move every time you have been recognized. You shoot and move; the enemy can't be allowed to track you. You have to be like a ghost in their midst.

'Leyla, is there another group we can give the munitions to? They won't be used here, as these guys are shooting directly at them. They even knew where we were crossing the street.'

Leyla called in Rozan and Hazan and spoke to them from a position of de facto leadership, as she was the highest-ranking commander on the front. Militan, the international fighter, was clearly impressed by her. 'This is not a *Rambo* film: what is going on here, *heval*?' Leyla asked. 'One mistake here and we all die, *hevals* – and this is a mistake. We need to move our spot.'

Hazan had been in Kobani four times kicking out *Daesh*, and I felt reassured that he was here, but I gave him the same hell as Leyla did, for their stupid spot.

A few of the Arab guys gathered around as Leyla was speaking, and I stepped back and took her in. I was so proud to be wearing the same uniform as her. She was so eloquent and gentle, yet she commanded complete respect. Having different cultures in our midst has always been something I love about the movement, and it was better than being surrounded by people who speak Turkish, which I still don't like. It was nice talking and joking with them. When you are with a stranger on the frontline, you are not strangers for long. That is another reason why it's important that we don't have romantic relationships.

Leyla had a bad leg from a previous injury, so she stayed back and we cleaned and oiled bullets for the SDF riles, polishing the same ones that we use for the PKM. Further back we had seen the sleeping quarters, where I assumed we were going to bed down at some point, as there was supposed to be a rotation going on, but so far everyone was refusing to leave. I gestured to a bed that I thought looked cosy and quiet for myself and Leyla, but she shook her head, so I knew we were going to be leaving that same night. Great, so I had to leave our munitions with these guys, who were about to be blown to smithereens any second now.

I spent some time talking with Militan; he wasn't rotating off, though I thought he should be. Militan was in love with our ideology and had spent a long time learning about the revolution. His Kurdish was good, and he said he thought our unit was more professional than his, which I had to agree with. At that time in Manbij, as elsewhere, *haraketli* were full of young people getting killed, and Militan was just recovering from the shock of his commander being killed, so we talked late into the evening.

We divided the food we had brought with us – bread, meat and cheese – and didn't take any ourselves. Our plan was to get back to our base, where there was plenty of food. The kitchen was disgusting, so I tidied it up and tried to clean it a little. Militan was teasing me for being an outsider, but he had a gentle way of speaking that I liked. Qatai still had our bag of munitions and had disappeared; we later learned that he went to take the guy who was shot ahead of me to one of the mobile health clinics run by the Americans. We were to make our way back to base, taking with us the mines, which they had deactivated to be inspected. Mijdar went first across the road again, and one of the SDF guys who was coming off the front drove, while a few more piled into the back with us. We returned to the main base, dropped the stuff with Rozan and went back to our sabotage unit's house to sleep.

Before bed we had tea and bread with cheese. Leyla and I were furious with Qatai for disappearing with our munitions bags; we hadn't managed to leave it where we were. 'Remember: any mistake on the frontline can kill. That bag has enough chemicals to kill a hundred people. We need to find out where it is – and fast.' We found out later that Qatai had made a simple mistake, but we couldn't understand why he didn't bring the bag back and present it to us. He had only two years of training in the mountains before he was sent out to battle after battle after battle, and by this stage he was tired of it. I didn't know this at the time, but it makes sense to me now that I do. He became really upset when Leyla and I shouted at him, storming out of the room dramatically and saying, 'I can't take this any more.'

When he apologized properly to Leyla, Qatai took her hand in his and kissed it and stroked it. They knew I could see them, yet they were brazen in their affection for each other: and my suspicions were confirmed. I knew it was not the first time he had held Leyla's hand. Qatai was on our base, in the boys' house, and he stayed up late with us after the apology, as we were all talking about ideology. We discussed the revolution and the war, and the differences between the job we were doing on the front and the job our commanders and the instigators of the revolution were doing from their safe distance in the mountains. Different people respond in different ways to the pressure of the frontline. Mijdar was very quiet while on the frontline, scurrying around, watching and being helpful – but when she was off the frontline she was more outgoing, always laughing and talking. Leyla had seen many battles and she was calm and collected; her face was fixed into a curious half-smile, half-frown, as if she couldn't quite decide how she felt.

Although Qatai had been involved in our movement for only a short time, he had impressed in his early trainings to the extent that he was promoted early, and was allowed to train at different mountain academies with some of our best commanders. But he couldn't take criticism, and criticism is an essential part of our movement; we learn from this kind of instruction. His explanation for what happened to the munitions bag wasn't good enough, and we told him that. 'Qatai,' I said, 'you could have got some of the other nine guys to drive the man to the hospital: we missed our mission, which was to deliver munitions as well as ammunition. We only delivered ammunition. Maybe we saved one friend's life, but we could have killed more of us.' Mijdar didn't say anything, but I could see that she was suspicious.

We went to bed and, as we were going to sleep, I whispered into Leyla's ear that I thought she needed to be careful with Qatai. 'It's obvious to me – and I have only just got here,' I said gently. She stiffened by my side and denied their relationship, so I just told her not to worry and we went to sleep.

The next day we were told to pack for our next mission: delivering munitions to a *haraketli* base on the other side of the city, where heavy fighting was still going on. On these journeys my mind was always on our explosives, where we were going and what we were going to encounter, so I don't remember every place we went. We prepared some food and took some sandwiches from the kitchen area; I decided to take a few extra, just in case we ran into the same kind of situation we had encountered a few days earlier.

We travelled towards the front, past the US Special Forces medical tent that helped us unofficially, past their forward positions and towards the house we were heading to. It was on another big corner, with a roundabout in the middle and at least three *Daesh* positions. We drove from behind our frontline, so *Daesh* were at our eleven o'clock, one o'clock and two o'clock positions. We weren't exactly surrounded, but their vantage point gave them a slight advantage over us. Our frontline was deep, though, and as we approached the area there were roadblocks and different barricades.

We came towards the roundabout and needed to go left, so we parked the car behind another van and made to go out. 'Get back inside!' a guy with a PKM gun said, as a bullet ricocheted past his head. We don't wear armour, we fight light; he didn't flinch, but I ducked my head rather dramatically, which briefly amused the others. We fired our PKM gun at them, and between our fronts there were a huge number of explosions. As we were in the car, a YPJ fighter hissed from the house on the left of us to get over and get in – now. I had the extra food in my bag, and my munitions bag firmly attached this time; everything was so heavy, but it was better than risking losing them again. We waited to hear if *Daesh* was going to return fire from nearby, and when they didn't, we ran across to the house. It was another scene from *Rambo*: about twenty-four people firing from the same line, clearly being seen by *Daesh*. One RPG and we would lose half of them, at least. Some of the fighters in Manbij didn't have much experience, which made me worried. I was really anxious not to do anything that endangered the lives of my friends, but many of the commanders were not as experienced as I expected.

The commanders had all got younger; in Kobani they were in their forties, whereas in Aleppo they had been in their fifties and sixties. Syrian Kurds – those who joined the revolution in Rojava – tend to die quite quickly in battle. Sniper training in Rojava only lasts around eight weeks, whereas in the Kurdish mountains it lasts six months. I took some sniper and general-shooting training in Denmark, which helped my practice, but you have to remember as well that I have been a hunter since I was child, hunting mammals of all descriptions. I was more focused initially on being in the sabotage unit than on being a sniper at Rojava, as I could see the sniper training was not complex, whereas the chemistry of making explosives is a wonder.

We got inside the house, and the smell of sweat hit me. All those bodies together, passing ammunition and helping each other, fighting to stay alive. I love that smell, because to me it smells like love. We are all fighting together and having an impact immediately. But I was also furious, when I entered, at the shooting formation and positions of the spots, so I went with Leyla to find the YPJ commander. Qatai and Mijdar eagerly joined the group near the windows, but Leyla and I went out the back. Leyla had to stay out of direct battle, as far as she could, because she was already injured in the leg and we needed her to stay safe. She was the best commander I have had, and I don't think I can tell you how much I loved this girl. She was also one of the few sabotage commanders we actually had left at this point.

It was absolute chaos in the room; I went to the back to organize my gun and begin to get ready, as Leyla and the commander talked. *Daesh* were using RPGs in Kobani, and we had learned that here we had to shoot and move: no crowds bigger than three per spot was the absolute rule. The problem with the rules is that the vast majority of people who make them aren't actually on the frontline; they are on phones or radios giving their updates. I found Mijdar and told her we needed to move down to another position.

I went behind a corner, near Leyla, and asked about knocking into the room next door. I couldn't see Militan, but I saw some of his other *haraketli* unit, so I was wondering why he was not there, but I thought the commanders probably wanted to keep the foreigner out of this suicide mission. No such luck for me,

I thought glumly, as I focused my scope and fired in the same direction as my friends. I put my head down to change the magazine, and Leyla came over and told me we were going to take the explosives to another house in the area.

'Where is the house?'

'Close by, sister,' she said with her mischievous half-grin again. We went back towards the kitchen, where my munitions bag was stacked. 'We will go in camouflage, to get nearer their positions.' The commander of the *harakatli* unit, the YPJ commander, said no, we weren't authorized to do this: *Daesh* were everywhere and we couldn't count on civilians being spared by them. Her YPG commander, who was about twenty-six, agreed, but Leyla was having none of it and pulled rank pretty bluntly. 'You follow our orders. We are sabotage, part of anti-terror; you are *haraketli*.'

Our house was connected to several others, so we went next door to see what we could find. There were already holes made in the walls, so someone had obviously been in looking for food. Some of the houses had been turned into de facto halls or sleeping areas, whereas others still had all their furniture exactly as it had been left. Leyla and I went into a bedroom to find clothes to wear over our uniforms for our mission. We each found an old *abaya* and threw them on. I also went into a bathroom in one of the houses and grabbed some of the make-up in the bathroom cabinet – someone had already been in for the painkillers. I still have the mascara from that house, and the scarf I wrapped over my head.

We went back to the main room and Qatai showed us the best route to take, so we scoped it out before changing into our clothes. We were working our way down the street of houses we were in, and would go out after five houses, then cross the road past a *Daesh* position and end up on the other side. We were disguised as covered women. Slowly we made our way through the houses. I only took a few magazines with me, and we carried our bag of munitions together between us, as if it was shopping, stuffing the top with plastic bags. We got through to the last house, beside the courtyard we were due to enter so we could go into the street from a different angle.

Here we met *heval* Amani, a commander who wanted to come with us to cover us from potential attack. He had been in position for a long time; he was a sniper, but was not one of those who goes behind enemy lines. I could see that he was exhausted; his eyes were red and bloodshot. He had been on guard duty every night for the past five days, but because the frontline he was stationed at was so hot, every night some kind of incident happened. He said he would come with us to provide cover, as his spot had been guarding the route we were due to take, but from his three o'clock angle – not the way we had planned it. He went back to the furthest house to get more ammunition, and we were waiting in the third house along when a volley of shots came towards our spot, just where he was heading. We immediately ducked into position beside the window and responded, Leyla and I still in our camouflage gear.

Amani had been shot and was screaming, so a few of the YPG guys went to get him. He had been shot in one leg, and was able to hobble with the other. He must have been shot by a sniper, because the opening was big. There are two ways to get shot in the leg: fairly minor or disastrously. His was the second, I think, because the blood was everywhere. They carried him to one of the cars under the hail of bullets and he was shot again; I'm not sure if this is where the big wound in his groin came from, or if it was just a flesh wound elsewhere, but there was blood everywhere. We all ran out to take him to the hospital, with Leyla grabbing Mijdar by the hair from her position in the second room, where she had remained during our time there. 'You are coming now,' she said, 'you are not with this group.'

It wasn't a good feeling to be leaving without delivering our munitions where they were most needed, but we left them in the house for the others to use at least; there were several dozen hand-grenades that should have been able to do some proper damage to *Daesh*. In our car, Qatai sped with Amani and his other friend, Ferhat, and us YPJ girls, straight to the American medical tent. It was close to the one they had on the north of Manbij at that time, which operated as a mini field-hospital.

Amani had been speaking in the car, but as the blood drained out of him, he became unresponsive. We got him out of the car and were screaming for a bed, but there were none, so the American medic just told us to lie him flat on the ground and he began CPR immediately. Amani went into cardiac arrest, I think, because next he had electric shocks to try and jolt him awake. They cut off all his clothes and he was completely naked, which is when I saw how large the hole in his leg was. It was a big bullet. There was still no sign of him waking up, and by now it was clear that he had bled out. The bullet must have hit an artery, and he had lost too much blood to survive. The American medic kept going, but we all knew Amani was gone. Ferhat was crying and saying, 'Again, again!' every time the poor American medic looked like stopping.

I walked back from the crowd a little and met a YPJ commander who was coordinating rotating the *haraketli* that we had just left off the front, for a few days of sleep and rest, and sending a new group of fighters to replace them. We sat down together, and I could see she was tired. Her radio was blaring constantly, and I thought to myself: She has never had a boyfriend, yet she is here with dying men. Leyla came by and asked me in English, 'Do you think he has a chance?'

One of the American medics turned to us: 'You speak English, great.'

We went back towards Amani, who was still lying on the ground as white as snow. 'He was going to leave,' Ferhat was saying over and over again, over the body. Apparently, Amani had finally had enough; he and a YPJ fighter were going to return to Turkey and get married.

We had some tea with Ferhat and called our commanders, to give them a report of details they may not have been clear on, and Leyla was tasked with finding this runaway bride-to-be. Ferhat knew they were planning to leave together, and who she was: a fighter from another *haraketli* unit, so of course she was sick of the war. Finally the medic had to stop his attempts to revive Amani, and his body was taken into one of the makeshift morgues, and we all went in with it. Calls went round on the radio informing everyone of his death. The American doctor asked me to get an official to sign that Amani was dead and asked me to tell everyone. I didn't want this to be my job, as he was a stranger to me. So I went to Ferhat and said, '*Heval*, your friend is dead.'

'He's not only my friend, *heval*, he is my brother.' I had guessed as much by this point, but it was painful to hear. Ferhat held

Amani's face and cried and cried, as we tried to comfort him. I later learned that they had run away together from their home in Turkey to join the movement.

While we were standing around his body, two girls from the sabotage unit fresh out of Derek pulled up in a car. Seeing their shock, Leyla took them away and gestured for me to come and help her. When someone from the academy sees the dead body of one of us on the frontline, we take them aside and make sure they are coping okay with the shock. It's a big deal the first time you see it. These girls had just turned sixteen, so it was all new for them.

We had to stick around to get all the different papers signed by the Americans, and the girl that Amani was supposed to run away with arrived with a driver. She was alone when she came, and she didn't speak to anyone as she walked with her Kalashnikov on her back. Leyla decided to take the younger girls back to the car.

Even though their relationship was not strictly permitted, in death those who love each other are given a moment alone together. Closer to the entrance, Leyla popped out of the car containing her two newbies and gently took the Kalashnikov from the girl's shoulder. The risk was that she would kill herself, or someone else. 'Sister,' Leyla cooed into her ear, 'let me hold your rifle, as you hold Amani's heart in your hands,' and the girl finally relented. She walked slowly to where his body was, and her breathing got deeper. Even though she was allowed that moment, I could see she was suddenly nervous of making a scene. When she got to his body she was overtaken by grief and wailed out in pain. Behind her, we could only watch as her shoulders convulsed and she let her sorrow overwhelm her small frame. Ferhat came towards her and they embraced, with him apologizing and apologizing. I learned later that he hadn't approved of their plans to leave, so he had been refusing to help them. It was as if we could feel the girl's pain as much as we could hear it.

The American medics offered us a hot shower before heading back to the front, but I didn't bother to take one. We were going back and I was hoping to go out on my first mission in Manbij with the sniper unit, so I wanted to keep the smell of nature and our surroundings on me. We travelled in silence in the car – just our unit and the two younger girls heading back to bed down for the night.

CHAPTER FIFTEEN

Munitions and Mind-Games

After Amani was killed, I went back in the car with Leyla and the new girls, who were still in shock. It was too late to travel to our sabotage base, because the area was too isolated, and to the west we were still repelling attacks. The threat of ambush was too high, so we went to another bigger base for the night. In this main house there was internet, so I went online and posted a picture of what had happened to my growing number of followers. That night we cooked some kebabs over the fire, and the others slowly started joking and laughing again.

When someone dies, we try to continue as if nothing has happened; we know the score, so we don't spend time mourning, when we ourselves are so close to death. I put Amani in that place where I put all my dead friends, deep inside me, not thinking of how or when they would come back to me. If you think about death too much, it overtakes you and you end up dead yourself. We had our delicious blackberry tea, and someone had Arden cigarettes from Qatar, which were shared around after the hot food. We slept together up on the roof of the house: the guys on one side and us girls on the other. I just wish I could sleep as soundly in the peace of Copenhagen as I did in chaos of Manbij.

The next day, after our early *takmil*, we returned to our sabotage base, taking the two newbies with us. We were informed that we were going to do some mine-clearing. It was an area that people wanted to return home to, so our job was to go round the area and make sure whatever mines *Daesh* had left were dismantled. We need to get the support of civilians immediately when we take over a town; particularly as we were fighting with Arabs and it was their area, not a Kurdish one. So part of this transition towards self-governing democratic confederalism is to clear the mines so that families can come back.

Where there is one mine, there are several, and the sophistication of the devices used by *Daesh* had increased fairly dramatically, even since Kobani. We were given the coordinates of the block we were clearing on our phone, and also an offline map. In our bag we had a variety of tools: screwdrivers, a lighter, different knives and lots of antibacterial and anti-chemical gel. You can get explosives poison on your fingers, so you have to clean your hands thoroughly with the gel, which is very cooling on your skin. Chemicals react to heat and movement, so if you have too much heat on your hands, it can trigger the explosive to combust. We wear special gloves as well, but not all the time. We tend to keep the best equipment for the younger ones, with less experience. In Manbij, Leyla and I worked without gloves on the vast majority of mine-clearings we did. This is not good practice, but we are a revolutionary army based in the mountains, not a pharmaceuticals laboratory. With mines, you have to have really good sight, and because Leyla's eye was damaged through injury, we would often work together, or she would have someone like Mijdar with her.

We arrived near our block in two cars; there were some YPG anti-terror guys with us, but Leyla, Mijdar and I were the only ones officially trained in sabotage. In missions like this, it's expected for all the *hevals* who aren't otherwise engaged to come and help out and learn. The best areas to bomb are crossroads, where artery roads join the main road, plus big infrastructural targets such as water mains or bridges, so these are the areas we have to search particularly carefully. We gather a lot of our own munitions by taking apart those that are left for us. We wandered around for a while, initially working our way very slowly through the streets and eventually through the houses.

Our area that day was mainly homes, with a few shops and hair salons. Inside a building the best bombs to use are dual devices, where one action sets off another. So by opening a door or stepping on a mat, the intended victim becomes the trigger. A YPJ girl had been killed just a few days before, when she saw an AK in one of the houses that *Daesh* had left. The act of her picking up the gun was the trigger; if she had found the lead she would have known this, but it was very cleverly hidden.

I went across the road to a group of bigger houses in a courtyard. It looked like somewhere significant, and had been lived in until very recently, so I knew it would be booby-trapped in some way and, sure enough, about a yard in front of the gate attached to the high wall, I saw the first wire. The first thing you do when you see a mine, or any kind of explosive, is follow your natural instinct: you stay back. Once at a safe distance, you have a quiet moment standing inside your fear, and taking strength from the urgency of your body's reaction. Controlled breathing helps here, and the younger ones are cute when they almost hyperventilate doing this step. Next, you become the eagle: you imagine all the fear inside you leaving your body and soaring above you, and you focus on looking at the device from that viewpoint. The eagle is the fiercest predator in the sky, not because he is the biggest, but because he is the smartest and strongest, with the most complete view. In our revolution we aim to be like the eagle, which is why our culture of *takmil* – reporting and self-criticism – is so important. We try to have a complete view of things, but this is always hard.

The next stage is to look around for any other clues and begin to make your approach. I went in a bit closer and removed some of the sand and stones from the wire, then traced it along the ground with my left hand. I was trying to see if it was a simple mine or an IED, or something more complicated connected to another device. In Kobani, *Daesh* had these elaborate daisy-chain mines that would trip a whole series of explosives with one trigger. The trigger would go off when you deactivated one device; we call this 'the fooler', as it makes you believe you are deactivating, but actually you are causing a much bigger explosion by becoming the trigger yourself.

The lead wasn't long, so it brought me to a box device very quickly. This immediately made me suspicious; this is what often happens with a fooler. There are normally two wires on an explosive; I learned them as red and blue, but that refers more to their qualities – they can be any colour of wire, and often are. Normally you are able to see both wires. This one only had a blue lead, which meant they were trying to trick me into believing this was the one to deactivate, when in fact it was probably the trigger.

I went closer and closer, and dug into the sand around the space where the device was. After carefully removing sand and stones with my hands, I could see a small grey box. Qatai was sulking around, and I shouted over to him gently that I thought I had found something, so not to come too close. 'We haven't seen any around where we are,' he replied, which made me even more suspicious of what I was dealing with.

Defusing munitions is like untangling an old necklace; you have to work backwards and exactly undo each knot and crease that has occurred. It's infuriating but totally engrossing, as you are trying to get inside your enemy's head, to outsmart them. It's quite different from shooting a gun, and the stakes are much higher as well; if I mess up a shot, I miss killing a *Daesh* fighter, but if I get the wrong lead, then there is a fairly high chance I will kill all of my friends. I sat down beside the explosive for a while and told Qatai to keep a watch, as I slowly dug around the sides of the device, looking for the trigger. I followed the wire out of the box to see where it was going: it entered the courtyard and went all round the room and through a wall in the courtyard that entered a smaller quad.

It was a long lead, it had been looped around a variety of different things in the courtyard and I couldn't see where it ended. There was a water tank near the further point of the lead, so it was an elaborately looped device. Normally we would shoot the mines from a distance, but this time I didn't want to do that, because if it was a fooler, then it could have exploded anywhere and everywhere. I had no idea what damage it could potentially do. I started digging down, to get to the bottom of the device, as a small crowd gathered behind me; Mijdar and Leyla were looking for mines elsewhere. Someone called Leyla over to me, but as she was round the corner she didn't hear. 'She's found one here,' one of the others called to her.

'Sshh. Don't say that yet. I'm not sure.'

'It must be: most of the other houses are clean,' was the reply. As I was clearing around the edges of the rectangle, I finally saw what I suspected: it was a fooler and the real device, a long, circular battery, was tucked beneath. I stood back again and observed this new device, before refocusing my breath to calm down, and slowly going in closer. By this stage a small crowd had gathered, and Leyla came up behind me. 'You have found a big one, you are a good hunter,' one of the *hevals* called out.

'I haven't deactivated it yet,' I responded, more than a little nervous of the task ahead.

Leyla came up behind me and patted my shoulder very gently. I could see she wasn't too concerned herself. 'Well done, keep going,' she said, raising her eyebrows and smiling, like it was nothing.

I had to cut the lead that linked the smaller fooler to the bigger bomb: this was the lead I couldn't find, when I was initially looking for the defuser wire. I was pretty certain it was the right lead to cut, but I told everyone to go away and stand back before doing so, in case I got it wrong. It was only one choice I had to make, but it was a big one. I took the chance, and thankfully nothing blew.

I moved back again and prepared for the next stage: taking the fooler away and deactivating the bigger explosive. I couldn't figure out where the trigger was, so after I cut the lead I unscrewed the top of the device; inside it was full of bits of shrapnel: old nails but no chemicals, and still no sign of the trigger. You have to think everything through very clearly, so I was asking myself the questions about the decisions the bomb-maker had made: What materials would he have had? Why would he use this material instead of another one?

Sabotage is completely fascinating; it's not the same as the thrill of sniping, and what's hard is that you end up respecting your enemy, or his mind at least. In our movement we have a lot of excellently trained saboteurs, and many different people with different specialisms. We work with highly dangerous materials, including nerve gas and chemical bombs. The better you are with chemicals and munitions, the more money you can demand from all around the world. And it can be significant amounts of money, depending on who is paying.

I took my chances and cut the lead that was connecting the bigger box to the smaller one that I had been removing shrapnel from, and then cut into the top of the real explosive to try and find out what was going on. You need to see every detail of a bomb and its circuits to understand how it works. And you have to be 100 per cent sure of every move. But the hardest thing I find in this situation is to take my time; once you have the bomb, you are halfway to deactivating it. It's not like a Bond film, where you have to cut the red lead by the time the clock ticks down. I didn't see any bombs with timers in Manbij, or anywhere else in Syria, as far as I remember. There is no rush, apart from the panic you are feeling by being in such proximity to it. The trick is to try and stay calm while this is happening. So I was slowly opening the fooler bomb and removing some of the little pieces of metal, and digging into the sides of the earth where the barrel of the main explosive was. I had the fooler bomb open, with the shrapnel exposed, and was cutting into the sides of the other device, when Leyla slowly approached. We sat together for a few moments, examining what was going on. 'Don't stress, Joanna. Just use your gut,' she told me. I put my torch into the hole I had made in the bigger bomb, to look around; still no chemicals.

I hadn't attempted to move the fooler yet, but I wasn't aware it was still attached. I dug deeper into the side so that I could see better, and held the torch in my mouth as I looked around to identify the different materials. There was some white powder directly under the fooler – an explosive that has a texture like sugar and water. It makes the explosion last longer, and it keeps the fire going after the explosion. I looked up and saw the trigger, finally, and the torch nearly dropped out of my mouth. The weight from the shrapnel of the fooler bomb was what was holding the trigger in place: it was being pushed down, and as I was taking the shrapnel off, the trigger was slowly rising. The bomb underneath was longer and deep, but thin, while the top bomb was a grey square box. It had risen about two or three inches – two or three more and everything would evaporate around me. By defusing the first, I had inadvertently (and slowly and carefully) been detonating the second. Fuck this, I thought. I needed help.

I decided to dig deeper into the hole to see the full depth of the bigger bomb, and to take both of the explosives – the fooler that was acting as the detonator, and the main explosive itself – back to our base. I needed some expert assistance to fully dismantle it, and it's fairly common in complicated cases like this to take the bombs back to our lab – or our bakery, as it was in this case. I put my sand gloves on; I find it easier to cut without them and hadn't been wearing them, but when I told Leyla of my plan, she smiled, raised her eyebrows in that funny way she did and told me to put them back on. I slowly dug out all around the bomb – and now I knew where the trigger wires were – then confidently clipped the other leads protruding from the bottom. I put my hands beneath it and showed Leyla the trigger.

'That was close,' was all she said. 'You need to put more weight on it, because the trigger is wobbly now,' she suggested. So I did, because I wasn't sure how to dismantle the bomb: this kind of weighted trigger was not something I had seen before. I needed to take it to one of our anti-terror vehicles. We make these cars from different materials: if we are lucky, it's a tank we have captured, but more often it's a van or a car reinforced with steel, so that if the bomb explodes, the explosion stays quite localized. Because the cars are reinforced and have no windows, travelling in them is like being inside an oven.

The roads in Rojava are flat, which is good for the cars, but they are full of potholes. Leyla brought a cool-bag and set it down beside me, and I carefully lifted the two explosives and placed them inside. I then placed a concrete block on top of the grey rectangular box. As we finished placing the concrete block, Leyla saw how far the trigger had come up.

And it could still rise further, I thought, though I didn't say that. I walked as carefully as possible, with the cool-bag in my hands, until we got to the car. One of the anti-terror guys followed behind me and insisted that he should carry it, because I hadn't been trained in how to walk with a mine, but Leyla insisted I keep it and bring it to the car. When walking with a bomb, you carry it in front of your heart, with your two arms wrapped around it. This means that should it explode, you die quickly and your body takes the full weight of the blast so it doesn't kill so many of your friends.

Leyla and Qatai left in a car to go and fetch an armoured vehicle to transport it in, as we didn't have one with us; I began walking to where they would be meeting me, with my hands wrapped around the mine. I was walking with a few of the *hevals*, who stopped to talk to several people on our way. That's the insanity of Rojava: you become very comfortable around mines, so instead of people shying away, everyone came to try and jokingly trip me up. 'Can I hug you?' a guy I hadn't talked to previously said, and I had to try my hardest not to laugh.

The car arrived – with Leyla and Qatai alone in it – and Leyla took out some bags of flour from the bakery. Opening the cool-box, she scattered the flour everywhere to stabilize the explosive further, before we got into the car together. We had to be careful to deprive it of oxygen, so she only opened the zip a little and poured the bag of flour in through this small opening. 'Be careful,' I warned her.

'Don't stress me, Joanna,' she said, in a weird sing-song voice. She was trying to sound cheerful, but we were both nervous. My hands weren't sweating, but my head was, and I could feel sweat trickling down my lower back. Qatai drove very slowly, but would tease us by pretending to rev up the car when we went around bends, while Leyla was calling back to our base to tell them to get ready for us, and what to expect.

We arrived and our most senior trainer was waiting for us, smoking a cigarette. I never really got over how the sabotage trainers could smoke; some even did so when they were dismantling devices. Everyone was excited to see what was so special about this bomb. It was very thoughtfully, though cheaply, made. If you are a really good saboteur, you can identify where a bomb comes from and who made it, who trained them and what kind of style it is. Each bomb says a lot about the person who made it. One of the older guys took it from me to lay it out for our senior commander. It was brought into our warehouse, as everyone gathered round excitedly. 'If you want to stay, you need to get your gear on,' the guy said, but no one moved.

We have special uniforms to wear while training: just plastic bags in yellow, white or completely clear. 'Why is everyone still here for this?' I asked one of the Kurdish commanders.

'Everyone has to learn,' he snapped back.

'You should tell them to step back,' I said, as many sabotage commanders have been killed by crowding around munitions during a learning occasion such as this.

'Okay, everyone who is not a trainer or doesn't have their chemical suits on, get out,' Leyla called out, and reluctantly the crowd dispersed. The units had also found some other smaller devices, and several maps that were in Russian, which made one of the commanders speculate that our device was made by Chechens. 'They are paying someone a lot of money to make these kinds of sophisticated devices,' Leyla said, as she had not seen one like this before, despite her many years of experience in the war by this point.

We went and had some tea, as the long process of dismantling the bomb began, and eventually went to find somewhere to sleep. 'The engineer who made this device has had a lot of learning,' the sabotage commander in charge of dismantling it told us the next morning at *takmil*, and others within the unit were told to go and study it.

Everyone on the frontline responds differently to life there. Mijdar, newly trained and always busy, was quiet and focused on the front. Leyla was always in good humour and making jokes. Qatai was ready to leave by the time I met him, and every new incident would make him more furious. For me, this tour was more difficult than the previous ones; I am not sure if it was because of the trolling beforehand, the events leading up to getting to the front, or what I saw once I was there. This time there were a lot more international special forces on the ground, and the gear, facilities and supplies they brought were a revelation to us in the YPG, who fight with so little. The Americans in their medical tents in the north of the city were kind to us, they gave us food rations and let us use their facilities. They were interested in talking to me all the time, and to the other YPJ fighters, as if they had never seen a woman in combat before.

When I was rotated off the Manbij frontline, there was a training camp in Kobani that I spent some time in. I used this as an opportunity to try and get back to Aleppo. I really wanted to go back to where I had started this war. In this training camp we were listening to a recording of sniper training, from one of our commanders in the mountains. Often we use tapes to listen to specific military instructions, as well as ideological teachings. After the weapons tape, a commander put on an ideological tape that was saying how bad capitalism and Europe were. 'Why are we listening to this?' I asked the trainer. 'Why do we only look at how bad capitalism is in Europe, and not at how we are also part of a capitalist system?'

'We never talk about capitalism within us, because it doesn't exist,' one of the other *hevals* replied.

'What about your cigarettes? Where do they come from?' I responded. Everyone was listening carefully as I continued. I was aware that I was being controversial, but I wanted to say my piece. 'In Europe,' I said, lowering my tone to be less aggressive, 'we eat better food than we have here. We go to the doctor's and we have free schools and free healthcare, and we have a better life. I'm not glad about capitalism, but you can't say a capitalist society doesn't function, because it does.' The commander in charge of this training got angry with me when I said this. So I asked her a question: What do you think of, when you think of Europe?

A girl called Bercha spoke up: 'I will answer.' We need permission to speak in class. 'Europe is the co-founder of capitalism and liberalism.'

'And when you think of the Middle East?'

'The struggle and resistance against capitalism.'

I looked around the room, at these young girls and boys with their uniforms and their weapons. 'Guys, you need to stop reading one book over and over again, and just repeating what it says. If we want support from Europe, look at ourselves. Look at what we have in our hands: cigarettes, weapons. Our movement is paying money for you to kill yourself. That is the ultimate capitalism. Look at our uniforms: they are bought from America and Eastern Europe. Look at our weapons? Where did they come from? Did someone not buy them? This is capitalism. We live within it.'

My little speech didn't go down very well, but I was glad I had made it, as I have always been honest with my *hevals*.

I asked to be moved to the sniper unit, since I had already had experience during my special-forces training, as well as in Denmark, before taking part in Operation Abu Leyla, which was the name of our operation in Manbij.

I went to the headquarters for the frontline commanders in Kobani and spoke with *heval* Sozdar, along with *heval* Leyla, who confirmed that I would be picked up by fighters from the sniper unit within a week. I went back to the base, which we nicknamed the White House because it was the most luxurious of the houses we had in that area at the time, with an internet connection. I was collected the day afterwards, by two YPG fighters whom I become very good friends with: *heval* Hozan, from the original battle of Kobani, whom I had met just before Amani was killed; and *heval* Vietnam. I wasn't ready to say goodbye to Mijdar and Leyla – we were a small unit and had become very close. Leyla was later sent to an ideological academy; Qatai eventually ran away from the YPG; Mijdar was moved to another unit.

Hozan's brother was a fighter from the mountains and was killed by the Turkish planes. He was a *cadra* and a leader of the sniper unit, and Hozan is from Kobani, just twenty minutes from where we were in Manbij. He served in the Syrian army before, but like many other Syrian Kurds, he joined the YPG when the movement became armed. Vietnam had taken his codename from the war, he was a huge fan of the Vietcong guerrillas and the most down-to-earth *heval* I have ever met. Hozan and Vietnam were very close, and remain so today, because Vietnam had saved Hozan's life on the frontline, when Hozan and some others were attacked by RPGs and Vietnam killed the attacking *Daesh* with his Zagros rifle.

Our first big fight was later that same day, when I was dispatched to be with a group of SDF fighters who were pushing *Daesh* back inside the city. My spot was inside an upstairs room in a house positioned slightly forward from where the *haraketli* fighters were. I was placed so that I had to wait for the fighters to run through a small alleyway. The SDF were behind me, at my four and five o'clock positions, and they were pushing *Daesh* into my street, where I was waiting for them. When I heard the gunfight behind me, I was ready to go. I was the only sniper in this street, and the only Kurd – the rest of the SDF were Arab fighters, so we had some communication issues. There were a lot of guys in this unit I was working with, and only a few of us from the YPJ. As the fight went on, some of *Daesh* dispersed a little, so I had to wait for hours in this house until they eventually came towards where I was hidden.

My hair was bright-yellow blonde back then, so I had to be totally camouflaged on the frontline, under my scarf and under a blanket, and my focus was solely on this one street. When I am in position as a sniper, I only shoot when I am sure I have my target; because once I fire, my position will be known. Every shot has to be successful. The SDF were shooting with their M-16s or PKMs, so they could move easily, but with the sniper rifle I didn't have this freedom. I had taken my position over from another sniper, and as I was waiting for *Daesh* to appear and was looking through my scope, suddenly a group of women and children appeared in the alley that the SDF guys were clearing *Daesh* into. One of the SDF guys, noticing what was happening, started screaming at the women to come towards us. 'Come here, come here, sister,' but of course they were too afraid to trust him, so they just remained on the street, totally exposed.

Looking at our position, I could see that these civilians were about to walk into a firefight, so in a split second I made the decision that I had to do something. Before I knew it, I had dropped my sniper rifle, taken my Kalashnikov and run out of the room, downstairs and out of the building towards the group. I took the scarf off my head and started to undo my hair as I ran towards them. I needed them to see that I was a woman, and not *Daesh*, so they would come with me and get out of harm's way. One of the children noticed me first and tugged on his mother's long black *abaya*. I was shouting at them: 'Come here, sister, come towards me,' and they ran to where I was standing. As they ran, *Daesh* started shooting in our direction, and the SDF guys behind me covered us and returned their fire.

I took the women and children to a safer side street, where I had to frisk them to make sure they didn't have anything on them, as there had been many occasions when *Daesh* hid as civilians, in order to blow themselves up once they got inside our compound. One by one, I searched the women and, after I found they had no explosives on them, I searched through their stuff, carefully. They had a lot of naan bread with them, along with sugar, some money and phone-charging cables. It was clear they were trying to escape the city to become refugees. The children were in shock, and I could see they didn't know whether they were even allowed to cry in front of us. After I searched them, I took them to a safer place, behind the street I was placed on, where the others came and gave them food and water, as the women and children slowly calmed down. Two SDF guys who spoke Arabic arrived and, with these guys translating, one of the women told me that *Daesh* had taken two of her daughters. 'We are here for you, and we are fighting to rid you of *Daesh*,' I told the woman, as she thanked me and hugged me. They were taken away to our safe house, and I went back to my spot to continue.

Much later, when I got back to our main coordination house on the frontline, I met *heval* Aras and *heval* Eylem, and they told me I had just missed the group of women and children, who had now left. These women had given us some good information about life under *Daesh*, but mostly they had wanted to tell us about their missing daughters.

Being a sniper, my days were spent staked out alone, working with different teams of *haraketli* as they pushed forward. I would have a bag with me to go to the toilet in, and some small pieces of food and water to keep me going. I didn't go behind enemy lines, but was part of teams taking back streets from *Daesh*; corner by corner, and at some points house by house. Towards the end of the summer, when it was still hot, I was situated at the top of the roof of a house, working with a large team near the south of the city; we had cleared them almost to the edge of the city by this stage, but they still had many pockets in the *canton* around the city.

In the heat, we continue to drink our tea, because actually it can help your body stay cool, and this one afternoon a *heval* called Dersim from the *haraketli* came up to the roof where my spot was, to see if I wanted some tea. I was lying in camouflage, behind two small holes I had made in the wall. In Syria the roof of the building is often used as just another space to dry clothes or whatever, so they have these little brick walls around the edge to stop people falling off. The wall was big enough for me to lie prone on the ground, or to sit behind it. The area was really hot, with lots of incomings and outgoings, so we had to crouch on the roof; we were in the direct line of enemy fire. I had a blanket over me and was absolutely roasting in the heat.

When Dersim came up again, I stood up to take the tea from him and to tell him to lie down. I heard some incomings closer to my spot, so I went back down to take up my rifle and have a look through my scope at what was going on. As I was crouching down to grab my rifle, Dersim was shot as he stood, with the tea still in his hand. He fell on top of me as I was crouched down, and his weight almost flattened me. He landed on my back and pushed my head forward, as I heard my neck crack. I had to try and stop him falling over the wall, so I pushed him back as hard as I could, but in doing so, I slipped and fell from the top of the building, head first.

I was on the second storey and, due to my position, I fell as if I was diving into a pool, somersaulting through the air and landed smack-bang in the rubble below. I went out cold, and the first thing I heard when I came round was the *hevals* shouting about what had just happened. I was dazed and completely confused momentarily, and couldn't stand by myself, so some of the YPG guys came over to help me up. One of the *hevals* noticed I was bleeding from my nose and ears, and I could taste blood in my mouth. My eyes were bloodshot, and when I opened my eyes it was painful: I could see colours and shapes, but everything was fuzzy. I remember asking about Dersim, but was told the others were going for him, and to concentrate on trying to walk.

Once I was upright, with the help of a YPJ *heval* and two of the YPGs, I slowly began to feel better, but as soon as I thought I was coming round, I started to throw up everywhere. This scared me a little, as it wasn't like I had been eating much; my vomit was yellow-and-white liquid, and I was projecting it everywhere. It just didn't stop.

I couldn't think straight and just started to apologize to everyone for being so sick, but my words came out slurred, as everything around me spun. Then I passed out completely.

When I came round again, the YPJ *heval* had her fingers in my mouth and was gently calling my name: '*Heval, heval* Joanna, wake up.' I was told I was to be taken back to the coordination house, and was picked up by some of the others from the sniper team. Our commander, Hozan, had already been informed, and in the car *heval* Edessa and *heval* Serya (who is dead now, so she is one of our *shehids*) asked me if I should see a doctor. I was embarrassed in some ways, because although I knew I was in shock, I had both my legs and both my arms, so I knew I would be okay, and our medics were already overwhelmed. But I was taken off the frontline and slept in the base that night.

The next morning my friends let me sleep for longer than normal, but when they eventually tried to wake me around midday, I wouldn't wake up and I had blood coming from my ears. They decided to put me in the car and take me to the military hospital run by the YPG, and I woke up in the car on the way, feeling woozy and confused. I couldn't think at all; everything hurt. It felt like my brain was too big for my head. At the hospital they said they believed I had fractured my skull in the fall, but it's not as if they did an X-ray or a scan. One of the other *hevals* who was in sabotage offered to operate on me. Often those who are trained in sabotage – having been through the most difficult aspects of our training – offer first-aid assistance on the frontline. After examining me, his idea was to drill a hole in my head to release the pressure. Having been through the same training as him, I was alarmed at his confidence, and there was absolutely no way he was getting near me. At first I thought he was teasing me, but he was seriously wanting to do it.

I rested for about four days, and went back to the frontline as a sniper, but my skull fracture got progressively worse, and I was worried it wasn't healing as it should have done. I ignored it initially, but one symptom I noticed straight away was that I needed to sleep more, which is dangerous as a sniper. My balance was also really bad, and I was still bleeding from my ears and nose. You have to relax as much as you can, when you are sniper, but you also need to stay alert. When you spend hours in one position, eventually it will be comfortable enough to sleep, so needing to sleep all the time and having poor balance was making the job I loved unusually tough. I just wasn't myself: I was often confused and became incredibly sensitive to everything. Loud noises, bright lights, everything you could expect on the frontline – the things that normally thrilled me – became excruciatingly difficult to bear.

I was hot all the time, and the dehydration didn't help my grinding headaches. I would cook in the different layers of my uniform and all my underclothes. A few weeks after the accident I was in the coordination house when I got an email from the police in my inbox, informing me that it was almost one year since the passport ban had been imposed on me and the twelve-month time-frame was due to expire; a decision was due to be made on whether it would be extended for another year or whether it would be lifted. It looked like it was time for me to get back to Denmark.

I really didn't want to leave my friends. Manbij was over, but I wanted to go on to Aleppo – back to where I started in this war. There was a Saudi Arabian sniper in Aleppo who had publicly stated his intention to come after me. The 'ISIS fighters are easy to kill' headline from the *Vice* article haunted me on the frontline with a vengeance I could never have expected. My commanders decided that I was not allowed back to Aleppo. I'm not sure why: maybe they didn't think I would have survived this sniper. I feel most safe in the lines between good and evil, so I am fairly confident I would have survived, but I wasn't given the opportunity to find out.

When you are on the frontline you have true friends and are bonded closely together, because you are so near to death. The camaraderie you have there is like nothing else; the friendships you make are incomparable, in terms of their honesty and intimacy. You don't think about materialistic things when you are at war; you think about the things that matter: the people you are with, the future you will have, the small amounts of food you can find. I'm happy to be alive on the frontline, in a way that is hard to explain. It's a feeling of contentment, acceptance and warmth that I don't get anywhere else. It intoxicates me like nothing else in the world.

CHAPTER SIXTEEN

Aftershocks

Getting out of a war zone can be as difficult as getting into one, and recently the Iraqi *Peshmerga* – the same ones I had been with – had been arresting YPG fighters and holding them in prison for violating the terms of their KRG entry visa. Many international fighters from the YPG spent weeks in jail, and some of them even months, on their way out.

There was a hearing about my passport in Copenhagen at the beginning of September 2016 and there was no guarantee that I would get back in time, but I spoke to my commander in Karacho and asked for advice on getting back to Denmark. The fact that I was born in Iraq should have helped me exit the country smoothly, we figured, as I wasn't subject to the same visa checks as other international volunteers travelling from Europe, but it was a risk, and I wasn't looking forward to the journey. I was still in sporadic touch with R, and I knew I could be arrested, if he wanted it. His commander, I heard, was furious at the attention I had brought in Denmark to the KDP *Peshmerga* – and was particularly annoyed that I had done an interview in Denmark where I showed the card that R had made me.

The date of my passport hearing came and went, with me still abroad. It took me about ten days to travel back to Copenhagen, and I wasn't given any hassle on the Iraqi side of the border, thankfully. I arrived in Denmark a few days after my hearing, scared following a conversation with my new lawyer about how I needed to get my butt back home. I didn't tell him where I had been, as I didn't feel I needed to.

I had changed lawyers, after the failure of the first court trial, getting rid of the lawyer who also represented *Daesh*. At that time Denmark had the highest rate of returning fighters in Europe, and I knew that if my first lawyer was to do my appeal, the chances were that I would be introduced to more of them. This was not something I could afford to risk; the notoriety that I had in Syria had already been too great. Everyone had seen my social-media posts, and the media interest was still swirling around me. My Instagram follower numbers had doubled and tripled while I had been on this trip, and then doubled and tripled again.

Back in Christiania, I stayed with my friend Maria. She is ten years older than me and runs around with biker gangs, but I liked her a lot and for a few months we were close. The deal was that I would stay with her until I got myself sorted and got some money together, so that I could rent a room or an apartment of my own. We had different value systems, though, which became apparent when I started looking for a job and she suggested I work in a brothel.

'I'm a female fighter, I'm not going into a brothel,' I told her.

'You don't have to have sex – you could work the phones.'

I now had a court case against me for breaking my travel ban, but I enrolled back in school anyway, and began attending different classes and looking for a job. This was more difficult than I expected, because for the work I wanted to do – for an NGO, or similar, working in the Middle East – you need to have police checks and a perfectly 'clean' record.

Eventually I got a job in Burger King, in one of the biggest malls in Copenhagen. The manager had seen me on television and read about me online in Denmark, and also in his home country, Sweden. So I started working there and initially I really enjoyed it, just having something to do all day, where I didn't have to think about the war or my dead friends.

It was weird to be known for a part of my life that I had previously hidden, particularly as I was suddenly – and completely unexpectedly – frozen out by the Kurdish movement. I went to the Kurdish community centre to tell them what was going on with my court case, but there was a certain reluctance to help me, perhaps due to my legal troubles. I never really got to the bottom of why they have not done more to support me, and it is a question that I still need to have answered.

The court case about breaking my travel ban was pending, and the legal point I was trying to stress was that I was not part of a terror group, so I could not have the law applied to me in the same way it was applied to those who went to join *Daesh*. The issue is the YPG's ideological links to the PKK, but this time round I wasn't going to hide what I was, and who I fought for. I had fought on the frontline with people from the international coalition to defeat *Daesh*, so there was no way any court could find that I wasn't a part of this sanctioned coalition; the YPJ and the

YPG are the founding members of the SDF, which is the main partner in the international efforts to dispel *Daesh* from Syria.

The court found me guilty of breaking my travel ban, and I was jailed on 11th December 2016 for six months. Initially I was held in the Vestre Fængsel, Denmark's oldest and, I am certain, coldest prison. As I was taken into custody, I managed to keep my phone on me, as always. They searched me, but I had it in my sock, and then I placed it in a plant pot on the ground as I went to tie my shoelaces, so I managed to sneak it past them.

From my cell I called Maria and told her to expect the police round to pick up my laptop and passport, and to tidy away anything she didn't want the police to see. She promised to protect my stuff and not hand it over. I had taken my laptop with me to the front and it had a lot of video material that I didn't want them to see. Their case against me was, and remains, that I am part of a category of people who are deemed a threat to the Danish state because I have participated in the Syrian war. The law doesn't differentiate on the ideology that we fight for: the law doesn't care why I fight, it just cares that I have the capacity to do so. The material on my computer would strengthen the prosecution's case that I could cause significant harm to a target inside Europe, but 'could' and 'would' are different things. I gave Maria permission to smash up my laptop, if she needed to, and urged her to hide my passport.

I keep my court hearings closed to the media as far as I can, because the prosecution has a history of using private details of my personal history against me – my mental-health diagnosis in particular, but also painful details about why I am estranged from my family. In court, the prosecutor tried to make me seem like a threat to Denmark, and initially the judge acknowledged her position and remanded me in custody until my next hearing. The first night in prison was a shock. I was hyper with frustration, as I paced up and down the tiny cell. Why was I in prison and *Daesh* fighters were not? I saw a few guys that I recognized as jihadis inside, but mainly I was kept by myself. When my phone ran out of battery I attempted to charge it using a teabag trick I learned in the mountains, but had no luck.

I would be lying if I said my time in prison was terrible; it wasn't. I was the only female prisoner being held where I was, and I didn't see many people, barring the guards. The food wasn't amazing, but there was a lot of it. I ate three times a day and I came out of prison having finally managed to put on some weight. It might sound weird, but being in jail – difficult as it was to have my freedom taken away – actually felt like a relief. I ate, read a few books and slept loads, more than I had in a while, and got into the routine of the place. The pressures I had experienced from being online all day and reading all the horrible things people were saying about me were removed, and it did me good to relax in this way. Not that the conditions were good or the guards were kind – they weren't.

While in prison, I had a visit from the PET – the usual thing of a female officer and a man. On my file I think they have some note that I respond better to women than to men, because they always get a woman to interview me. They informed me that in Iraq it was being reported that *Daesh* had offered a $1m bounty for my head, and that I couldn't assume I was safe from their threats just because I was home in Denmark. 'Quite the opposite: our rate of returning jihadis continues to grow, Joanna,' I remember the male officer saying. Great. I knew *Daesh* were after me, and had heard rumours from Iraq and Syria when I was there, but the PET telling me this made me take the threat more seriously than I had previously. I'm not sure where their information came from, but I know they have some undercover agents inside the group. I was also informed that Maria had readily handed over my laptop and passport, despite her promises.

Around the same time, unfortunately, a member of my organization put out a statement saying that I was indeed a member of the YPJ and had, in the course of my several tours of the region, killed about 100 *Daesh* fighters. This figure has been scoffed at and I have been ridiculed, but this count is not just from my sniper kills – it is from all of my positions within the organization. I have not counted the number I have killed, and I will never confirm or discuss the toll of lives that I have taken. I'm not a psychopath; I don't take pride or pleasure in the numbers of my dead. No fighter with honour boasts of their kills, as we do not speak of these things. Once *Daesh* soldiers are killed, they become human again to me, and although I do not mourn their death, I certainly do not celebrate it or try and use it to flatter myself. This is why I'm really confused as to why my organization would reveal this information; normally this happens only after a fighter has died, and I'm not quite dead yet.

Later during my prison stay, two officers from Denmark's police ombudsman came to visit me; two women. They took me into an interview room and we had tea and biscuits, so I knew they were going to be asking me to help them. The male PET officer who had been asigned to my case was being investigated for abusing his position of power, and for entering into sexual relationships with those he was supposed to be mentoring. I nearly spat my tea out when they told me, but managed to cough and recover my calm.

They were so earnest, these two police officers, so concerned. It almost made me laugh: their absolute faith in the system, and their horror that something like this could occur. 'We realize this might be hard for you, Joanna, and we want to apologize to you sincerely, on behalf of the PET, for any mistreatment that may possibly have occurred.' I took some more tea with sugar and let them continue, as they outlined – in the vaguest possible terms – the allegations against him, which he denied, of course. 'Was he ever inappropriate towards you?'

'Define "inappropriate".' I was beginning to enjoy watching them squirm. 'Inappropriate – like dating my sister, and then forging a relationship behind my back?' They looked alarmed. I continued, 'Inappropriate – like coming into the bathroom on the thinnest excuse so he could see me naked? Inappropriate – like commenting positively on my physicality, telling me I had a good body?'

By this stage the younger woman had started taking notes. 'Did you ever report him?' the blonde one asked.

'Of course not. To whom exactly?'

'Well, there's—'

'Who would believe a girl like me, over a man like him?' I interrupted before she could finish. What a preposterous idea. Of course I didn't report him. I wasn't believed the first time I reported a man, or the second time, or the fucking tenth time, so what would have made this time any different?

They lowered their eyes to their pages, because they knew I was right. And I was glad they were ashamed.

On 21st December, just before Christmas, I was released after an appeal. I went back to Christiania and avoided Maria; she had turned my stuff over to the cops and had betrayed me, so our friendship was over. I stayed with a group of older guys from the squatters' rights group called BZ, which has now disbanded, but a number of them still lived in a warehouse squat in Christiania and allowed me to stay in a storeroom they had. As well as clashing with the police in Denmark over forced evictions, BZ worked with various other militant left-wing organisations, and many of them had been in Libya fighting to defeat Gaddafi. They allowed me to stay as a favour to Maria, because apparently she did feel bad about giving all my stuff over to the cops. These guys were kind and liked to try and impart their wisdom on reintegrating into civilian life.

I was offered protection from the PET when I was released from prison, due to the threat *Daesh* had made, but I refused it. I believe it was just the PET's way of trying to follow my movements, as they believed the lies my family told them about me being in the PKK. Not having protection meant I could disappear for a while and sometimes, while lying in my sleeping bag in the tiny storeroom, I felt like I had. No one noticed me and no one was waiting for me. Increasingly my social contact was performed online instead of off.

My headaches were still crippling me, and the cold failed to bring the respite it should have done, but I don't trust painkillers now, so I just rested as much as I could when I wasn't working at Burger King, and hoped it would heal. I didn't dare risk going to hospital or the doctor's because on my file was the diagnosis from the OPUS clinic, and then my admission that I had lied just to get painkillers, and I was worried they would use it against me in court.

I started having nightmares living in the storeroom, because I wasn't always sure I was safe: any noise would wake me and I would sit bolt upright, covered in sweat and trembling. Initially the nightmares were not vivid, and would feature basic things that I had been through before: scenes that had gone badly on the battlefield would play out and I would be back there, trying to make a better decision this time. This kind of dream is just a natural way for your body to process trauma and grief, and although it wasn't pleasant, I didn't find myself thinking of it during the day. I tried to read as much as I could about how to cope after being on the frontline, and I stayed in touch with friends who were also combatants.

Soon enough, the type of visions I was seeing changed. I would be with my friend back in the house in Kobani, and he was begging me to save him. Or I was in the room sleeping with my friends, when suddenly I would feel warm blood draining out of them onto me. The blood in my dreams was always warm, and I would wake up covered in sweat, thinking I was covered in blood. It was terrifyingly lonely: I didn't tell the guys I was staying with what was happening, because I wasn't sure if I could trust them and I didn't really know how to begin. Some of them had been in battle too, but I didn't want them to think I was weak or couldn't cope. I have this public persona where everyone thinks I am fierce (which I am), and I didn't want their view of me to change, so I struggled on alone, initially keeping these apparitions to myself. I would wake from the dreams, but still be there in my head. Sometimes the dreams would even carry on when I was awake; conversations would continue, and my dead friends were with me as if they were real flesh and blood.

I started to avoid falling asleep and instead would walk around Christiania late at night, talking to different people and slowly making contacts. The community there was kind to me, and I fell in with some girls who ran a tea shop that would stay open late each night. More than once I slept on a park bench, as I tried to come to terms with what was happening to me. I had no money, no family support, a bounty from *Daesh* on my head in one of the most jihadi-loving countries in the world, and very few people I could call friends. Online friends and followers were still growing every day, but offline my circle was thin, and the furious outbursts that I started having with everyone didn't help. The trolling had made me distrust people, in a new way. And it wasn't like I trusted people so easily before.

I did an interview with a UK newspaper in February 2017, because I desperately needed the money it was willing to pay. No one else was helping me, so I needed to stand up for myself, and it was a relatively easy way to make a lot of money, or I thought it would be. But the cost of going public on my health and well-being has been much greater than I ever anticipated. It's hard, because once I speak and put what I think out into the world, I have no control over how others will react.

My lawyer wasn't happy with me speaking to the press and confirming things I hadn't yet admitted in court, but I told him about my financial and living situations and he saw my point of view. The interview gave rise to another wave of trolling, but slowly I started to stand up for myself online and call people out for what they were saying.

It was not the lies of my enemies that hurt me as much as the silence of my friends. Beyond the comment reported in the Iraqi media about *Daesh* putting a bounty on my head – and I still find it unlikely that this information would have been leaked – my army had said nothing on my behalf. The Kurdish community in Copenhagen was weary of the media attention I was bringing, and of the bounty on my head, so I was seldom invited to speak at events about the war. I watched as male volunteers, who had spent half as much time as I had on the front, were invited to speak to large crowds.

There was an occasion in March 2017 when I was due to speak at a rally, with two YPG guys protecting me, but they cancelled my appearance, out of safety concerns. I felt like this was just an excuse: they were annoyed about the pictures of me on social media. I was being punished for embracing the camouflage of being a young woman at college in Europe. Who did I think I was, to behave in this way? – that seemed to be the response from the community. 'You are just too liberated,' my friend Sholan would say, when I asked her why they did this to me.

The pictures from my social-media pages left a lasting impression on many Kurdish men in the community, and several took the opportunity to invite me out to meetings, which would be these weird dates where they would try to hold my hand and ask me personal questions, as if they were trying to negotiate a relationship. I was hungry, and I respected these men as members of my movement and had hoped they would offer some kind of financial support to help me. A few people online offered to donate money, and one or two people I was in contact with did, but many others said they would but it never materialised.

I sometimes slept in the main church in Copenhagen, which had opened its doors to refugees travelling over from the same

Syrian war I had just left. I got many different clothes from them, but staying overnight made me fearful, because I was sure *Daesh* were among the refugees. The storeroom was freezing, but I knew it was secure and private, so it became my little cave. I didn't think about myself much, but spent my time missing my friends in Kurdistan and thinking of how little they had over there, yet so much more than I had. I had nothing but the memories of my friends, which became my everything. I hope they know how much I want to improve my personal situation, and the work I am doing on their behalf while here in Denmark.

A girl I had been talking to online, whose family was from Afghanistan, had a room in shared student accommodation, but wasn't using it, so I moved into her room and paid her some rent, although it was still her name on the lease. The room was small, but I had my own shower and the use of a large communal kitchen; and Charlie from the church refugee programme cleaned all my clothes for me when I first moved in. I had so much washing, as everything stank from my months in the storeroom. The small acts of kindness that I received during this year were precious few.

It was so great to have my own space: a double bed, a coffee table and some cushions, a huge fridge and enough space for all the boxes of my stuff, collected in one place. I bought candles and sheepskin mats, and started to look after myself better and tried to put on some weight. By this stage I had also finally gone back to finish my *gymnasium* education, and I quit my job in Burger King, which allowed me to start the process of putting together my crazy life story for this book.

It's hard to talk about an experience that is difficult for others to believe. It is privilege that makes a person blind; for those whose own life experience is safe and protected, they cannot conceive that life is not like that for everyone. When some people say that my story is unbelievable it means they clearly have not been paying attention to what has been going on in the world. I am just one girl from the Middle East who grew up in Europe and went to join the Syrian war. There are hundreds like me, and many thousands more Muslim girls who are silently enduring much worse than I have described in these pages. It's time for those who say they find my story unbelievable to stop posting selfies and start actually engaging with the world around them. Or at least do what I do, and post selfies and politics side by side.

There were eight of us who shared the kitchen and living area in the student flat, and I enjoyed our communal space. I would watch TV with my flatmates and we would talk together, but even though it was nice to be around people my own age, it was sometimes hard to find common ground because our life experiences had been so different. I didn't really talk to the others about my experiences, because I was feeling so unsteady from my months of basically being homeless that I just nested for a while. I was safe and warm, and the view out my window of the cityscape was beautiful. I loved to make all kinds of herbal tea with cream and honey for myself, smoke a cigarette and light candles for my dead friends. I light my cigarettes with the lighters that we used there – lighters belonging to people no longer on our Earth. I'm healing, I suppose, but some days it doesn't really feel like it. Some days I just wish I was back there.

This all ended when the girl I rented the flat from was kicked out of the student accommodation because she was being kicked out of school, and she demanded that I pay much more money than she did for the flat, as she was in debt. I transferred her the money she wanted, and went to the administration office of the apartments to tell them I was living there and that I needed to remain there, as otherwise I was homeless. They were annoyed I was there, and told me I had five days to clear all my stuff out: I had no right to be there because, even if I fitted the criteria, the waiting list for this kind of student accommodation was more than two years. So I had to leave.

I had become friendly with some guys in Christiania, and one of them offered me a room in his house. I was reluctant to accept and asked lots of different people if they knew anywhere else, but apartments are not easy to find in Copenhagen, and I wanted a place to myself. The flat I was in before I went to Syria in 2014 had been sublet by someone who didn't pay their rent, so I also had this on my record, which made it difficult for me to find somewhere new. And I suddenly owed money to the government, because I had received money to be in school during periods when I had been away, and I had large fines to pay, not to mention legal fees. I had no identification and no means of getting any, because my passport had been taken away, so I had to take the legal charge sheet from my arrest in Turkey to the bank in order to get money out, because they wanted some form of ID. Every corner I turned, I could see only ugly faces.

My family doesn't want anything to do with me, and they have never helped me financially. I was talking to my mother and she came to my flat in the university accommodation, but we fought and she left. I've spent the last year fighting with a lot of people, as I have fought my court case. I have had two trials: one to decide whether I broke the passport ban, and one to decide what my punishment would be.

In court for my first trial, I was hoping the judge would accept that I shouldn't have had the passport ban imposed in the first place, and therefore I didn't do anything wrong by breaking it. My whole legal case has been based on this basic principle, which anyone who knows anything about the conflict can quickly grasp: as part of the YPJ, I am on the frontline of the SDF coalition, which is backed by the international coalition.

I am the one who actually fought *Daesh* fighters in real life; I am the one who has made that sacrifice, who has tasted that blood, who has to live with that experience in my heart for the rest of time. I cannot be prosecuted as one of them, when I have given up everything to destroy them. 'They are my enemy, and I am not yours' – this is what I wish I could have said to the judge.

I testified at my first trial, but not at my second. My new lawyer in these cases was arguing that the law was improperly applied, but it came down to the fact that no matter how improperly applied, it had been applied and I had travelled outside Denmark. I had to admit some things: that I had travelled as far as Qatar on 6th June 2016, breaking the terms of the ban. My lawyer argued that there was no substantive evidence that I had both broken the ban and had gone back to war, but I had laid my own trail in videos, pictures and updates on Instagram. The prosecutor used my social media against me, and used the articles that had been written as evidence. I was found guilty, and on 22nd November 2017 I was sentenced to nine months in prison. It was longer than I hoped, but less than I had feared.

I fought for love and friendship, but for the past year I have felt abandoned by the movement whose love and friendship I fought for. I understand that they are busy with the war, but I have still been hurt and could do with some support in my legal case. My understanding of our deal was incomplete; I believed that if went to fight and was willing to sacrifice myself on the frontline, I would be taken care of, if I survived. I don't mean taken care of financially; I mean I didn't think I would be left alone with all the deaths.

On the frontline everything is shared: we spend all our time together and we share our food, our fears, our hopes and our dreams. Off the frontline, nothing is shared, because no one else understands. I miss feeling a part of something that is bigger than me and my small life, something that makes the world better. The world needs to be better, so back here in Denmark I sometimes wonder what is wrong with everyone else.

Fighting for my future on the frontline was much easier than fighting for it off the frontline. On the frontline you can see who your enemies are, but in civilian life I find it's sometimes unclear. I know how to fire a gun and make and defuse a bomb, and I know how to kill someone. I know who I need to kill, but I haven't graduated yet; and there are a lot of things I don't know that I wish I did. I almost died in Kobani, and I almost died in Manbij, several times, and it made me see what I actually wanted.

Now that I have lived, I have made myself a promise that I will try to fulfil my own dreams. The dreams I have for myself: to have a family, to have a baby, to have a career and to be independent. I have lots more classes to take before I can begin to study to become a nurse, and with my court case and the attention it will bring, I am nervous that I will drop out of school again, as I was forced to last year. I have only so many chances at my own life, so I'm not nervous about being in prison. I have survived worse places before, and I probably will again.

I have wars in my own life to fight, but I went to fight the war against *Daesh* on behalf of the world. This is what the YPG has done for the world; what my friends have done for the world. When I came back from the war I had many projects planned for myself that would take me back to the frontline, but I have decided to put aside these plans and projects now. Let me explain why: in the many times I have been close to death in combat, I've never regretted what I've done – and I know I have done many bad things. What I regret are the things I have *not* done: fighting my own personal wars, against the monsters under my bed.

I have tried to chase death, but apparently death doesn't want me. So close to losing my life, it was the ghosts of what I had not yet done that surrounded me: my personal dreams and an inner voice, asking me why I was hunting death when I hadn't really lived yet. So close to death, I didn't feel proud or successful, as if I could look back on my achievements; instead I felt full of shame that I didn't have better deeds to present to God, if he or she exists, on Judgement Day. I could of course say that I was trying to change the world for the better, but the question I couldn't answer was whether I had tried to change *myself* for the better.

I should at least have a taste of life before I die. A life that is about more than the trauma I experienced as a daughter of the war. Kurdistan has never left me, though I have physically left Kurdistan many times, and it will always be a part of me; but I am more than this experience, and I wish to have a life that is more than I had before. A life where I honour my lost friends by appreciating being alive and by telling my story, one that many Kurdish and Middle Eastern people have to tell.

One of the most difficult parts of this year, and the process of writing this book, has been trying to imagine myself as an old woman, reading this book. I've always just assumed I will be dead before I'm old. People like me don't generally get to plan for a future, or a personal life, because we give all of that to our movement when we join. The experience I now have has isolated me from my friends in Europe, most of whom only remind me of those friends I lost in Syria; and I feel flattened by the trolling. My family believes I am too different from them, too Danish; and yet the Danish government sees me as too Kurdish for them, and therefore a risk.

Many of those I left behind in Syria are now gone for ever, and nothing I can do will bring them back. Almost every week I hear the news on Facebook that another fighter has died. So many have died it's as if we don't even matter. Not all of us Kurds who come to Syria to defeat *Daesh* are being counted, for political reasons. Our sacrifice cannot be forgotten easily, and I hope the international community does not renege on its pledges to us. If the West wants a democratic partner in the Middle East, then Kurds must be given their rights to self-govern, across the four corners of our as-yet-unrealized nation.

As for my own fight, I will take some time to recover, to rest and get my head back to being in Denmark; to see how I can work, off the frontline, for women's rights. I have some sisters in Afghanistan that I want to visit, who are fighting for women's rights. I do think women should be armed, as part of a wider democratic and equality movement. I do believe women are entitled to defend and protect themselves with weapons from ideologies that seek their absolute destruction, because what other choice do we have?

It was not death that haunted me on the battlefield, it was my life. I don't regret anything I've done: there is no longer an Islamic State, and there is no longer a caliphate, so we achieved our aims – we won. My prize is to be alive still: to see what age I will actually make it to, and to find out how else I can spend my life.

Acknowledgements

Many people have helped me to write this book and without their support I could not have done it. I would like to say a special thank you to Lara Whyte who worked tirelessly with me and continued to believe in my story during the difficult times. Also to my agent Maggie Hanbury and Harriet Poland who made it all happen and guided me through the process. And thank you to my friends Dave, Emily and Catherine who have been so generous with their support and kindness.

Thank you to the many people in Denmark who helped me when I had nowhere to live, their generosity is not forgotten.

A special thank you to James Nightingale, my publisher at Atlantic, who commissioned the book and who has worked hard on the text. Also, a big thank you to my Danish publisher JP/Politikens Forlag and my editor Tonie Yde Højrup, and my Swedish publisher Polaris Forlag.

Joanna Palani was born in 1993 in a UN refugee camp outside of Ramadi in Iraq. She spent the first three years of her life there, before her family were moved to Denmark. Joanna first travelled to Syria in 2011, as part of the Kurdish battalions that supported the Free Syrian Army volunteers against the Assad regime. She played a variety of roles for the YPJ – the female battalion of the Syrian Kurdish militia group YPG – the Peshmerga and as part of coalition forces, including the Syrian Democratic Forces, supported by US and UK special forces. Her last position in the YPJ was in a sniper unit. She lives in Copenhagen.

Lara Whyte is a reporter, producer and editor from Belfast.